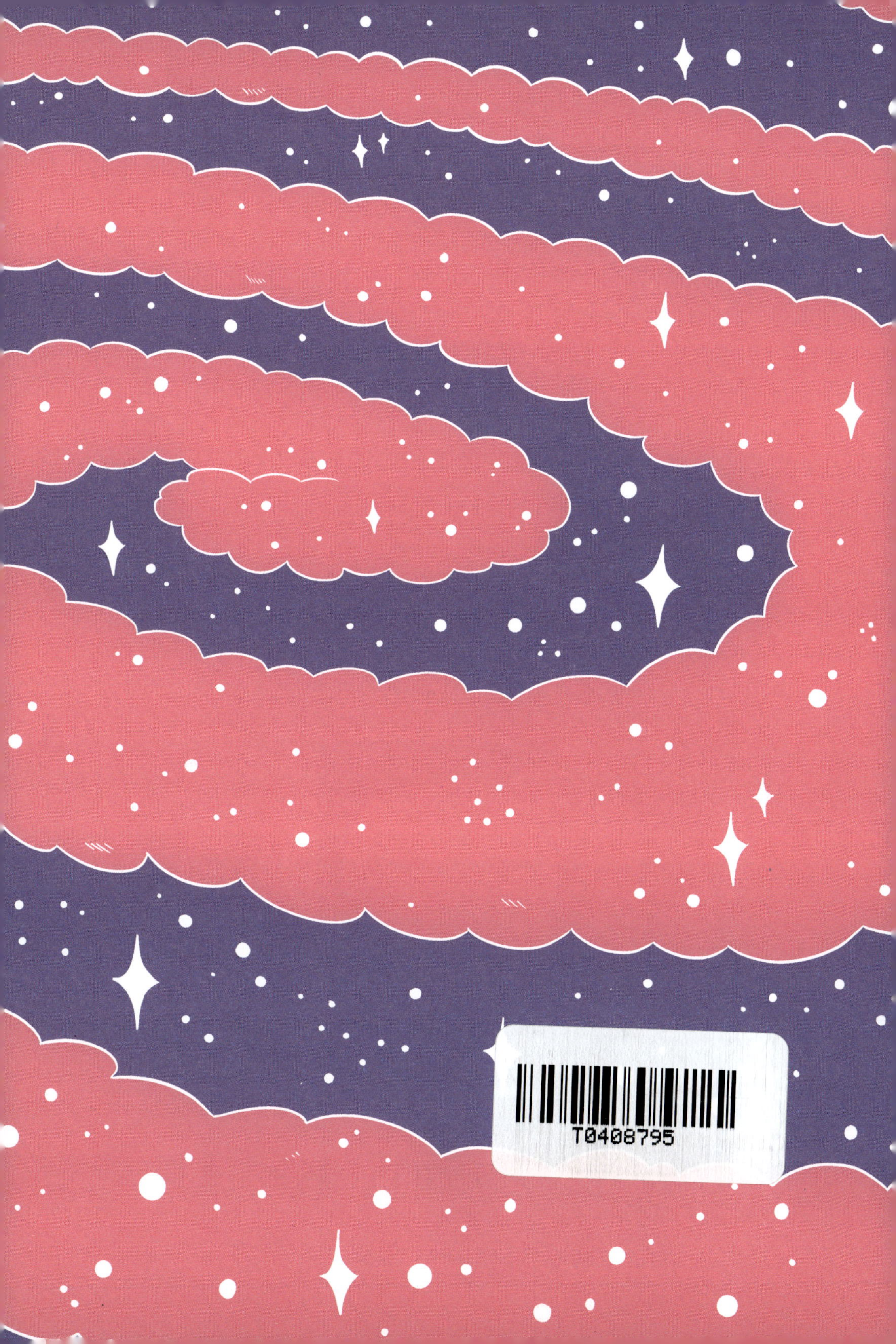

TO EVERYONE WHO HELPED ALONG THE WAY,
BOTH HUMAN AND FELINE, THANK YOU.
—MADELEINE

TO MUM, DAD, OLIVER, MADI,
AND THE TEAM AT FLYING EYE.
—TOM

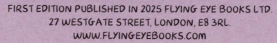

FIRST EDITION PUBLISHED IN 2025 FLYING EYE BOOKS LTD.
27 WESTGATE STREET, LONDON, E8 3RL.
www.flyingeyebooks.com

REPRESENTED BY: AUTHORISED REP COMPLIANCE LTD.
GROUND FLOOR, 71 LOWER BAGGOT STREET,
DUBLIN, D02 P593, IRELAND.
www.arccompliance.com

TEXT © MADELEINE FINLAY 2025
ILLUSTRATIONS © TOM DEARIE 2025

MADELEINE FINLAY AND TOM DEARIE HAVE ASSERTED THEIR
RIGHT UNDER THE COPYRIGHT, DESIGNS AND PATENTS ACT, 1988,
TO BE IDENTIFIED AS THE AUTHOR AND ILLUSTRATOR OF THIS WORK.

ALL RIGHTS RESERVED. NO PART OF THIS PUBLICATION MAY
BE REPRODUCED OR TRANSMITTED IN ANY FORM OR BY ANY MEANS,
ELECTRONIC OR MECHANICAL, INCLUDING PHOTOCOPYING, RECORDING
OR BY ANY INFORMATION AND STORAGE RETRIEVAL SYSTEM,
WITHOUT PRIOR WRITTEN CONSENT FROM THE PUBLISHER.

CONSULTANT: PROFESSOR BEN MAUGHAN
EDITED BY NIAMH JONES
DESIGNED BY ELOISE GROHS

1 3 5 7 9 10 8 6 4 2

ISBN: 978-1-83874-130-3
US LIBRARY ISBN: 978-1-83874-934-7

PUBLISHED IN THE US BY FLYING EYE BOOKS LTD.
PRINTED IN POLAND ON FSC® CERTIFIED PAPER.

MADELEINE FINLAY TOM DEARIE

« WARNING, MAY CONTAIN METEOR SHOWERS, GREEDY BLACK HOLES, AND SPACE-TIME SECRETS »

FLYING EYE BOOKS

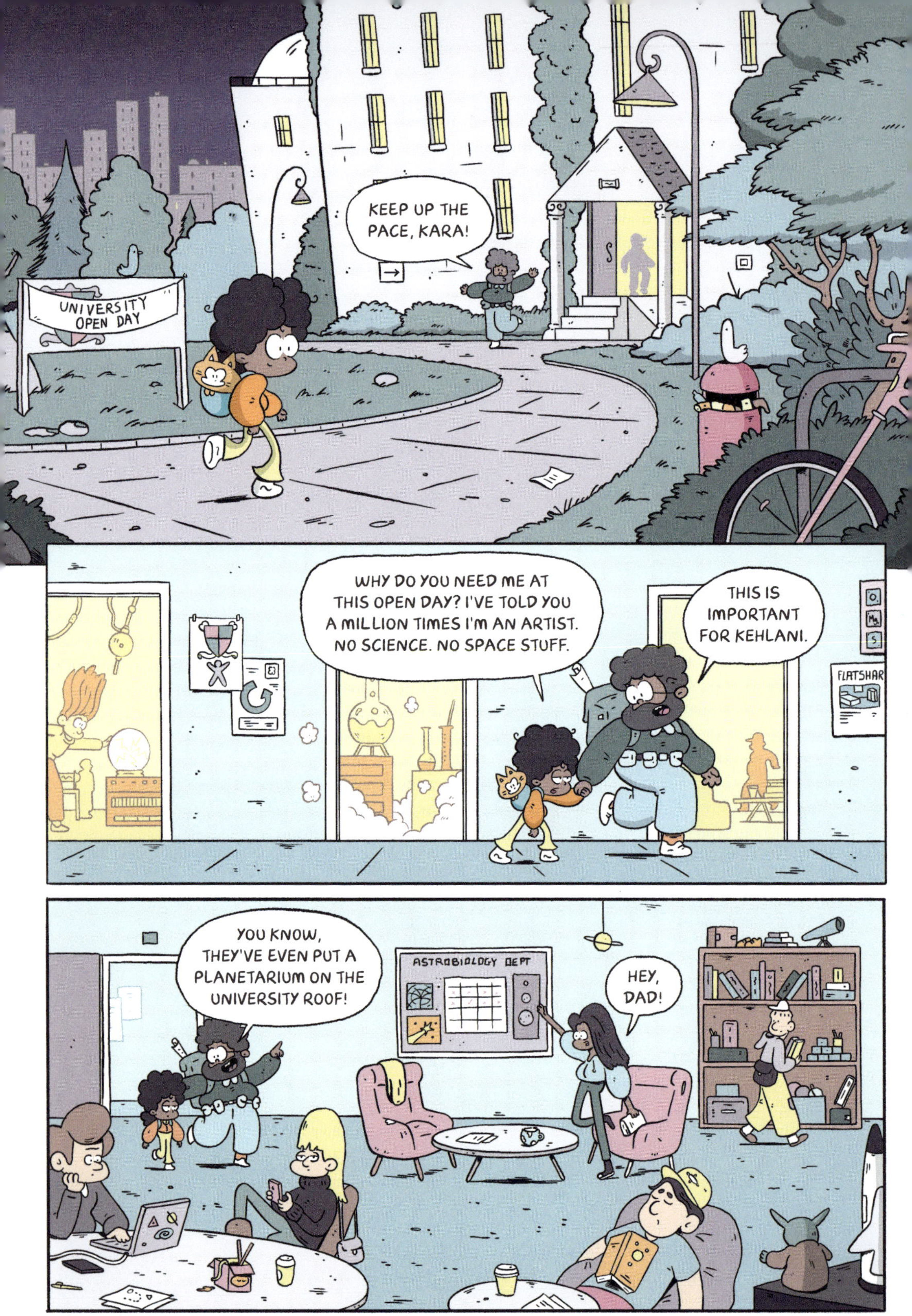
UNIVERSITY OPEN DAY
KEEP UP THE PACE, KARA!
WHY DO YOU NEED ME AT THIS OPEN DAY? I'VE TOLD YOU A MILLION TIMES I'M AN ARTIST. NO SCIENCE. NO SPACE STUFF.
THIS IS IMPORTANT FOR KEHLANI.
YOU KNOW, THEY'VE EVEN PUT A PLANETARIUM ON THE UNIVERSITY ROOF!
ASTROBIOLOGY DEPT
HEY, DAD!

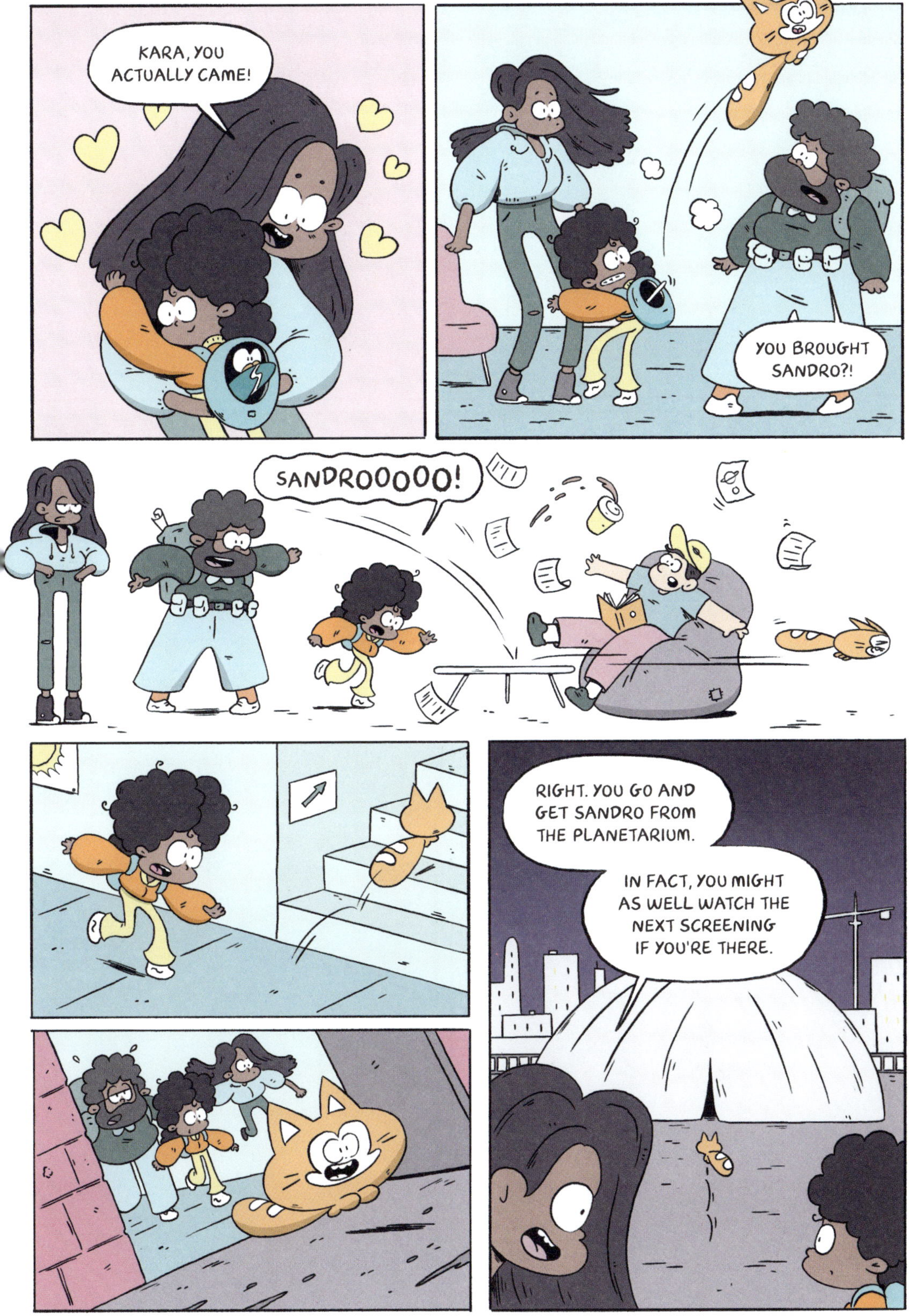
KARA, YOU ACTUALLY CAME!
YOU BROUGHT SANDRO?!
SANDROOOOOO!
RIGHT. YOU GO AND GET SANDRO FROM THE PLANETARIUM.
IN FACT, YOU MIGHT AS WELL WATCH THE NEXT SCREENING IF YOU'RE THERE.

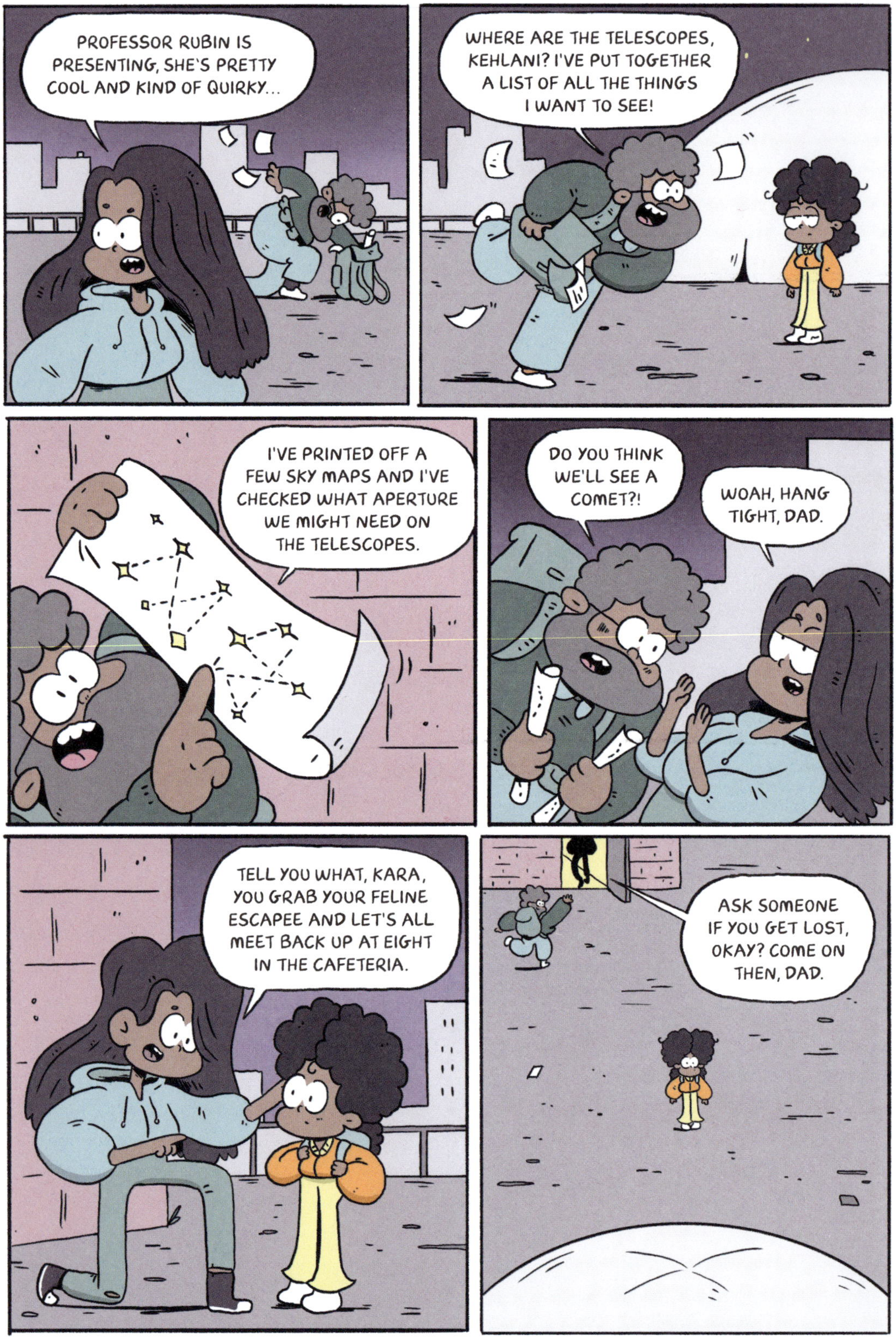
PROFESSOR RUBIN IS PRESENTING, SHE'S PRETTY COOL AND KIND OF QUIRKY...
WHERE ARE THE TELESCOPES, KEHLANI? I'VE PUT TOGETHER A LIST OF ALL THE THINGS I WANT TO SEE!
I'VE PRINTED OFF A FEW SKY MAPS AND I'VE CHECKED WHAT APERTURE WE MIGHT NEED ON THE TELESCOPES.
DO YOU THINK WE'LL SEE A COMET?!
WOAH, HANG TIGHT, DAD.
TELL YOU WHAT, KARA, YOU GRAB YOUR FELINE ESCAPEE AND LET'S ALL MEET BACK UP AT EIGHT IN THE CAFETERIA.
ASK SOMEONE IF YOU GET LOST, OKAY? COME ON THEN, DAD.

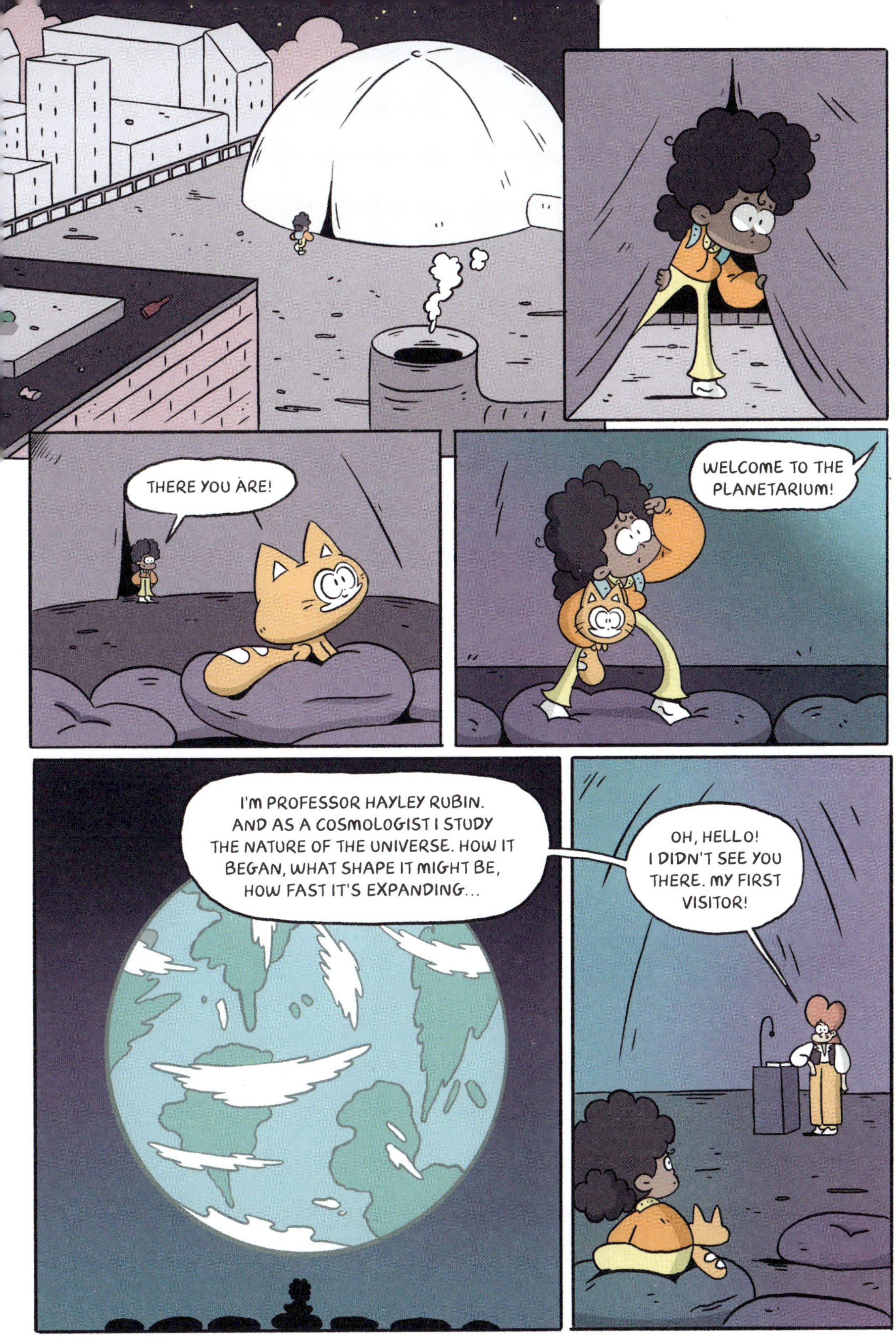
THERE YOU ARE!
WELCOME TO THE PLANETARIUM!
OH, HELLO! I DIDN'T SEE YOU THERE. MY FIRST VISITOR!
I'M PROFESSOR HAYLEY RUBIN. AND AS A COSMOLOGIST I STUDY THE NATURE OF THE UNIVERSE. HOW IT BEGAN, WHAT SHAPE IT MIGHT BE, HOW FAST IT'S EXPANDING...

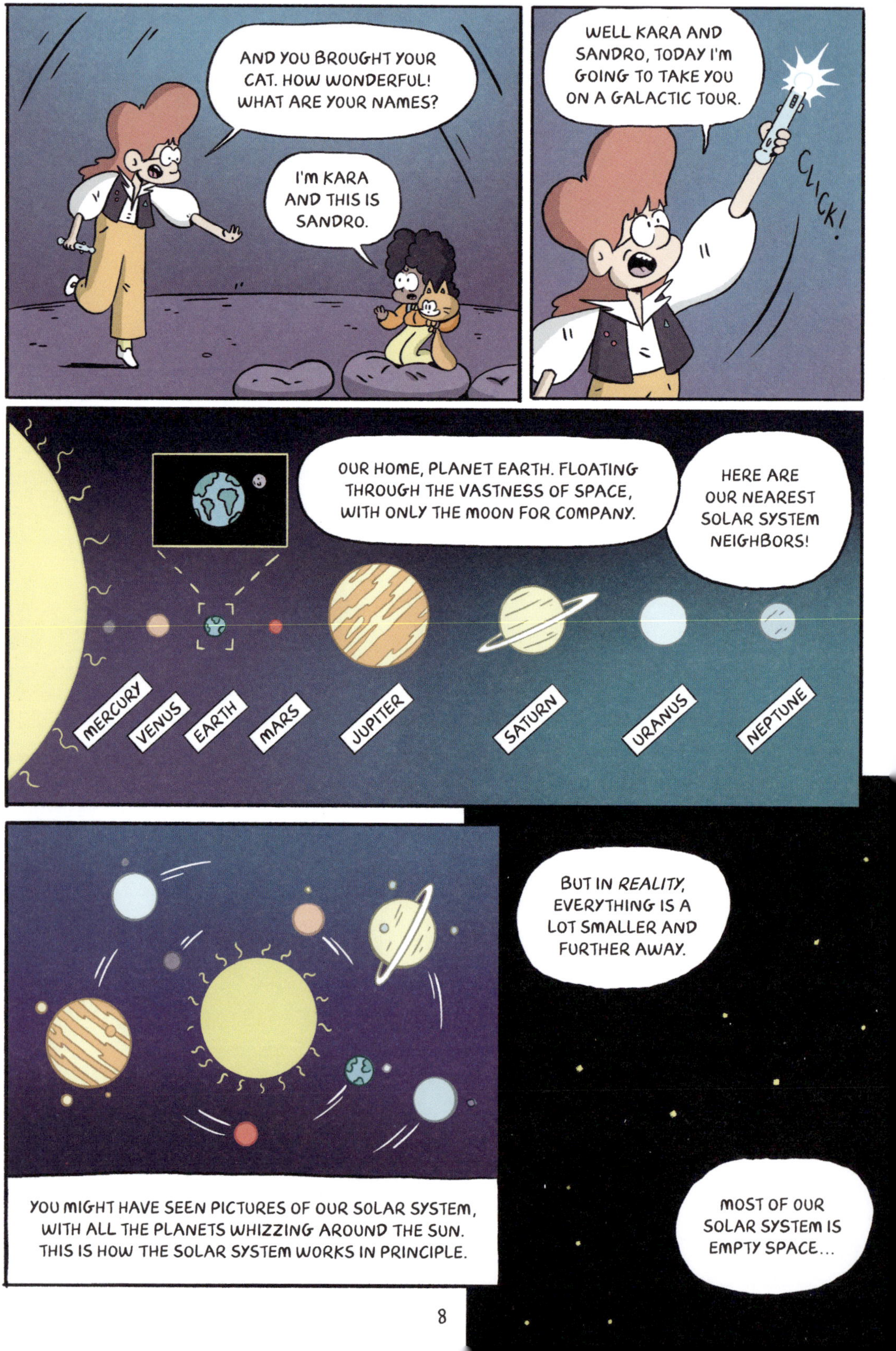
AND YOU BROUGHT YOUR CAT. HOW WONDERFUL! WHAT ARE YOUR NAMES?
I'M KARA AND THIS IS SANDRO.
WELL KARA AND SANDRO, TODAY I'M GOING TO TAKE YOU ON A GALACTIC TOUR.
CLICK!
OUR HOME, PLANET EARTH. FLOATING THROUGH THE VASTNESS OF SPACE, WITH ONLY THE MOON FOR COMPANY.
HERE ARE OUR NEAREST SOLAR SYSTEM NEIGHBORS!
MERCURY
VENUS
EARTH
MARS
JUPITER
SATURN
URANUS
NEPTUNE
YOU MIGHT HAVE SEEN PICTURES OF OUR SOLAR SYSTEM, WITH ALL THE PLANETS WHIZZING AROUND THE SUN. THIS IS HOW THE SOLAR SYSTEM WORKS IN PRINCIPLE.
BUT IN *REALITY*, EVERYTHING IS A LOT SMALLER AND FURTHER AWAY.
MOST OF OUR SOLAR SYSTEM IS EMPTY SPACE...

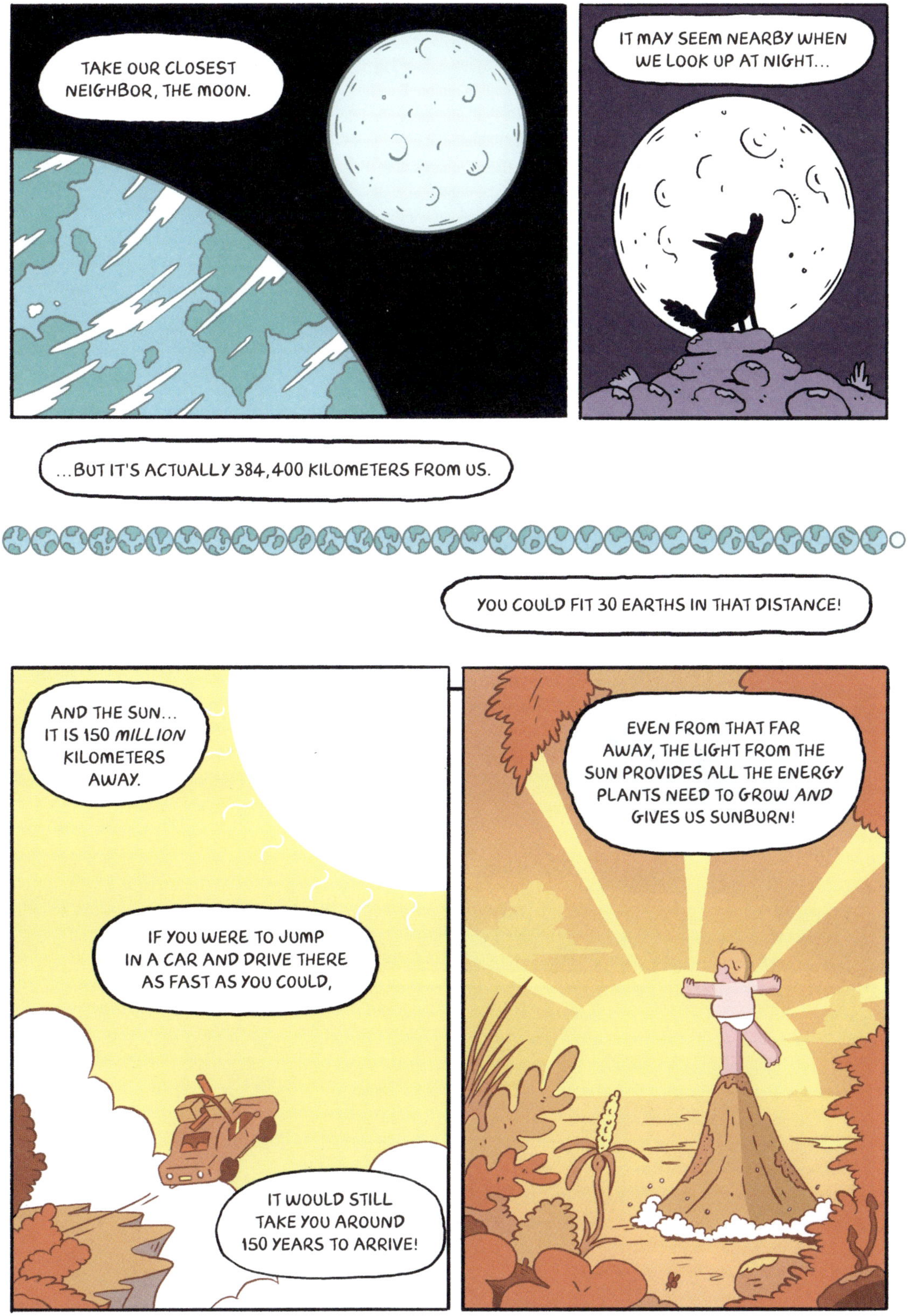
TAKE OUR CLOSEST NEIGHBOR, THE MOON.
IT MAY SEEM NEARBY WHEN WE LOOK UP AT NIGHT...
...BUT IT'S ACTUALLY 384,400 KILOMETERS FROM US.
YOU COULD FIT 30 EARTHS IN THAT DISTANCE!
AND THE SUN... IT IS 150 MILLION KILOMETERS AWAY.
IF YOU WERE TO JUMP IN A CAR AND DRIVE THERE AS FAST AS YOU COULD,
IT WOULD STILL TAKE YOU AROUND 150 YEARS TO ARRIVE!
EVEN FROM THAT FAR AWAY, THE LIGHT FROM THE SUN PROVIDES ALL THE ENERGY PLANTS NEED TO GROW AND GIVES US SUNBURN!

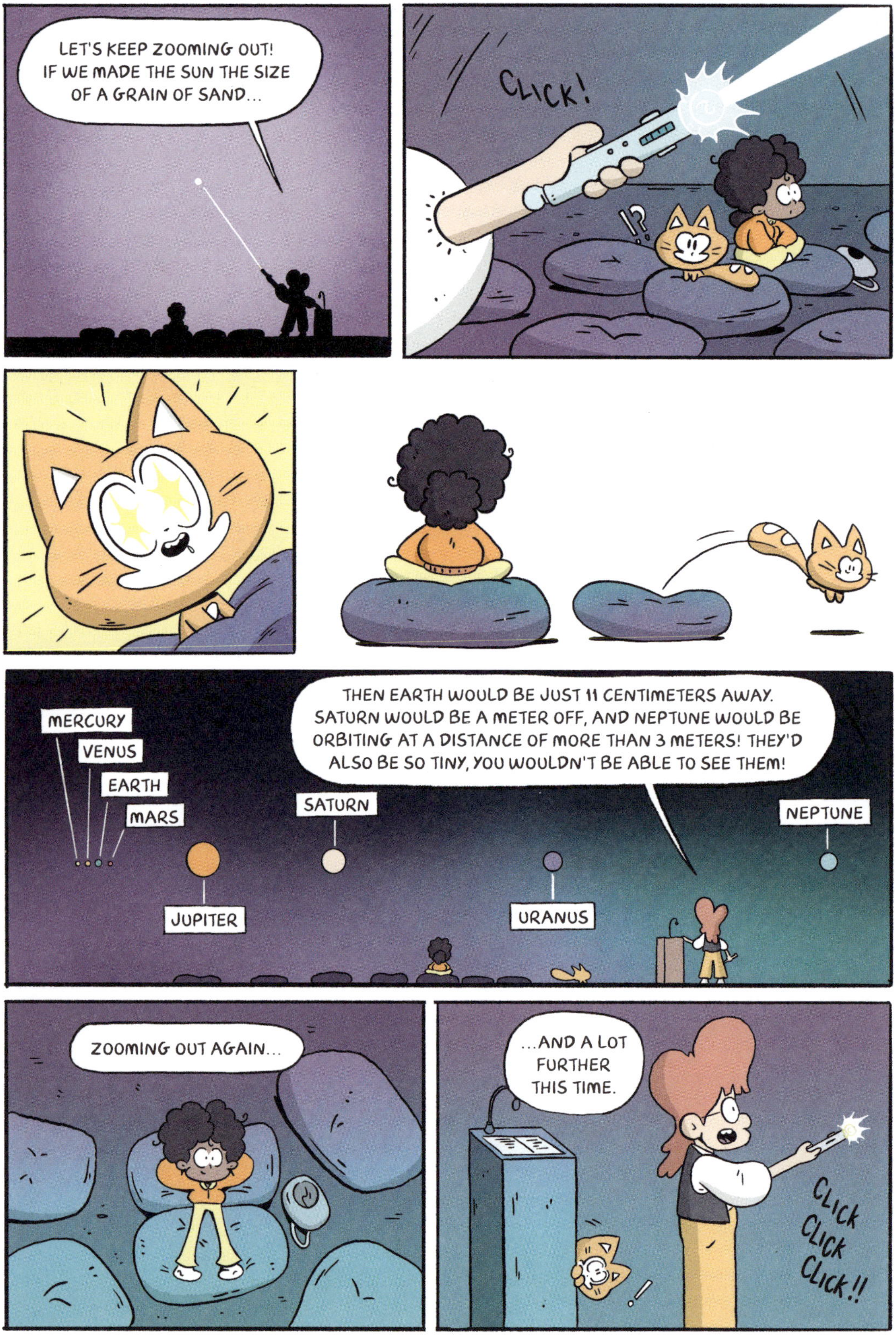
LET'S KEEP ZOOMING OUT! IF WE MADE THE SUN THE SIZE OF A GRAIN OF SAND...
CLICK!
!?
THEN EARTH WOULD BE JUST 11 CENTIMETERS AWAY. SATURN WOULD BE A METER OFF, AND NEPTUNE WOULD BE ORBITING AT A DISTANCE OF MORE THAN 3 METERS! THEY'D ALSO BE SO TINY, YOU WOULDN'T BE ABLE TO SEE THEM!
MERCURY
VENUS
EARTH
MARS
JUPITER
SATURN
URANUS
NEPTUNE
ZOOMING OUT AGAIN...
...AND A LOT FURTHER THIS TIME.
CLICK CLICK CLICK!!

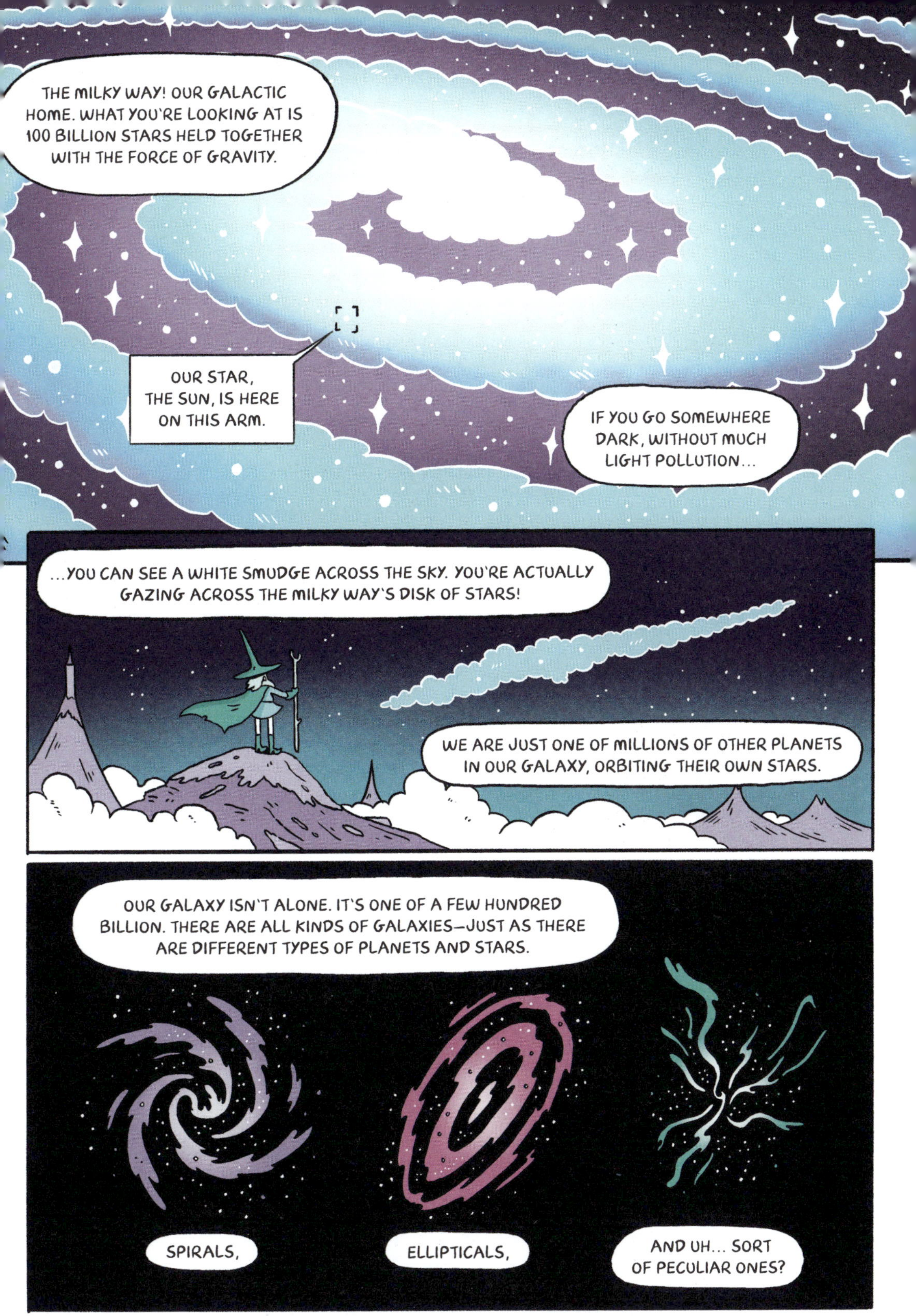
THE MILKY WAY! OUR GALACTIC HOME. WHAT YOU'RE LOOKING AT IS 100 BILLION STARS HELD TOGETHER WITH THE FORCE OF GRAVITY.
OUR STAR, THE SUN, IS HERE ON THIS ARM.
IF YOU GO SOMEWHERE DARK, WITHOUT MUCH LIGHT POLLUTION...
...YOU CAN SEE A WHITE SMUDGE ACROSS THE SKY. YOU'RE ACTUALLY GAZING ACROSS THE MILKY WAY'S DISK OF STARS!
WE ARE JUST ONE OF MILLIONS OF OTHER PLANETS IN OUR GALAXY, ORBITING THEIR OWN STARS.
OUR GALAXY ISN'T ALONE. IT'S ONE OF A FEW HUNDRED BILLION. THERE ARE ALL KINDS OF GALAXIES—JUST AS THERE ARE DIFFERENT TYPES OF PLANETS AND STARS.
SPIRALS,
ELLIPTICALS,
AND UH... SORT OF PECULIAR ONES?

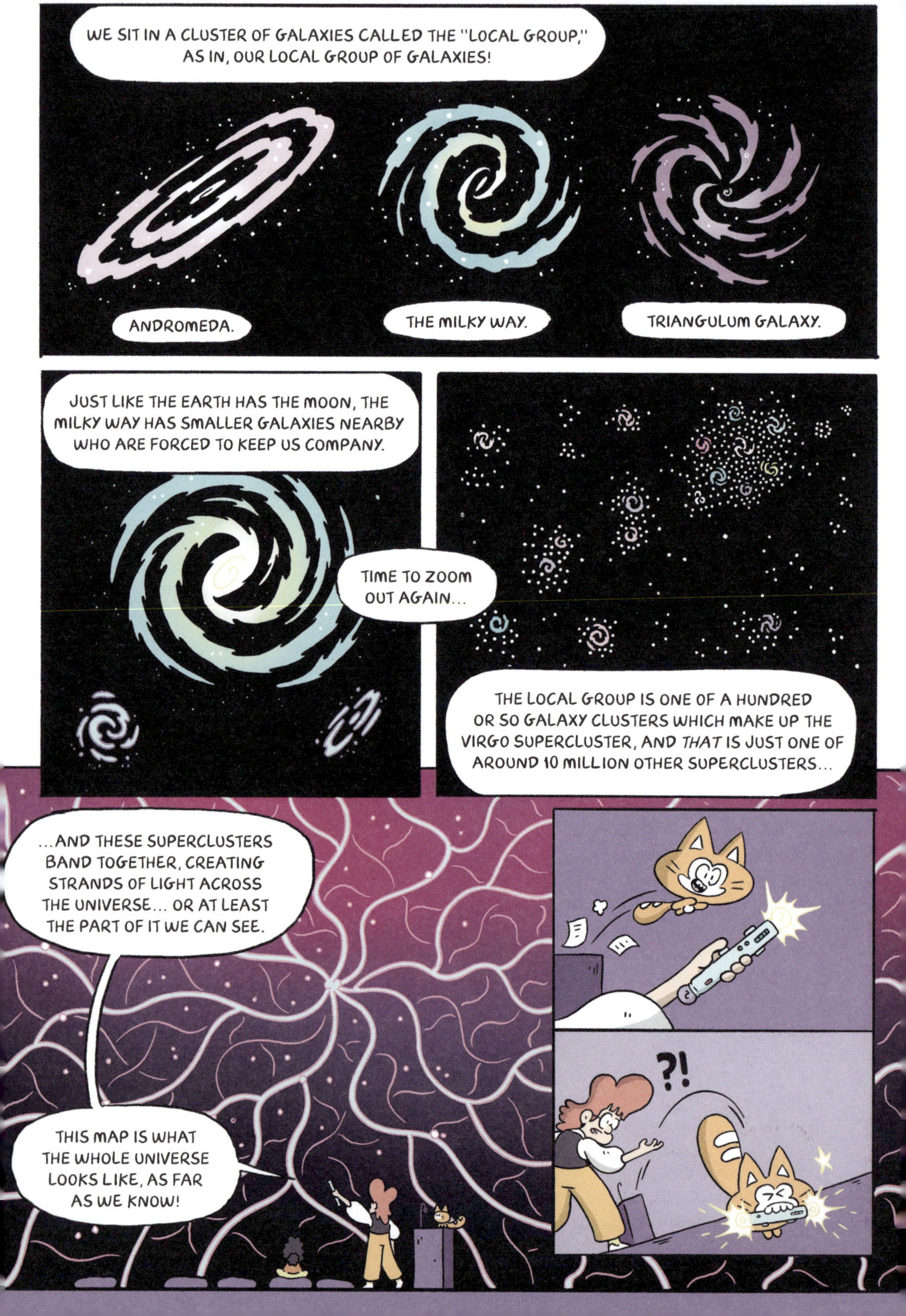
WE SIT IN A CLUSTER OF GALAXIES CALLED THE "LOCAL GROUP," AS IN, OUR LOCAL GROUP OF GALAXIES!
ANDROMEDA.
THE MILKY WAY.
TRIANGULUM GALAXY.
JUST LIKE THE EARTH HAS THE MOON, THE MILKY WAY HAS SMALLER GALAXIES NEARBY WHO ARE FORCED TO KEEP US COMPANY.
TIME TO ZOOM OUT AGAIN...
THE LOCAL GROUP IS ONE OF A HUNDRED OR SO GALAXY CLUSTERS WHICH MAKE UP THE VIRGO SUPERCLUSTER, AND *THAT* IS JUST ONE OF AROUND 10 MILLION OTHER SUPERCLUSTERS...
...AND THESE SUPERCLUSTERS BAND TOGETHER, CREATING STRANDS OF LIGHT ACROSS THE UNIVERSE... OR AT LEAST THE PART OF IT WE CAN SEE.
THIS MAP IS WHAT THE WHOLE UNIVERSE LOOKS LIKE, AS FAR AS WE KNOW!
?!

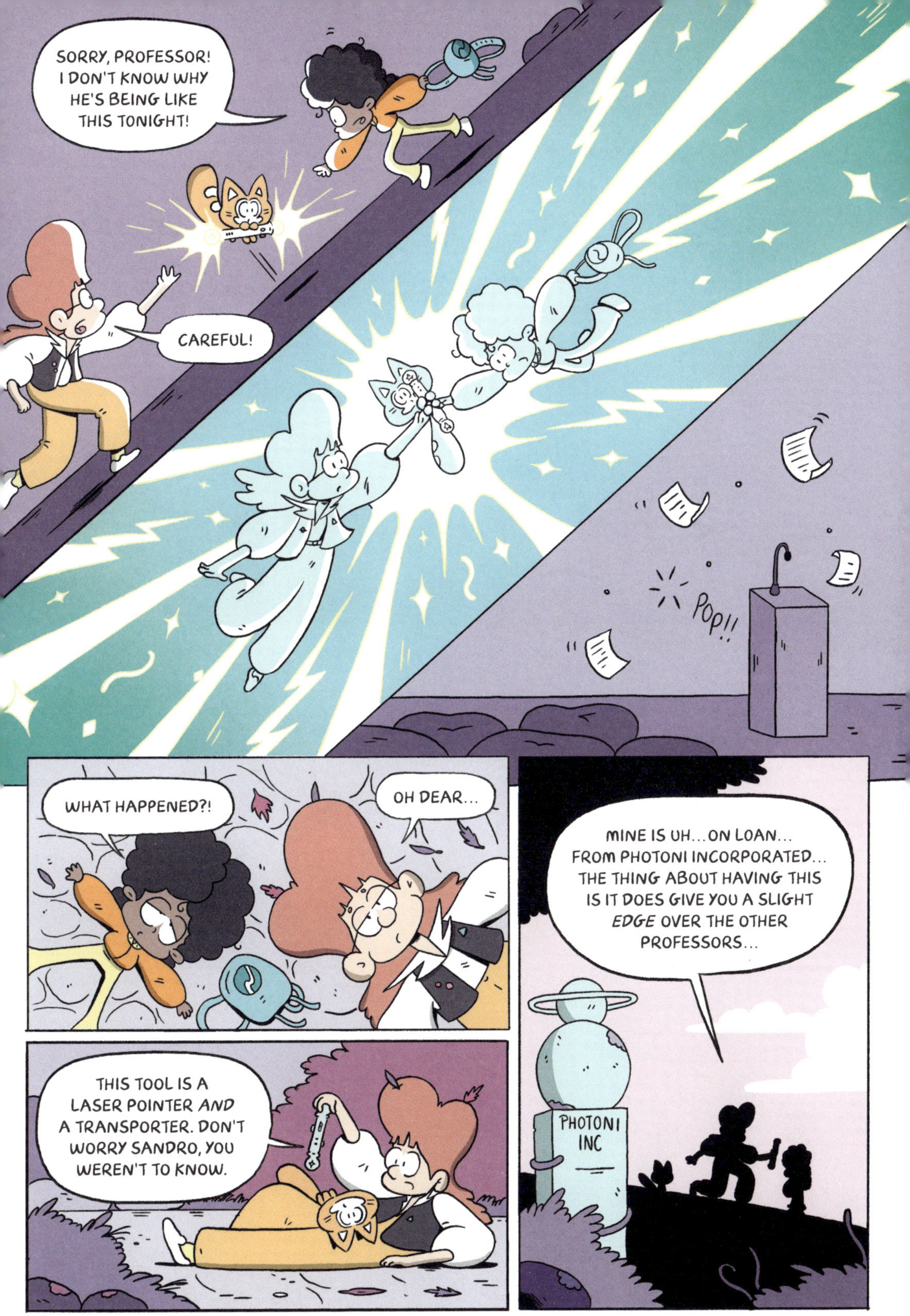
SORRY, PROFESSOR! I DON'T KNOW WHY HE'S BEING LIKE THIS TONIGHT!
CAREFUL!
POP!!
WHAT HAPPENED?!
OH DEAR...
MINE IS UH...ON LOAN... FROM PHOTONI INCORPORATED... THE THING ABOUT HAVING THIS IS IT DOES GIVE YOU A SLIGHT *EDGE* OVER THE OTHER PROFESSORS...
THIS TOOL IS A LASER POINTER *AND* A TRANSPORTER. DON'T WORRY SANDRO, YOU WEREN'T TO KNOW.
PHOTONI INC

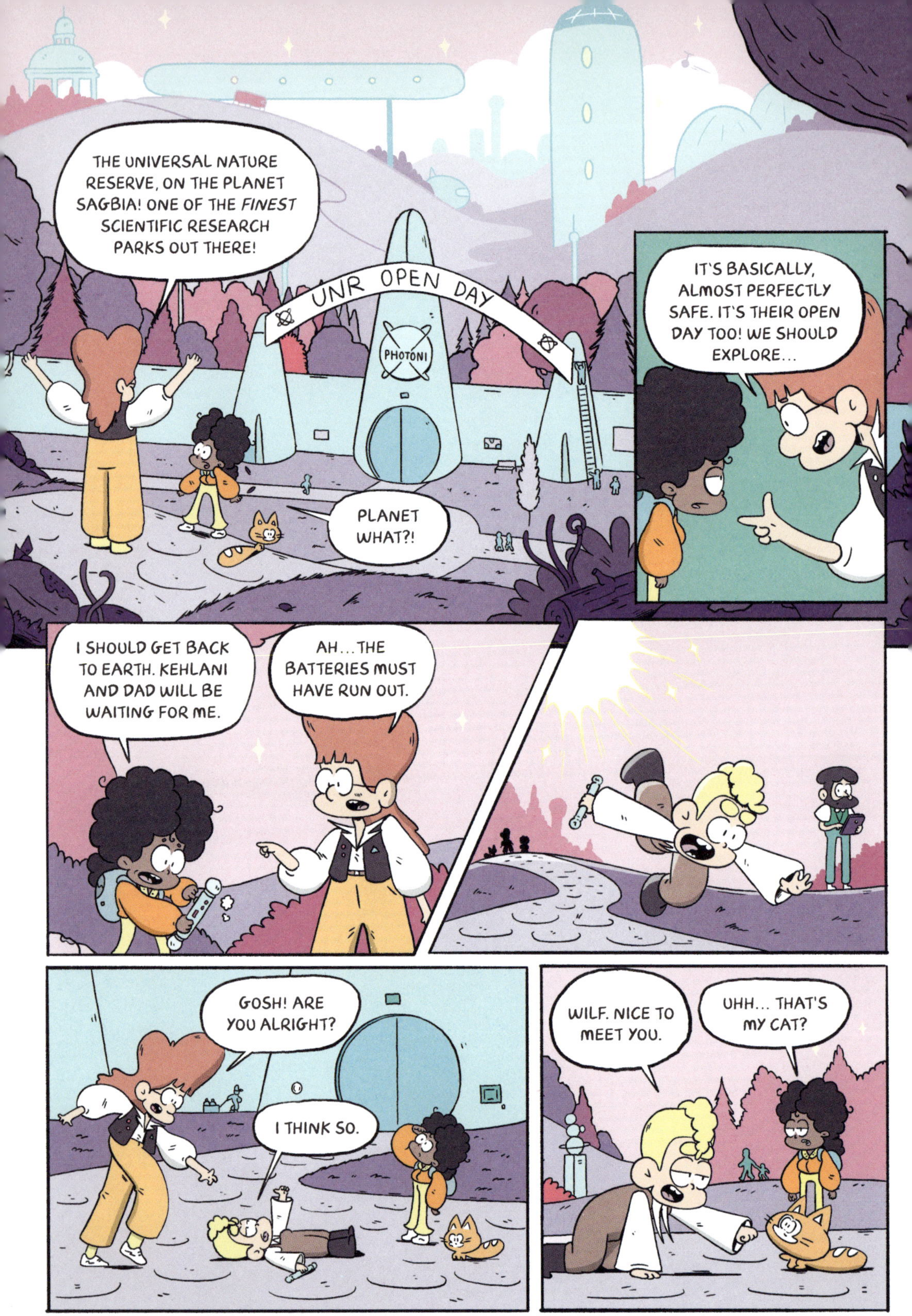
THE UNIVERSAL NATURE RESERVE, ON THE PLANET SAGBIA! ONE OF THE *FINEST* SCIENTIFIC RESEARCH PARKS OUT THERE!
UNR OPEN DAY
PHOTONI
PLANET WHAT?!
IT'S BASICALLY, ALMOST PERFECTLY SAFE. IT'S THEIR OPEN DAY TOO! WE SHOULD EXPLORE...
I SHOULD GET BACK TO EARTH. KEHLANI AND DAD WILL BE WAITING FOR ME.
AH... THE BATTERIES MUST HAVE RUN OUT.
GOSH! ARE YOU ALRIGHT?
I THINK SO.
WILF. NICE TO MEET YOU.
UHH... THAT'S MY CAT?

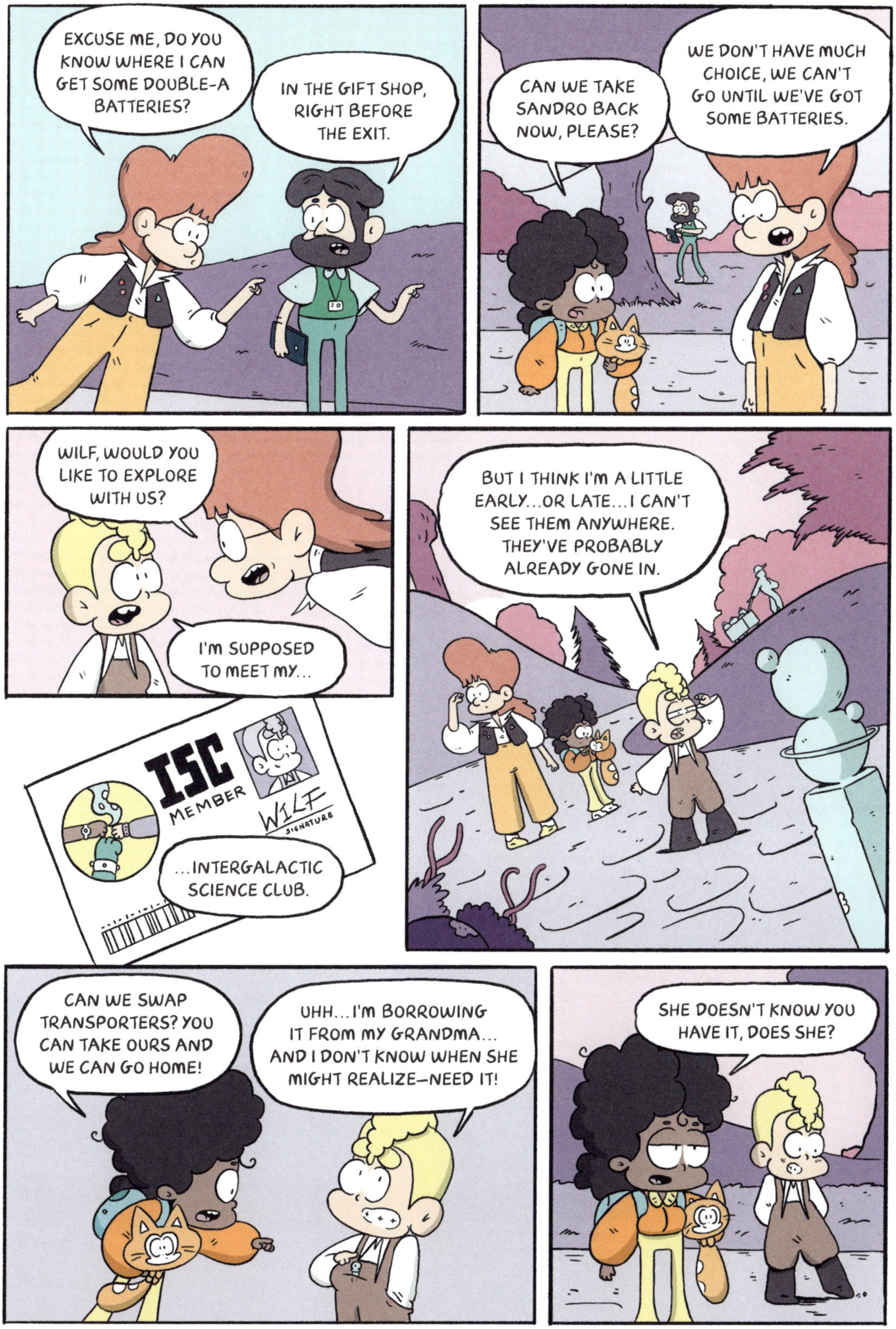
EXCUSE ME, DO YOU KNOW WHERE I CAN GET SOME DOUBLE-A BATTERIES?
IN THE GIFT SHOP, RIGHT BEFORE THE EXIT.
CAN WE TAKE SANDRO BACK NOW, PLEASE?
WE DON'T HAVE MUCH CHOICE, WE CAN'T GO UNTIL WE'VE GOT SOME BATTERIES.
WILF, WOULD YOU LIKE TO EXPLORE WITH US?
I'M SUPPOSED TO MEET MY...
ISC
MEMBER
WILF
SIGNATURE
...INTERGALACTIC SCIENCE CLUB.
BUT I THINK I'M A LITTLE EARLY...OR LATE...I CAN'T SEE THEM ANYWHERE. THEY'VE PROBABLY ALREADY GONE IN.
CAN WE SWAP TRANSPORTERS? YOU CAN TAKE OURS AND WE CAN GO HOME!
UHH...I'M BORROWING IT FROM MY GRANDMA... AND I DON'T KNOW WHEN SHE MIGHT REALIZE—NEED IT!
SHE DOESN'T KNOW YOU HAVE IT, DOES SHE?

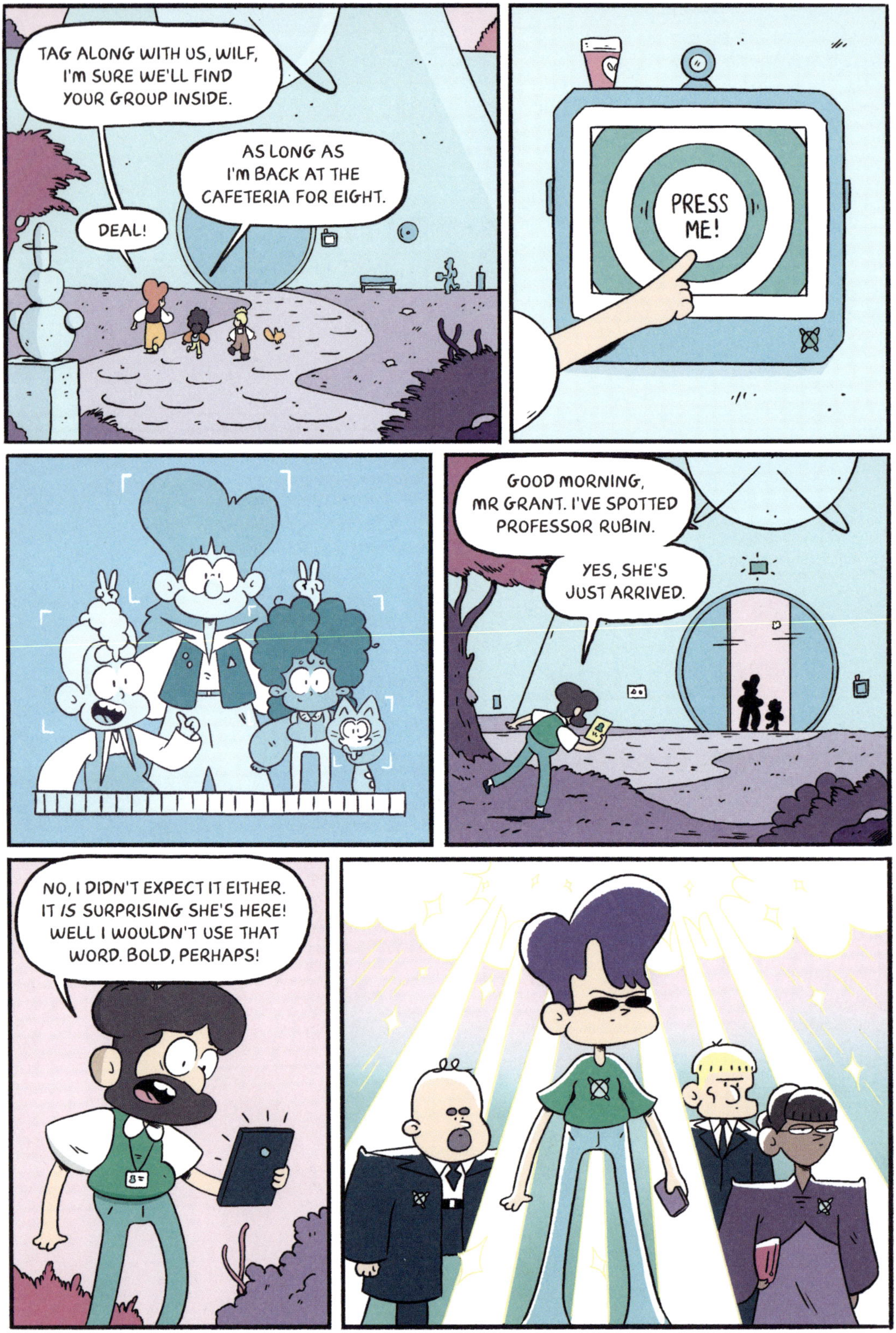
TAG ALONG WITH US, WILF, I'M SURE WE'LL FIND YOUR GROUP INSIDE.
AS LONG AS I'M BACK AT THE CAFETERIA FOR EIGHT.
DEAL!
PRESS ME!
GOOD MORNING, MR GRANT. I'VE SPOTTED PROFESSOR RUBIN.
YES, SHE'S JUST ARRIVED.
NO, I DIDN'T EXPECT IT EITHER. IT IS SURPRISING SHE'S HERE! WELL I WOULDN'T USE THAT WORD. BOLD, PERHAPS!

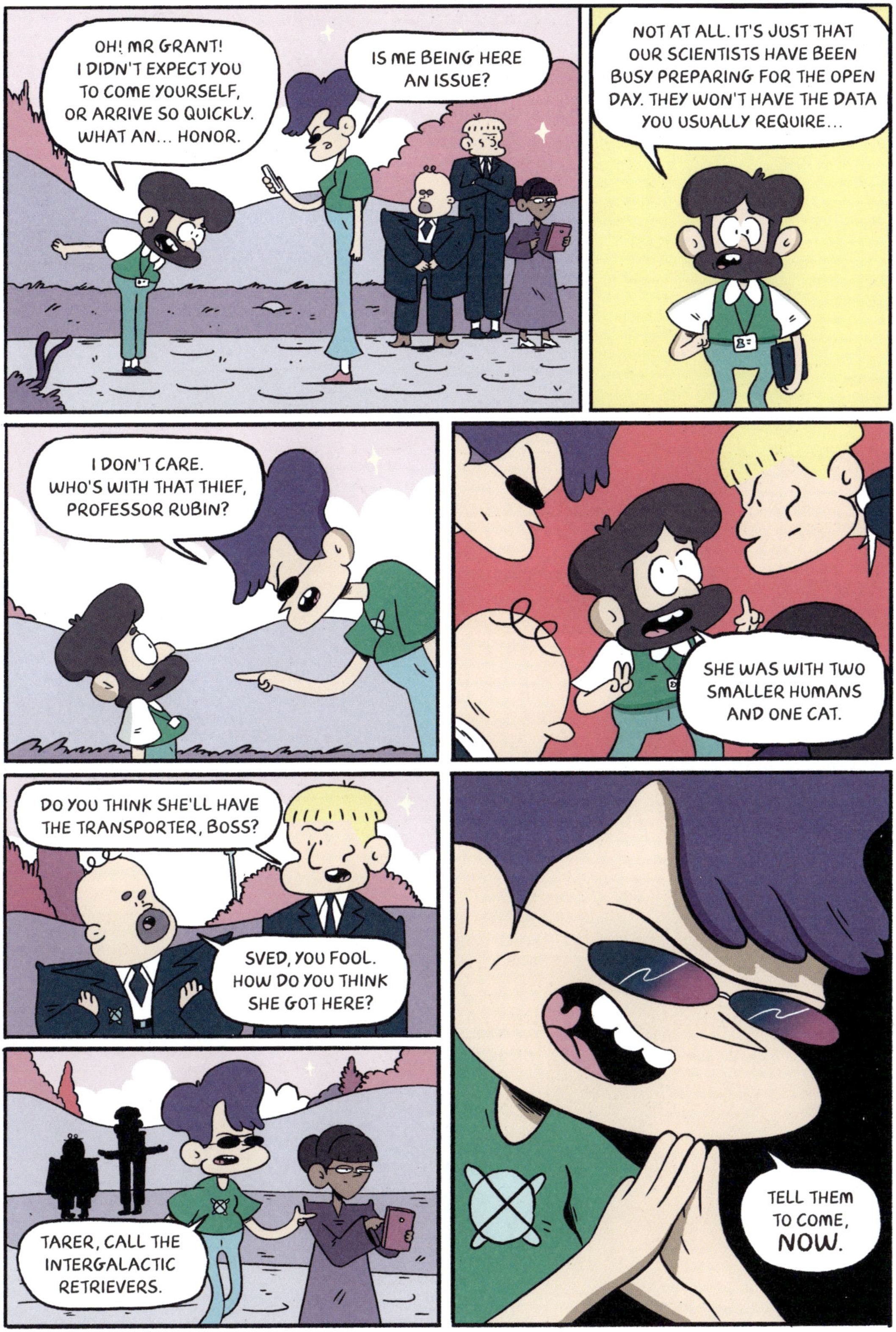
OH! MR GRANT! I DIDN'T EXPECT YOU TO COME YOURSELF, OR ARRIVE SO QUICKLY. WHAT AN... HONOR.
IS ME BEING HERE AN ISSUE?
NOT AT ALL. IT'S JUST THAT OUR SCIENTISTS HAVE BEEN BUSY PREPARING FOR THE OPEN DAY. THEY WON'T HAVE THE DATA YOU USUALLY REQUIRE...
I DON'T CARE. WHO'S WITH THAT THIEF, PROFESSOR RUBIN?
SHE WAS WITH TWO SMALLER HUMANS AND ONE CAT.
DO YOU THINK SHE'LL HAVE THE TRANSPORTER, BOSS?
SVED, YOU FOOL. HOW DO YOU THINK SHE GOT HERE?
TARER, CALL THE INTERGALACTIC RETRIEVERS.
TELL THEM TO COME, NOW.

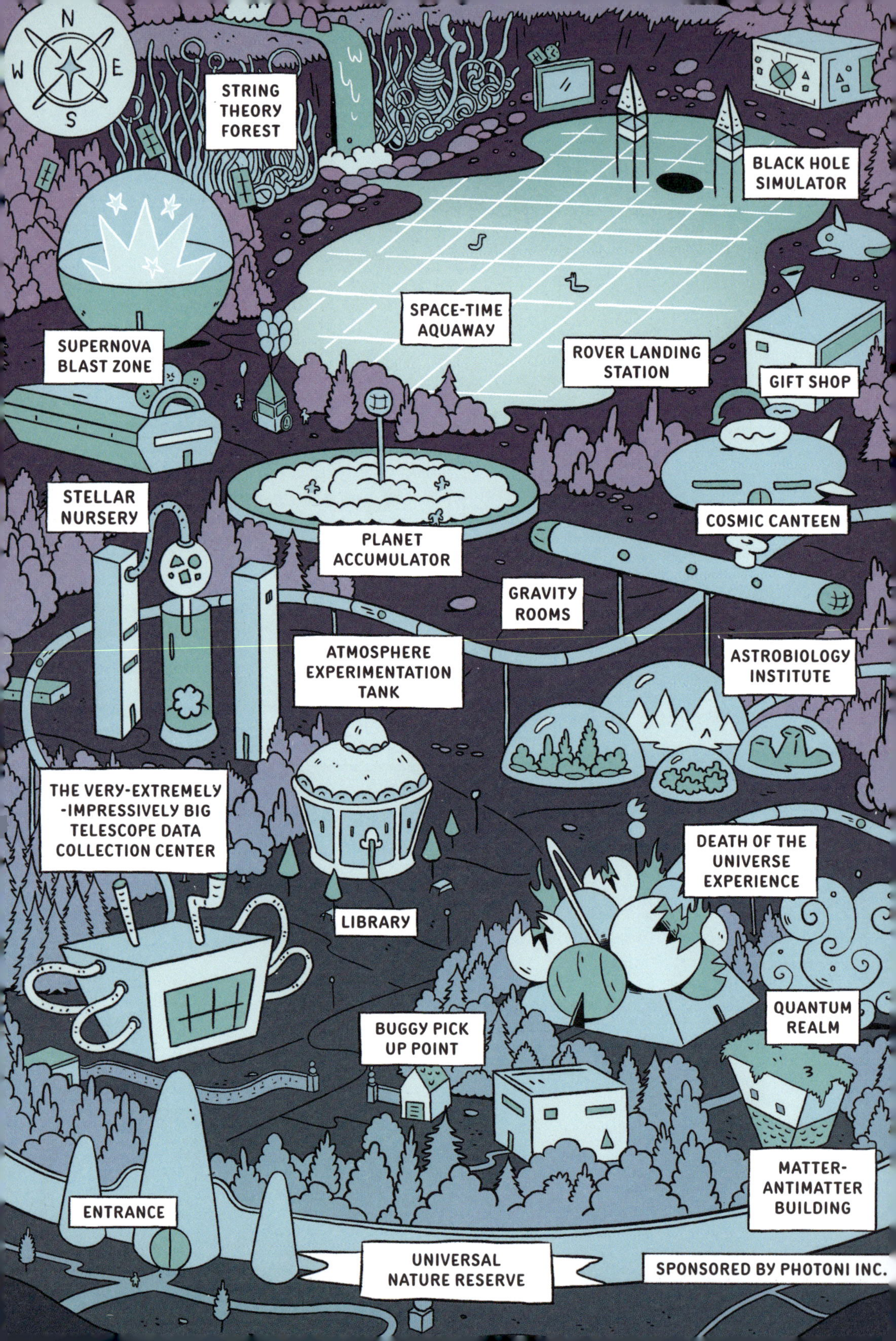
N
W
E
S
STRING THEORY FOREST
BLACK HOLE SIMULATOR
SUPERNOVA BLAST ZONE
SPACE-TIME AQUAWAY
ROVER LANDING STATION
GIFT SHOP
STELLAR NURSERY
PLANET ACCUMULATOR
COSMIC CANTEEN
GRAVITY ROOMS
ATMOSPHERE EXPERIMENTATION TANK
ASTROBIOLOGY INSTITUTE
THE VERY-EXTREMELY -IMPRESSIVELY BIG TELESCOPE DATA COLLECTION CENTER
DEATH OF THE UNIVERSE EXPERIENCE
LIBRARY
QUANTUM REALM
BUGGY PICK UP POINT
MATTER-ANTIMATTER BUILDING
ENTRANCE
UNIVERSAL NATURE RESERVE
SPONSORED BY PHOTONI INC.

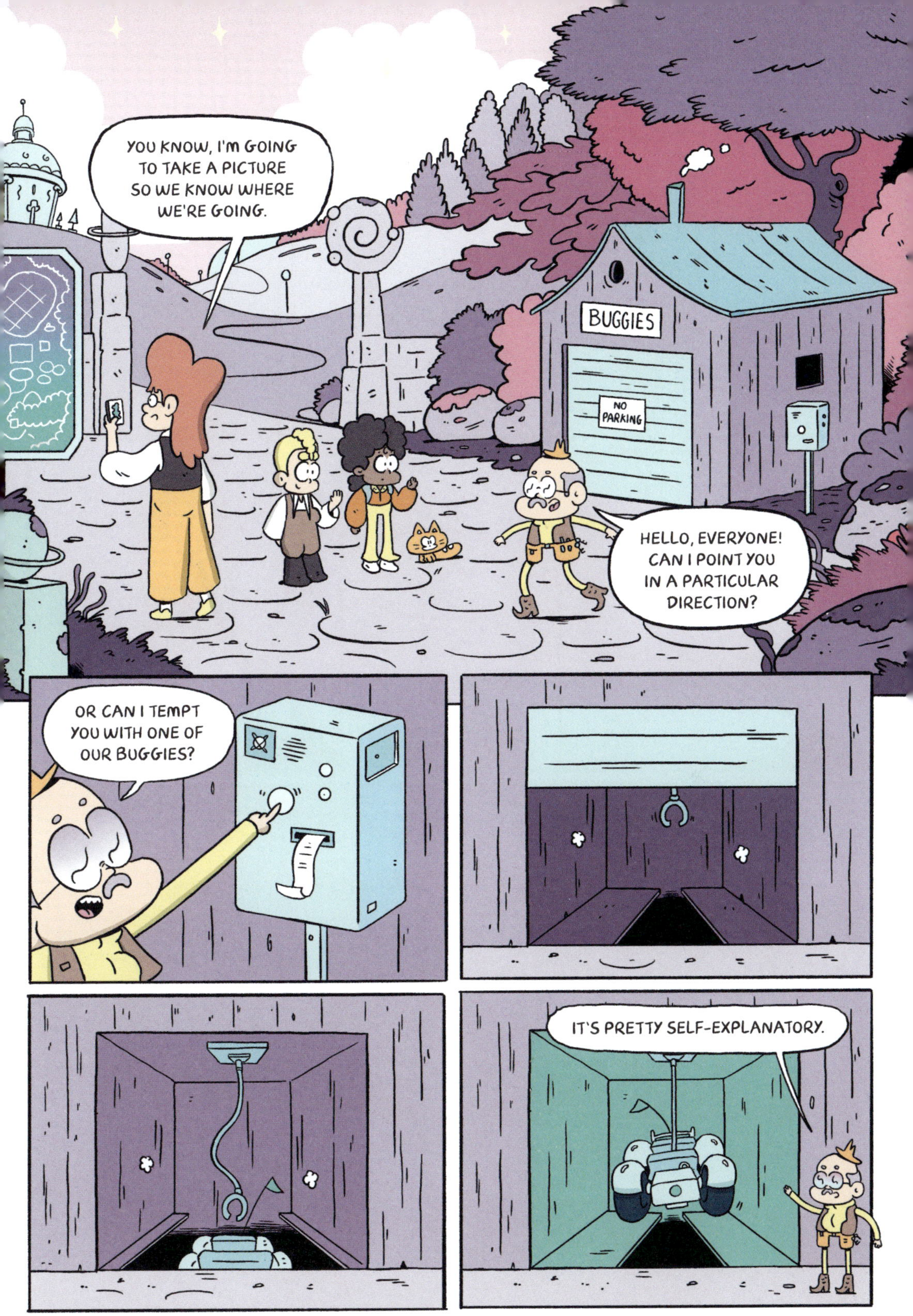
YOU KNOW, I'M GOING TO TAKE A PICTURE SO WE KNOW WHERE WE'RE GOING.
BUGGIES
NO PARKING
HELLO, EVERYONE! CAN I POINT YOU IN A PARTICULAR DIRECTION?
OR CAN I TEMPT YOU WITH ONE OF OUR BUGGIES?
IT'S PRETTY SELF-EXPLANATORY.

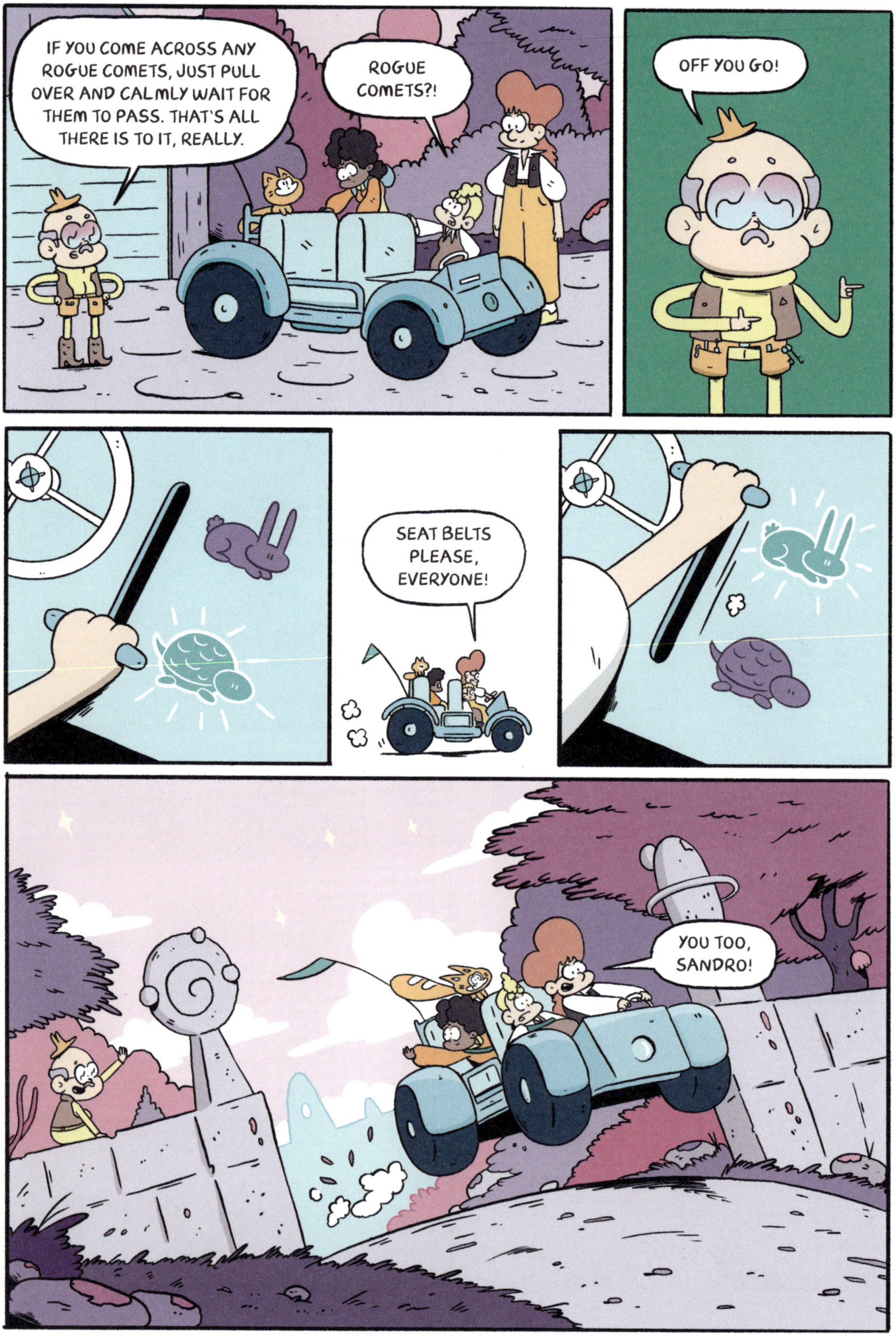
IF YOU COME ACROSS ANY ROGUE COMETS, JUST PULL OVER AND CALMLY WAIT FOR THEM TO PASS. THAT'S ALL THERE IS TO IT, REALLY.
ROGUE COMETS?!
OFF YOU GO!
SEAT BELTS PLEASE, EVERYONE!
YOU TOO, SANDRO!

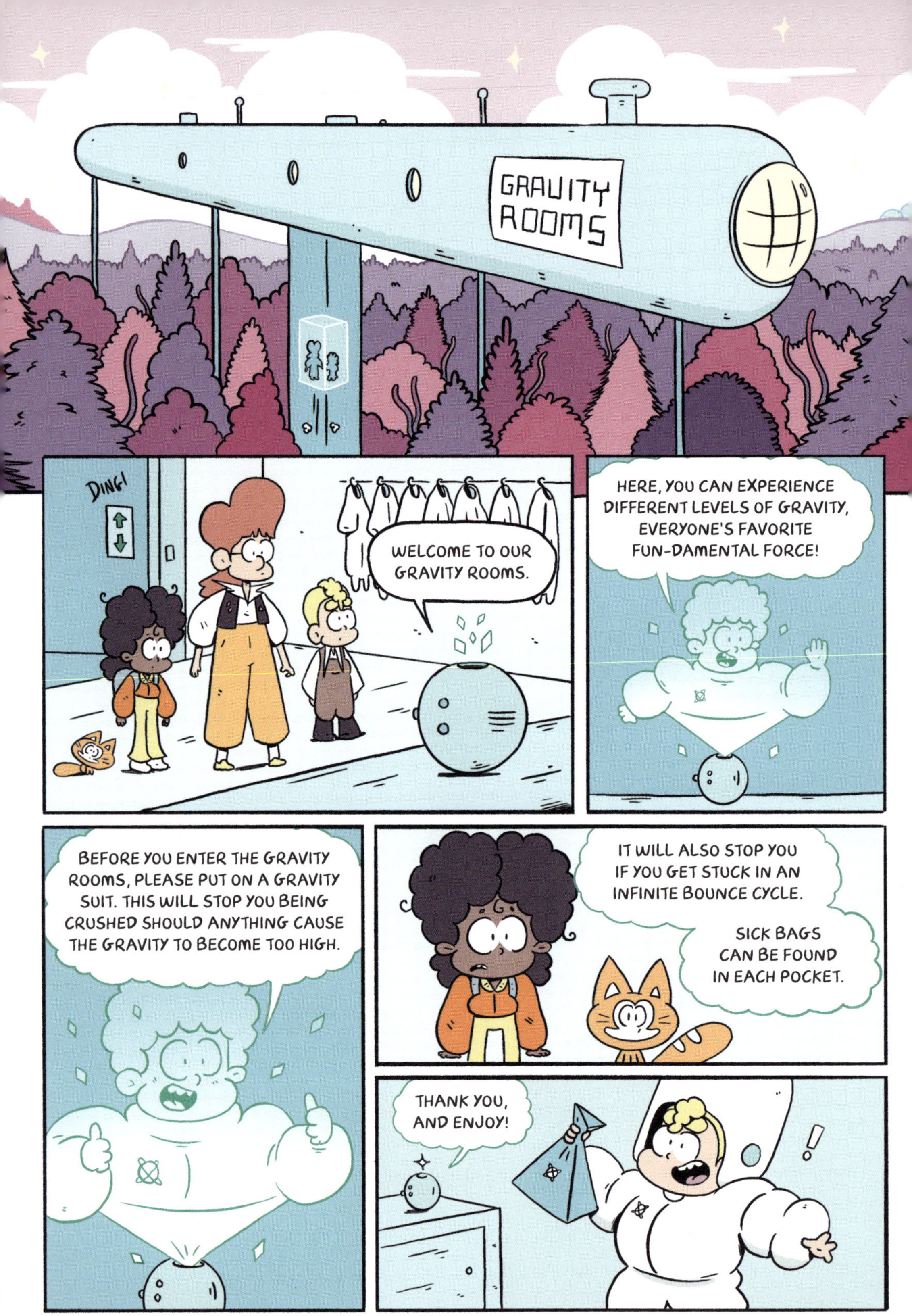
GRAVITY ROOMS
DING!
WELCOME TO OUR GRAVITY ROOMS.
HERE, YOU CAN EXPERIENCE DIFFERENT LEVELS OF GRAVITY, EVERYONE'S FAVORITE FUN-DAMENTAL FORCE!
BEFORE YOU ENTER THE GRAVITY ROOMS, PLEASE PUT ON A GRAVITY SUIT. THIS WILL STOP YOU BEING CRUSHED SHOULD ANYTHING CAUSE THE GRAVITY TO BECOME TOO HIGH.
IT WILL ALSO STOP YOU IF YOU GET STUCK IN AN INFINITE BOUNCE CYCLE.
SICK BAGS CAN BE FOUND IN EACH POCKET.
THANK YOU, AND ENJOY!
!

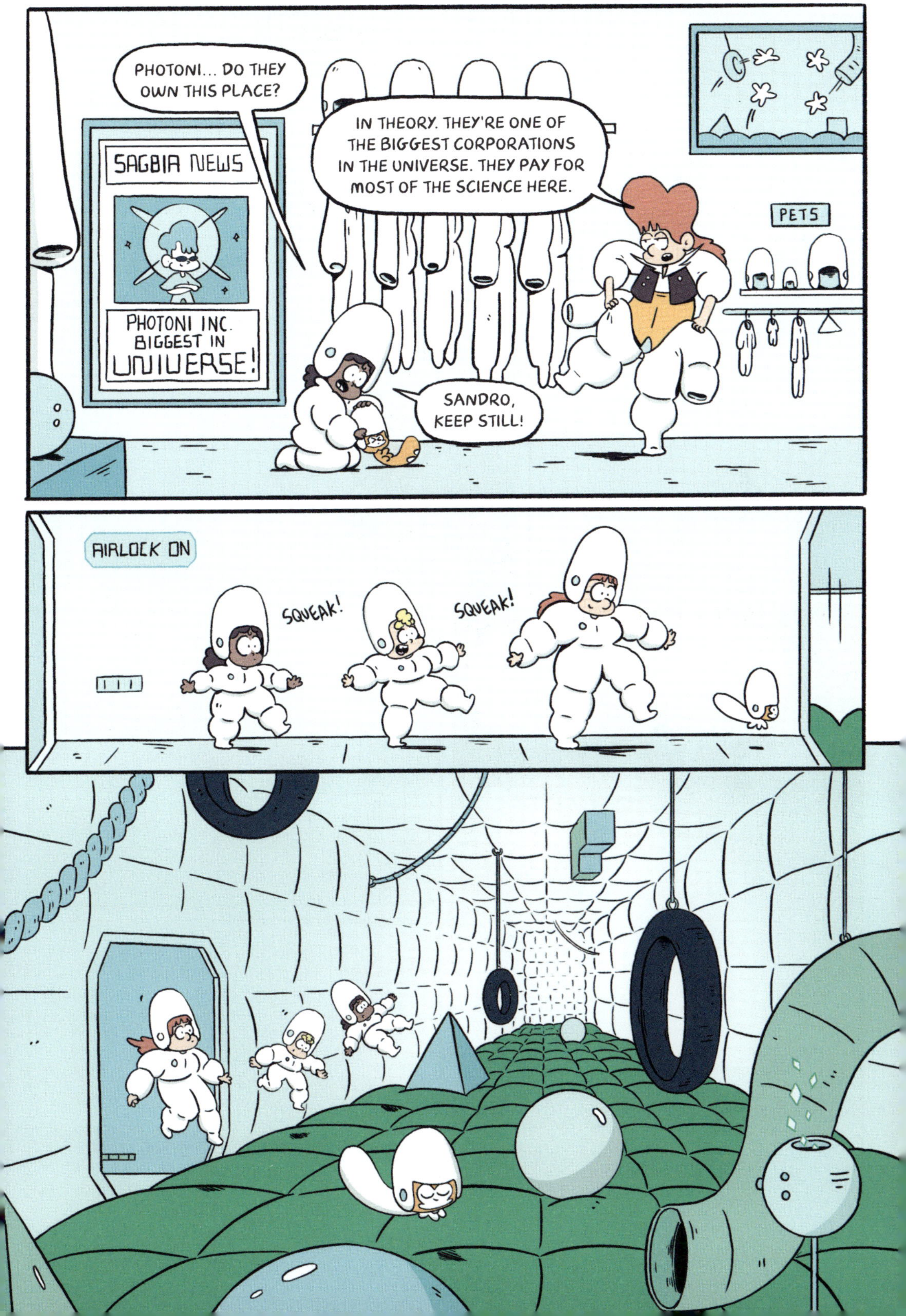
PHOTONI... DO THEY OWN THIS PLACE?
SAGBIA NEWS
PHOTONI INC. BIGGEST IN UNIVERSE!
IN THEORY. THEY'RE ONE OF THE BIGGEST CORPORATIONS IN THE UNIVERSE. THEY PAY FOR MOST OF THE SCIENCE HERE.
PETS
SANDRO, KEEP STILL!
AIRLOCK ON
SQUEAK!
SQUEAK!

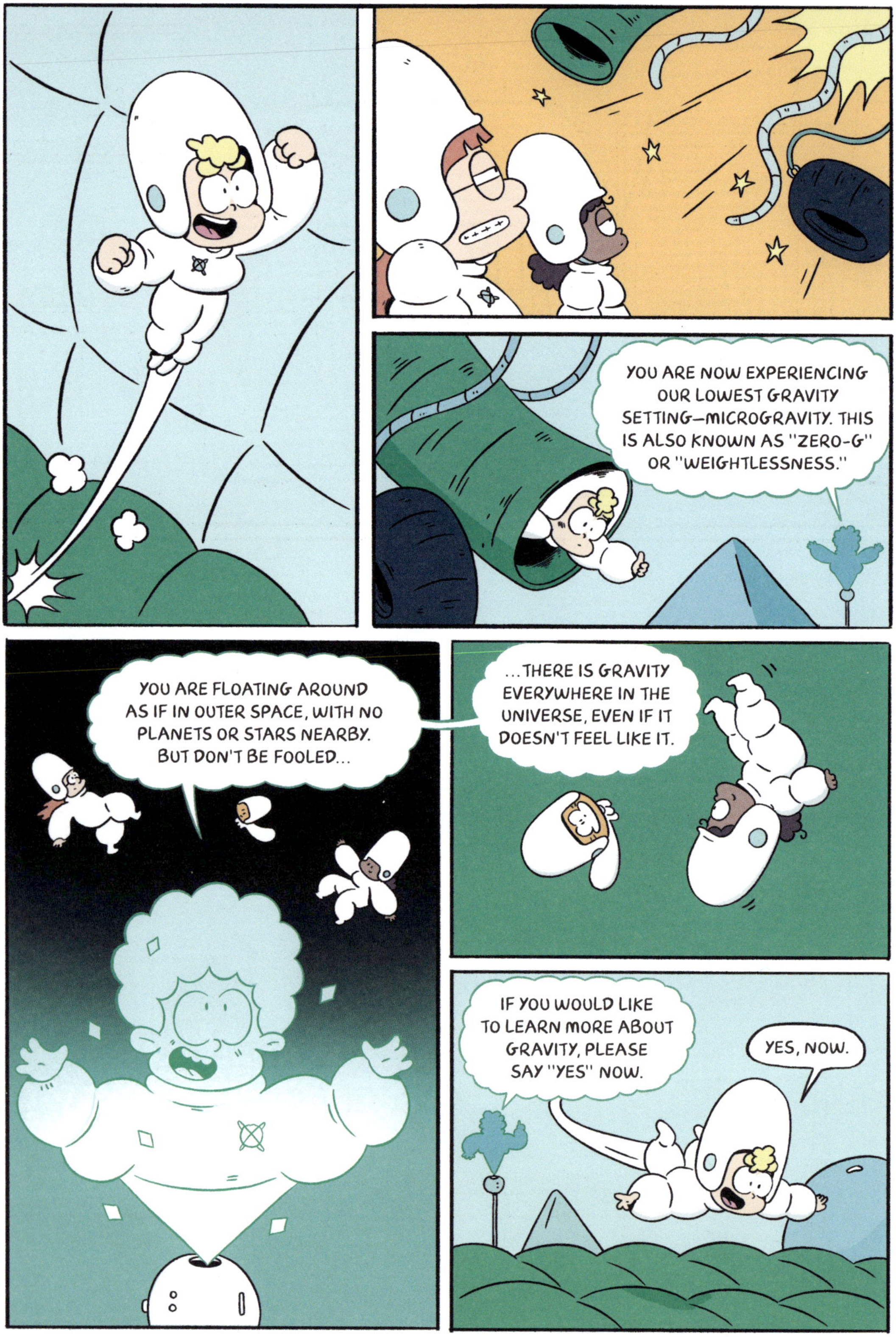
YOU ARE NOW EXPERIENCING OUR LOWEST GRAVITY SETTING—MICROGRAVITY. THIS IS ALSO KNOWN AS "ZERO-G" OR "WEIGHTLESSNESS."
YOU ARE FLOATING AROUND AS IF IN OUTER SPACE, WITH NO PLANETS OR STARS NEARBY. BUT DON'T BE FOOLED...
...THERE IS GRAVITY EVERYWHERE IN THE UNIVERSE, EVEN IF IT DOESN'T FEEL LIKE IT.
IF YOU WOULD LIKE TO LEARN MORE ABOUT GRAVITY, PLEASE SAY "YES" NOW.
YES, NOW.

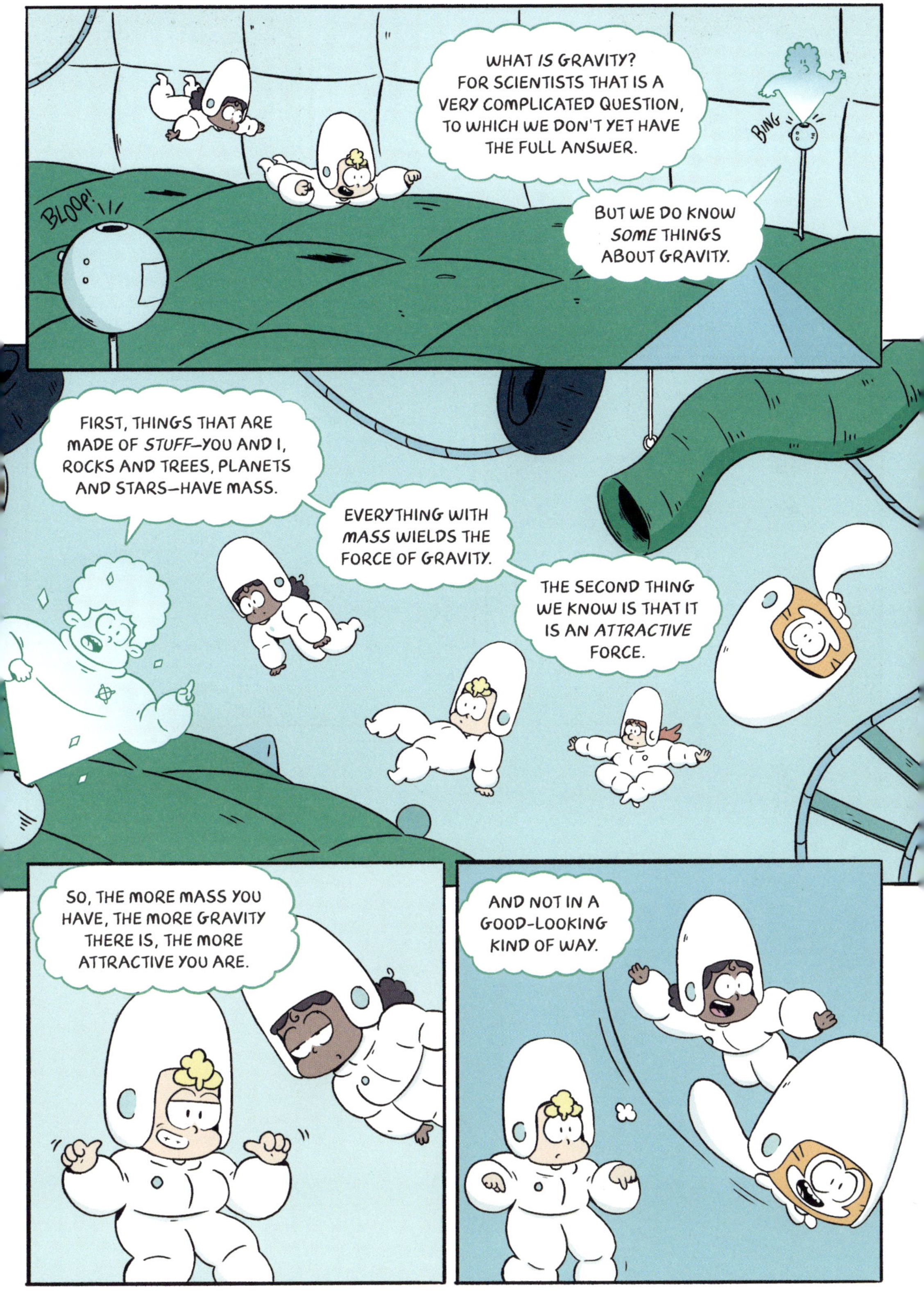
WHAT IS GRAVITY? FOR SCIENTISTS THAT IS A VERY COMPLICATED QUESTION, TO WHICH WE DON'T YET HAVE THE FULL ANSWER.
BUT WE DO KNOW SOME THINGS ABOUT GRAVITY.
BLOOP!
BING
FIRST, THINGS THAT ARE MADE OF STUFF—YOU AND I, ROCKS AND TREES, PLANETS AND STARS—HAVE MASS.
EVERYTHING WITH MASS WIELDS THE FORCE OF GRAVITY.
THE SECOND THING WE KNOW IS THAT IT IS AN ATTRACTIVE FORCE.
SO, THE MORE MASS YOU HAVE, THE MORE GRAVITY THERE IS, THE MORE ATTRACTIVE YOU ARE.
AND NOT IN A GOOD-LOOKING KIND OF WAY.

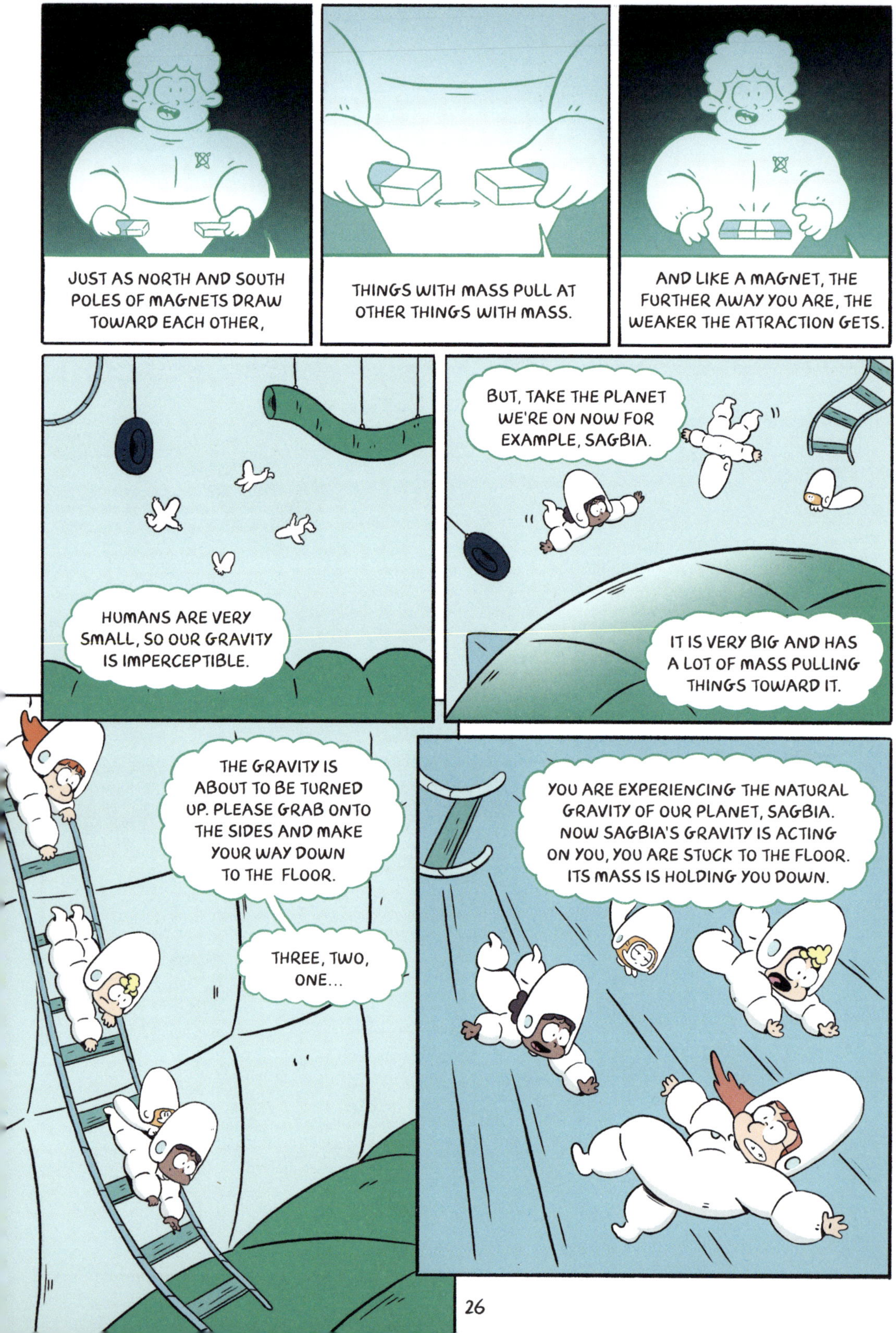

JUST AS NORTH AND SOUTH POLES OF MAGNETS DRAW TOWARD EACH OTHER,
THINGS WITH MASS PULL AT OTHER THINGS WITH MASS.
AND LIKE A MAGNET, THE FURTHER AWAY YOU ARE, THE WEAKER THE ATTRACTION GETS.
HUMANS ARE VERY SMALL, SO OUR GRAVITY IS IMPERCEPTIBLE.
BUT, TAKE THE PLANET WE'RE ON NOW FOR EXAMPLE, SAGBIA.
IT IS VERY BIG AND HAS A LOT OF MASS PULLING THINGS TOWARD IT.
THE GRAVITY IS ABOUT TO BE TURNED UP. PLEASE GRAB ONTO THE SIDES AND MAKE YOUR WAY DOWN TO THE FLOOR.
THREE, TWO, ONE...
YOU ARE EXPERIENCING THE NATURAL GRAVITY OF OUR PLANET, SAGBIA. NOW SAGBIA'S GRAVITY IS ACTING ON YOU, YOU ARE STUCK TO THE FLOOR. ITS MASS IS HOLDING YOU DOWN.

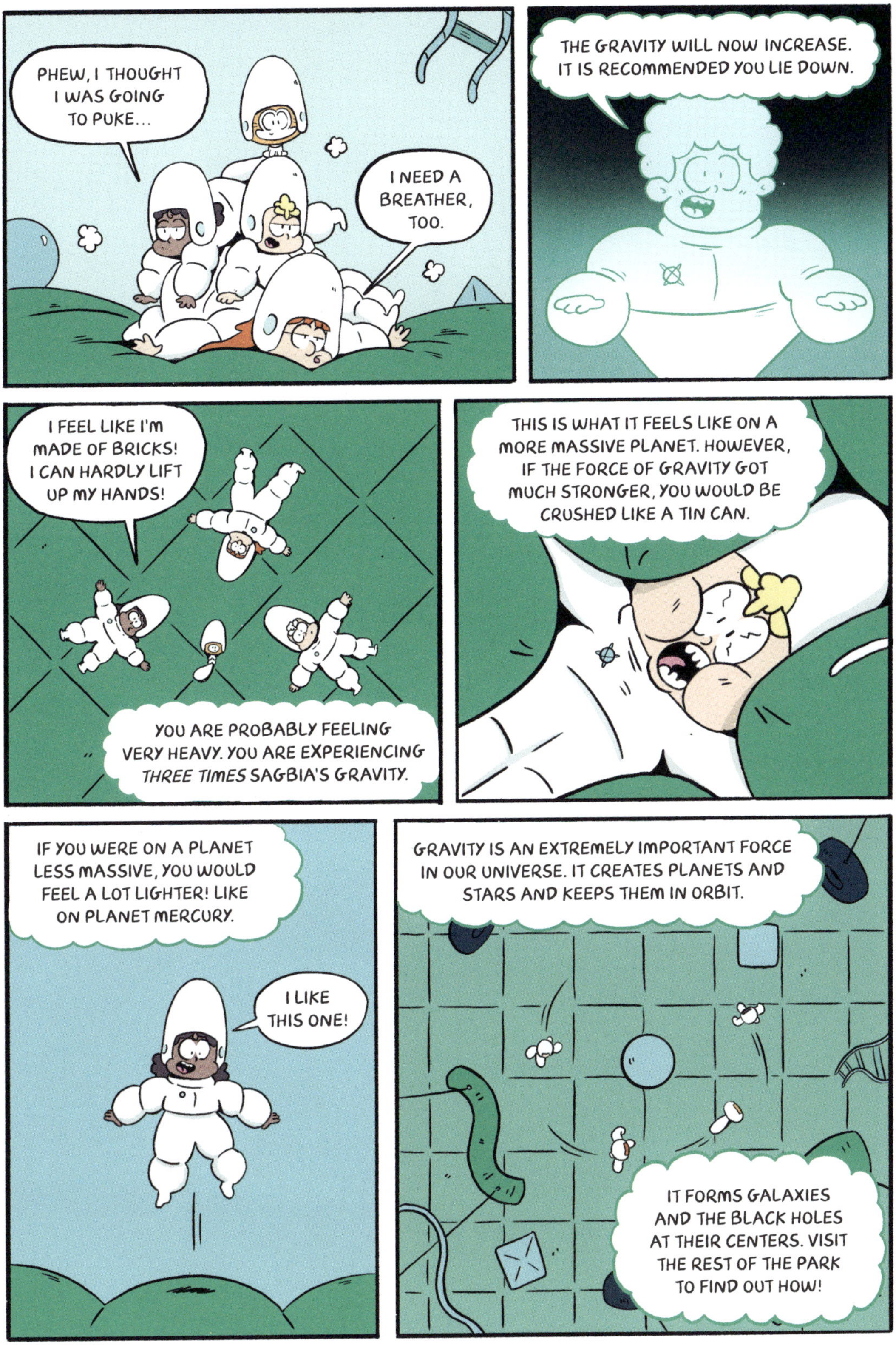
PHEW, I THOUGHT I WAS GOING TO PUKE...
I NEED A BREATHER, TOO.
THE GRAVITY WILL NOW INCREASE. IT IS RECOMMENDED YOU LIE DOWN.
I FEEL LIKE I'M MADE OF BRICKS! I CAN HARDLY LIFT UP MY HANDS!
YOU ARE PROBABLY FEELING VERY HEAVY. YOU ARE EXPERIENCING *THREE TIMES* SAGBIA'S GRAVITY.
THIS IS WHAT IT FEELS LIKE ON A MORE MASSIVE PLANET. HOWEVER, IF THE FORCE OF GRAVITY GOT MUCH STRONGER, YOU WOULD BE CRUSHED LIKE A TIN CAN.
IF YOU WERE ON A PLANET LESS MASSIVE, YOU WOULD FEEL A LOT LIGHTER! LIKE ON PLANET MERCURY.
I LIKE THIS ONE!
GRAVITY IS AN EXTREMELY IMPORTANT FORCE IN OUR UNIVERSE. IT CREATES PLANETS AND STARS AND KEEPS THEM IN ORBIT.
IT FORMS GALAXIES AND THE BLACK HOLES AT THEIR CENTERS. VISIT THE REST OF THE PARK TO FIND OUT HOW!

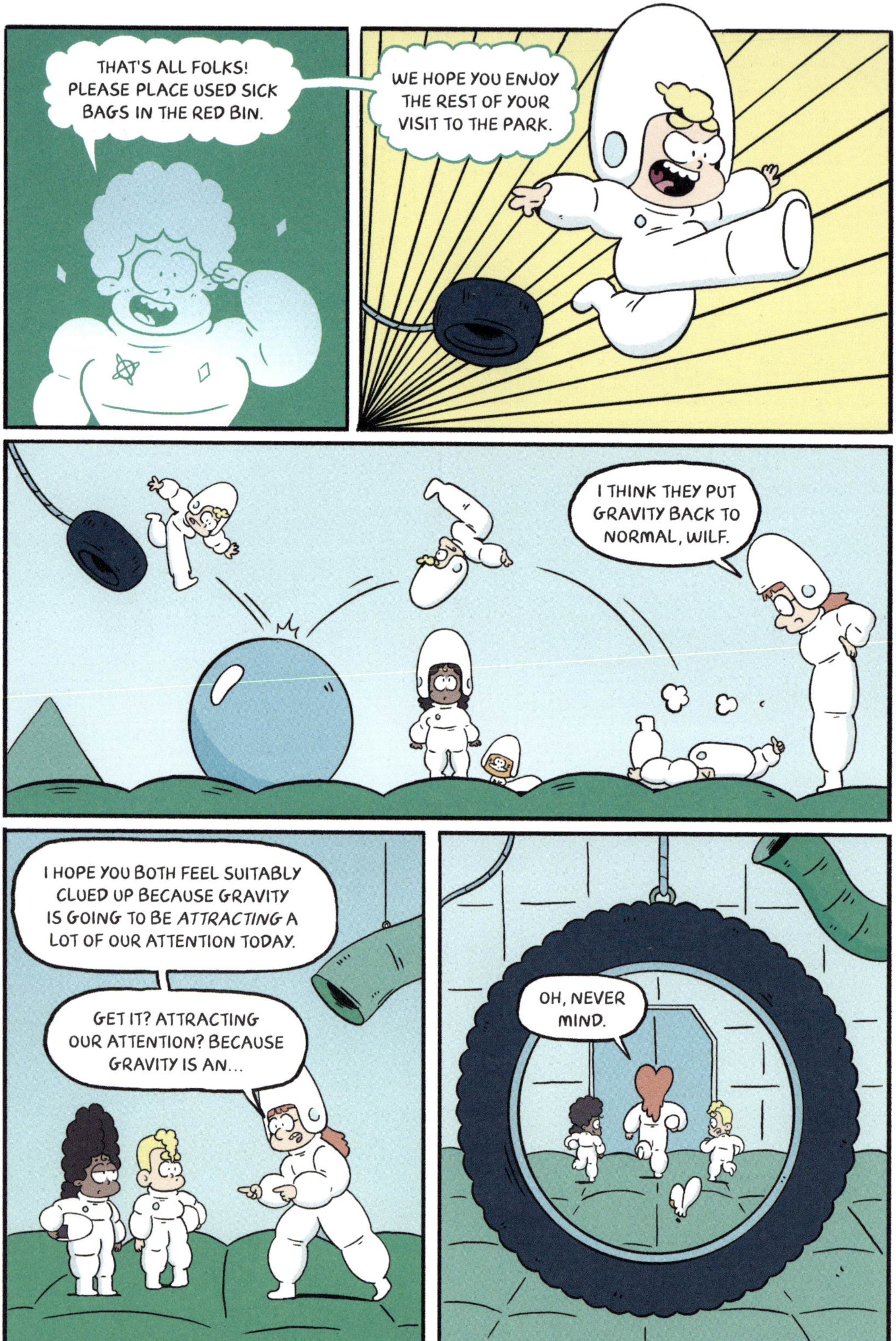
THAT'S ALL FOLKS! PLEASE PLACE USED SICK BAGS IN THE RED BIN.
WE HOPE YOU ENJOY THE REST OF YOUR VISIT TO THE PARK.
I THINK THEY PUT GRAVITY BACK TO NORMAL, WILF.
I HOPE YOU BOTH FEEL SUITABLY CLUED UP BECAUSE GRAVITY IS GOING TO BE *ATTRACTING* A LOT OF OUR ATTENTION TODAY.
GET IT? ATTRACTING OUR ATTENTION? BECAUSE GRAVITY IS AN...
OH, NEVER MIND.

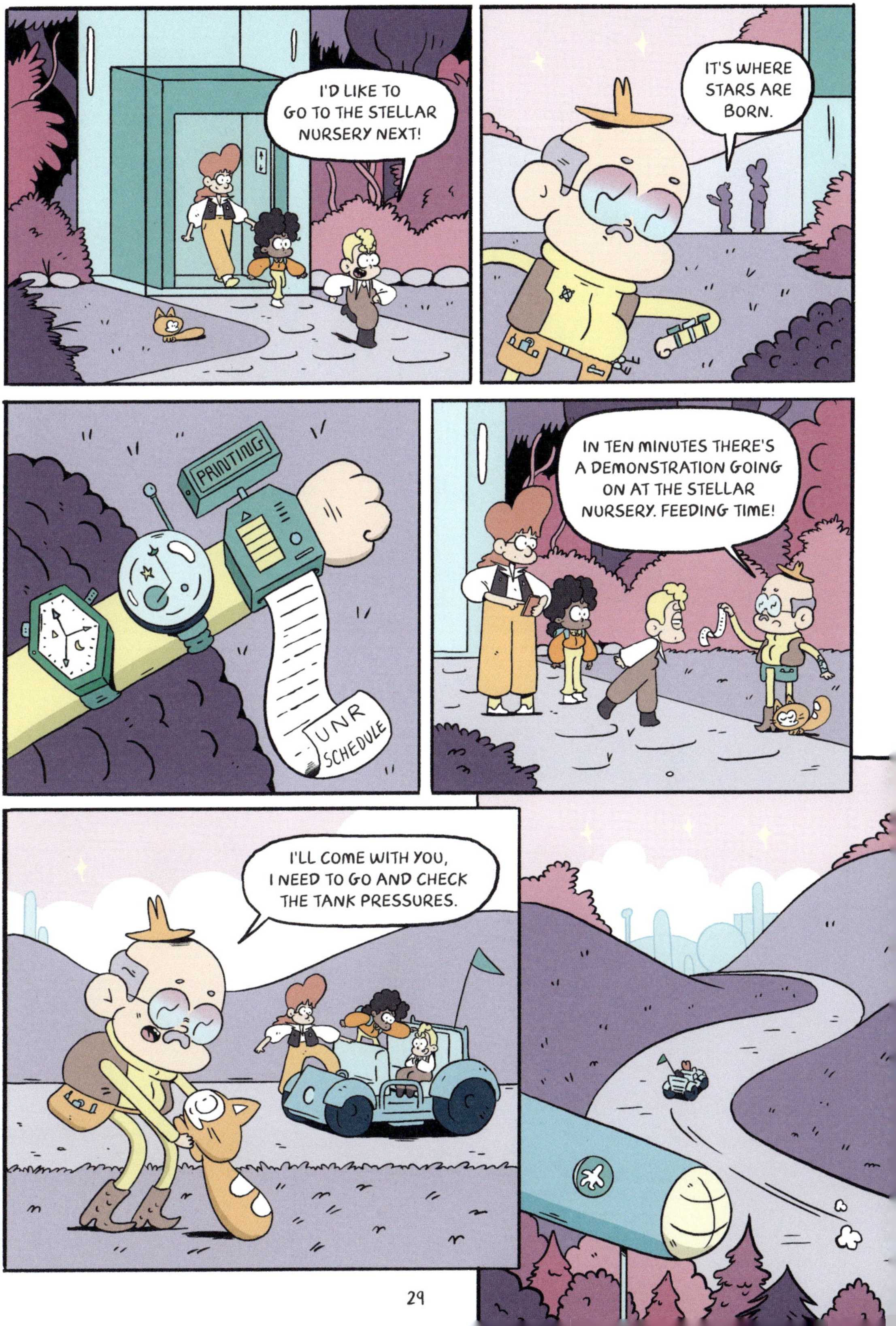
I'D LIKE TO GO TO THE STELLAR NURSERY NEXT!
IT'S WHERE STARS ARE BORN.
PRINTING
UNR SCHEDULE
IN TEN MINUTES THERE'S A DEMONSTRATION GOING ON AT THE STELLAR NURSERY. FEEDING TIME!
I'LL COME WITH YOU, I NEED TO GO AND CHECK THE TANK PRESSURES.

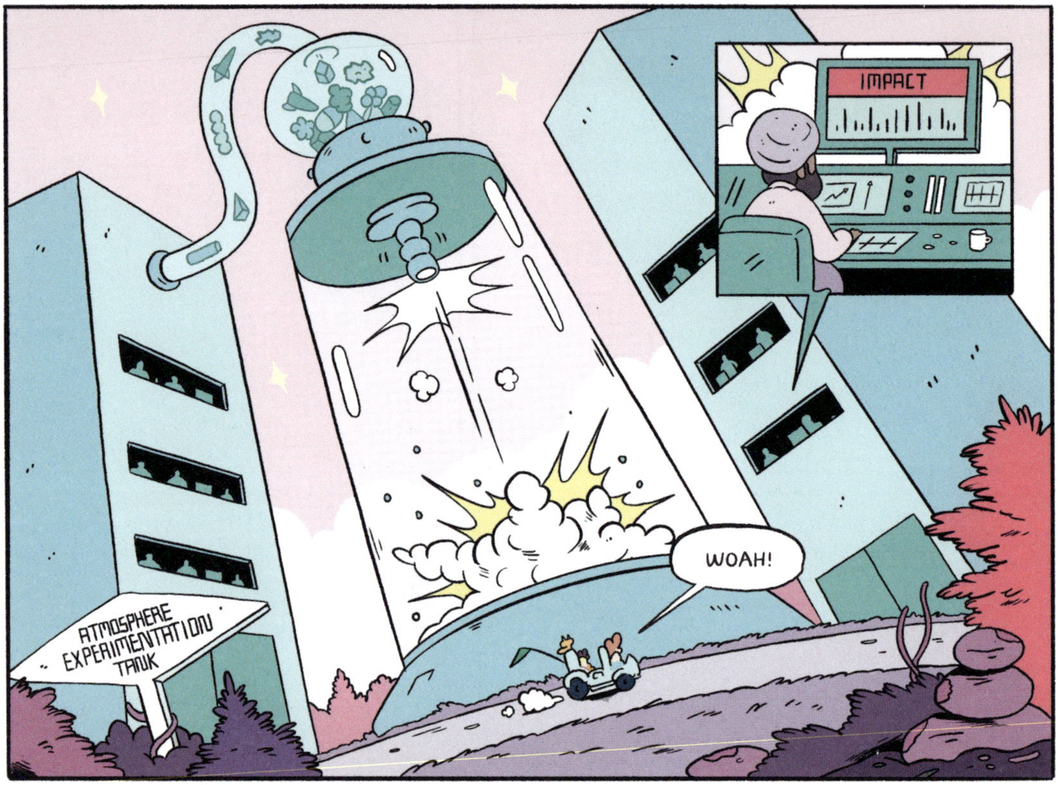
IMPACT
WOAH!
ATMOSPHERE EXPERIMENTATION TANK

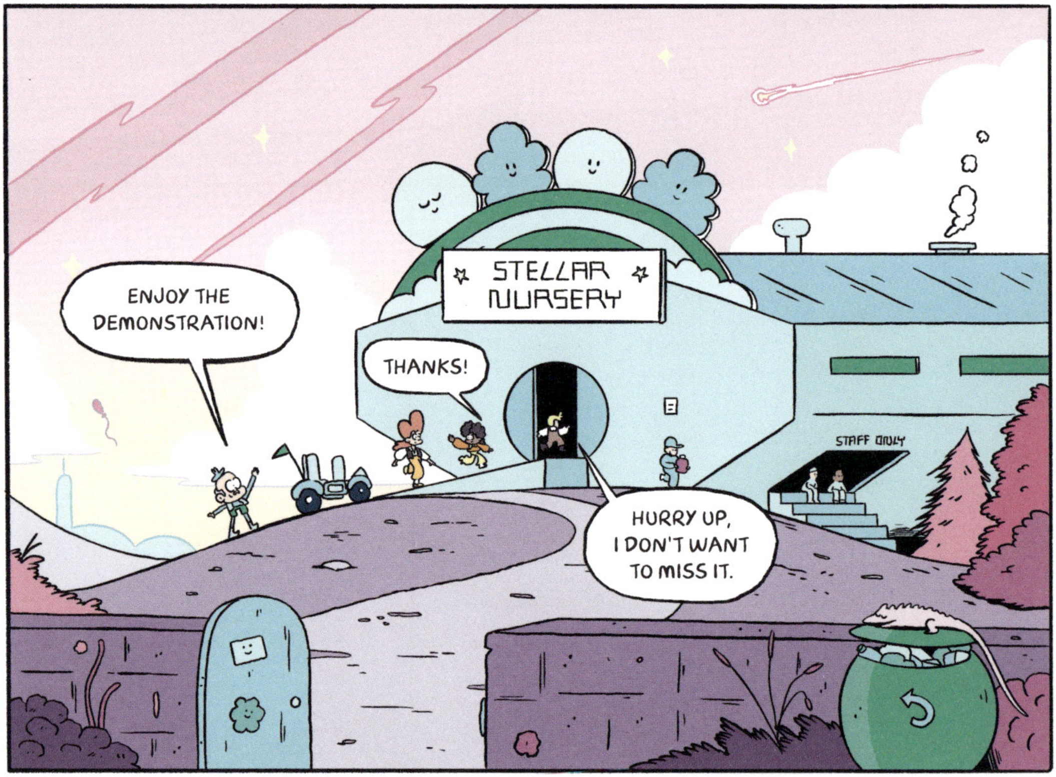
STELLAR NURSERY
ENJOY THE DEMONSTRATION!
THANKS!
HURRY UP, I DON'T WANT TO MISS IT.
STAFF ONLY

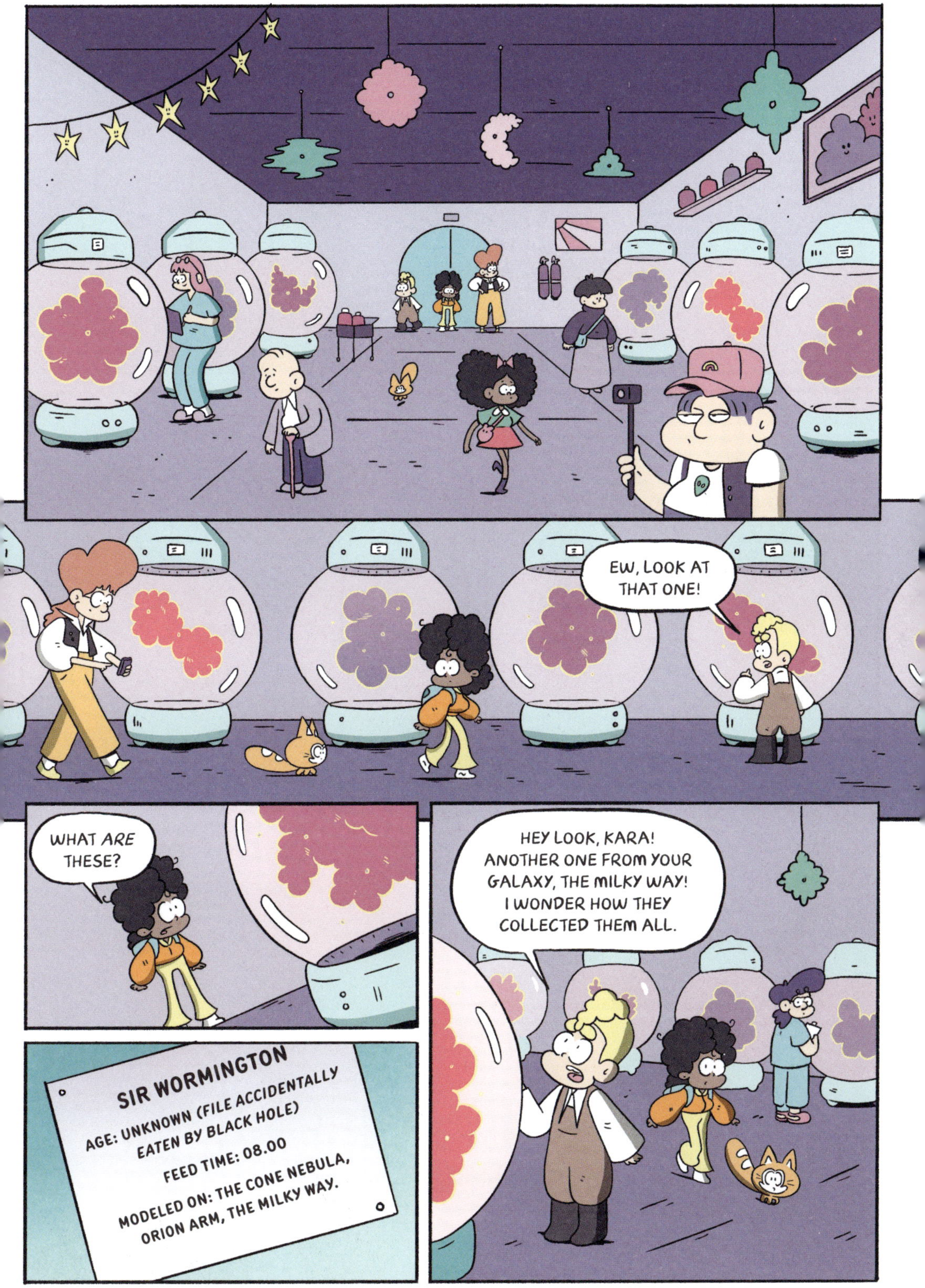
EW, LOOK AT THAT ONE!
WHAT ARE THESE?
HEY LOOK, KARA! ANOTHER ONE FROM YOUR GALAXY, THE MILKY WAY! I WONDER HOW THEY COLLECTED THEM ALL.
SIR WORMINGTON
AGE: UNKNOWN (FILE ACCIDENTALLY EATEN BY BLACK HOLE)
FEED TIME: 08.00
MODELED ON: THE CONE NEBULA, ORION ARM, THE MILKY WAY.

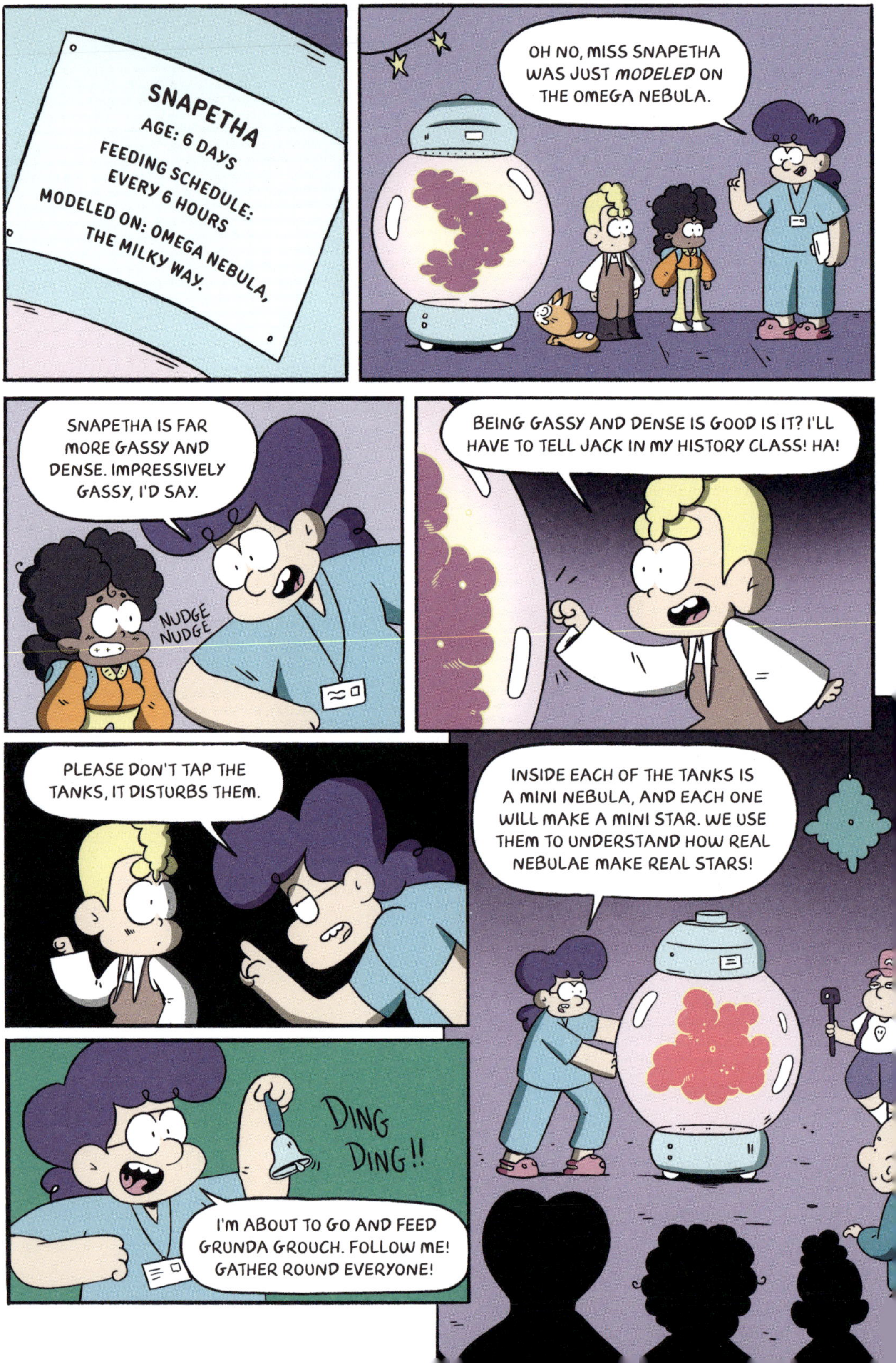
SNAPETHA
AGE: 6 DAYS
FEEDING SCHEDULE: EVERY 6 HOURS
MODELED ON: OMEGA NEBULA, THE MILKY WAY.
OH NO, MISS SNAPETHA WAS JUST *MODELED* ON THE OMEGA NEBULA.
SNAPETHA IS FAR MORE GASSY AND DENSE. IMPRESSIVELY GASSY, I'D SAY.
NUDGE NUDGE
BEING GASSY AND DENSE IS GOOD IS IT? I'LL HAVE TO TELL JACK IN MY HISTORY CLASS! HA!
PLEASE DON'T TAP THE TANKS, IT DISTURBS THEM.
DING DING!!
I'M ABOUT TO GO AND FEED GRUNDA GROUCH. FOLLOW ME! GATHER ROUND EVERYONE!
INSIDE EACH OF THE TANKS IS A MINI NEBULA, AND EACH ONE WILL MAKE A MINI STAR. WE USE THEM TO UNDERSTAND HOW REAL NEBULAE MAKE REAL STARS!

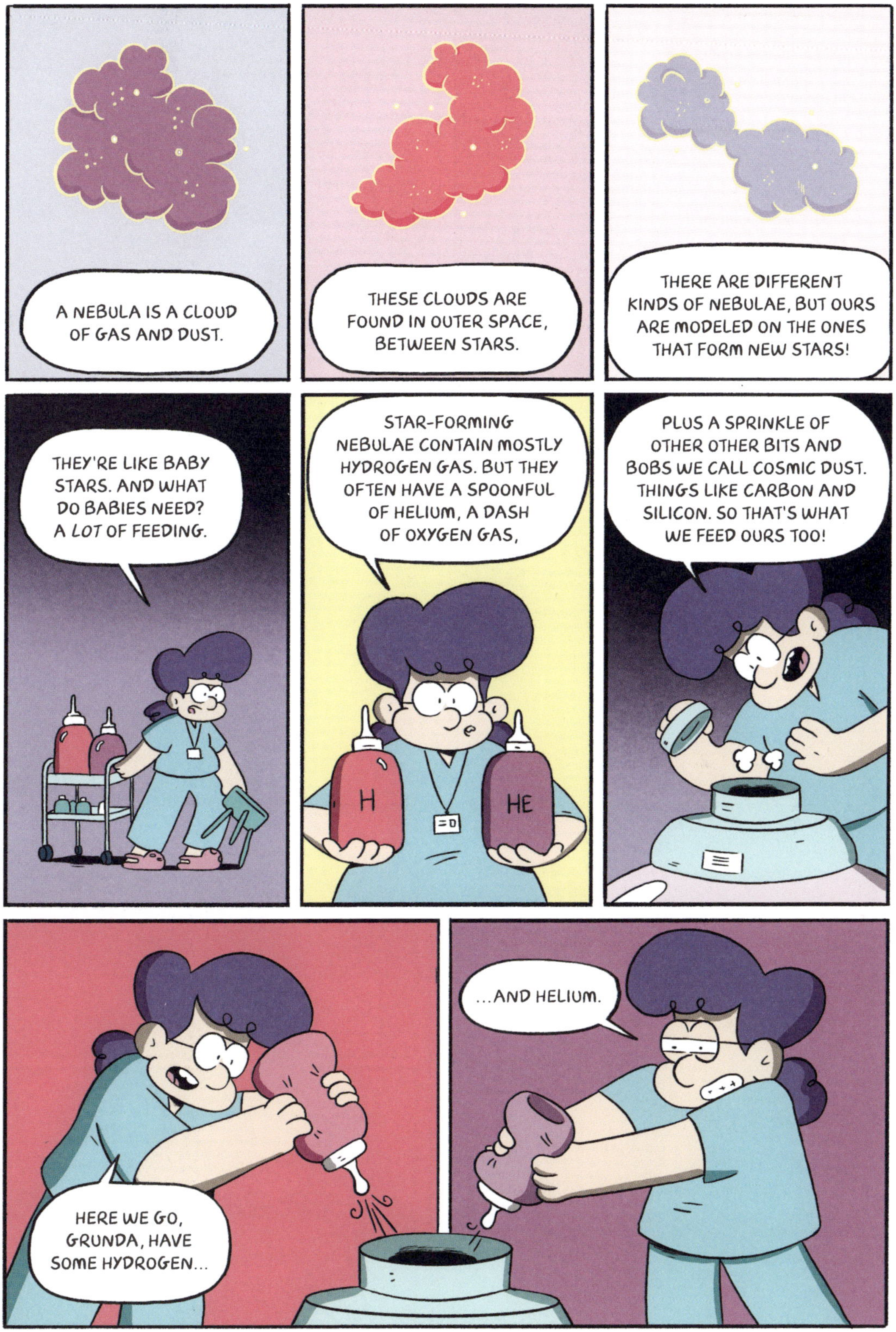
A NEBULA IS A CLOUD OF GAS AND DUST.
THESE CLOUDS ARE FOUND IN OUTER SPACE, BETWEEN STARS.
THERE ARE DIFFERENT KINDS OF NEBULAE, BUT OURS ARE MODELED ON THE ONES THAT FORM NEW STARS!
THEY'RE LIKE BABY STARS. AND WHAT DO BABIES NEED? A *LOT* OF FEEDING.
STAR-FORMING NEBULAE CONTAIN MOSTLY HYDROGEN GAS. BUT THEY OFTEN HAVE A SPOONFUL OF HELIUM, A DASH OF OXYGEN GAS,
H
HE
PLUS A SPRINKLE OF OTHER OTHER BITS AND BOBS WE CALL COSMIC DUST. THINGS LIKE CARBON AND SILICON. SO THAT'S WHAT WE FEED OURS TOO!
HERE WE GO, GRUNDA, HAVE SOME HYDROGEN...
...AND HELIUM.

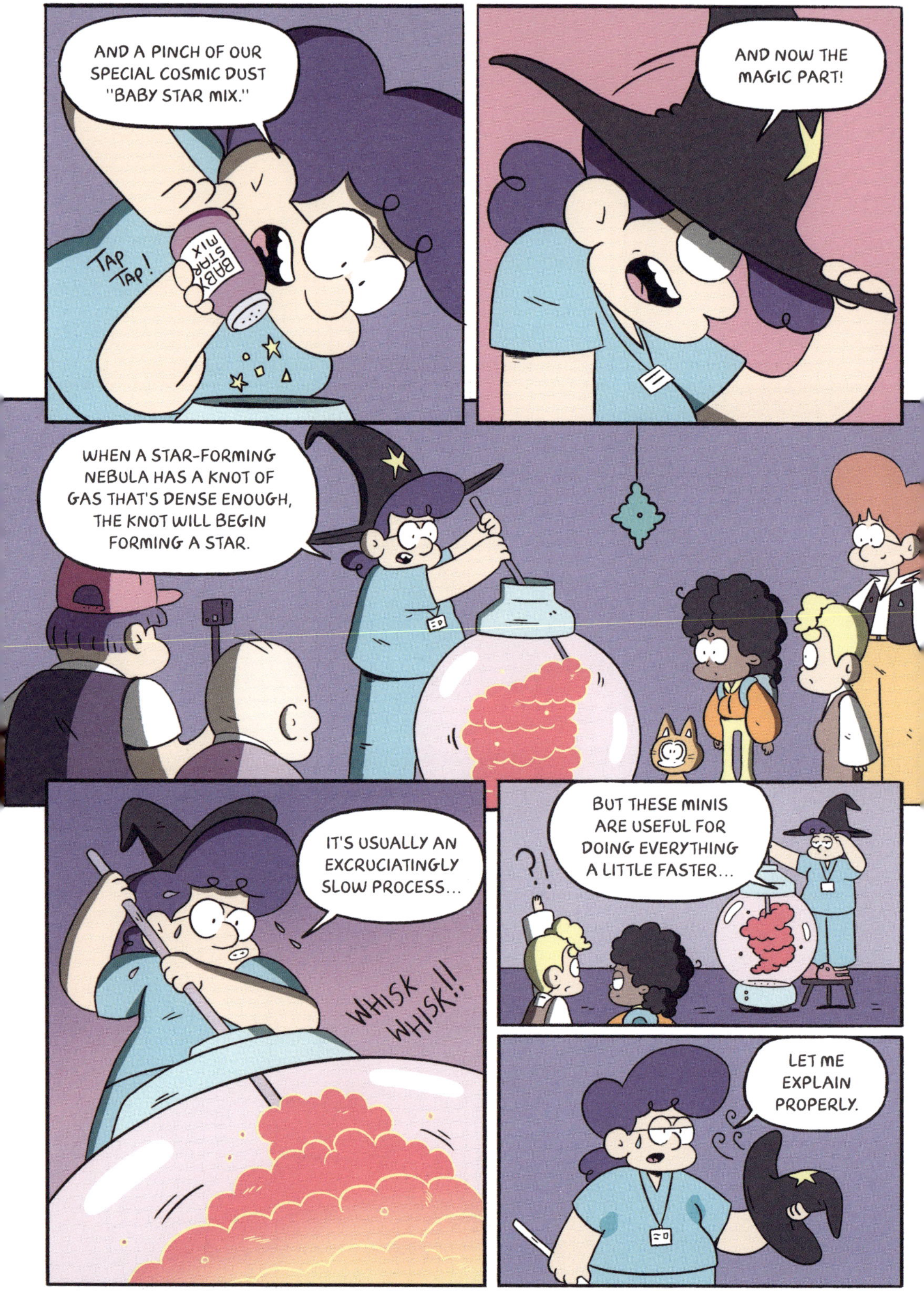
AND A PINCH OF OUR SPECIAL COSMIC DUST "BABY STAR MIX."
TAP TAP!
BABY STAR MIX
AND NOW THE MAGIC PART!
WHEN A STAR-FORMING NEBULA HAS A KNOT OF GAS THAT'S DENSE ENOUGH, THE KNOT WILL BEGIN FORMING A STAR.
IT'S USUALLY AN EXCRUCIATINGLY SLOW PROCESS...
WHISK WHISK!!
?!
BUT THESE MINIS ARE USEFUL FOR DOING EVERYTHING A LITTLE FASTER...
LET ME EXPLAIN PROPERLY.

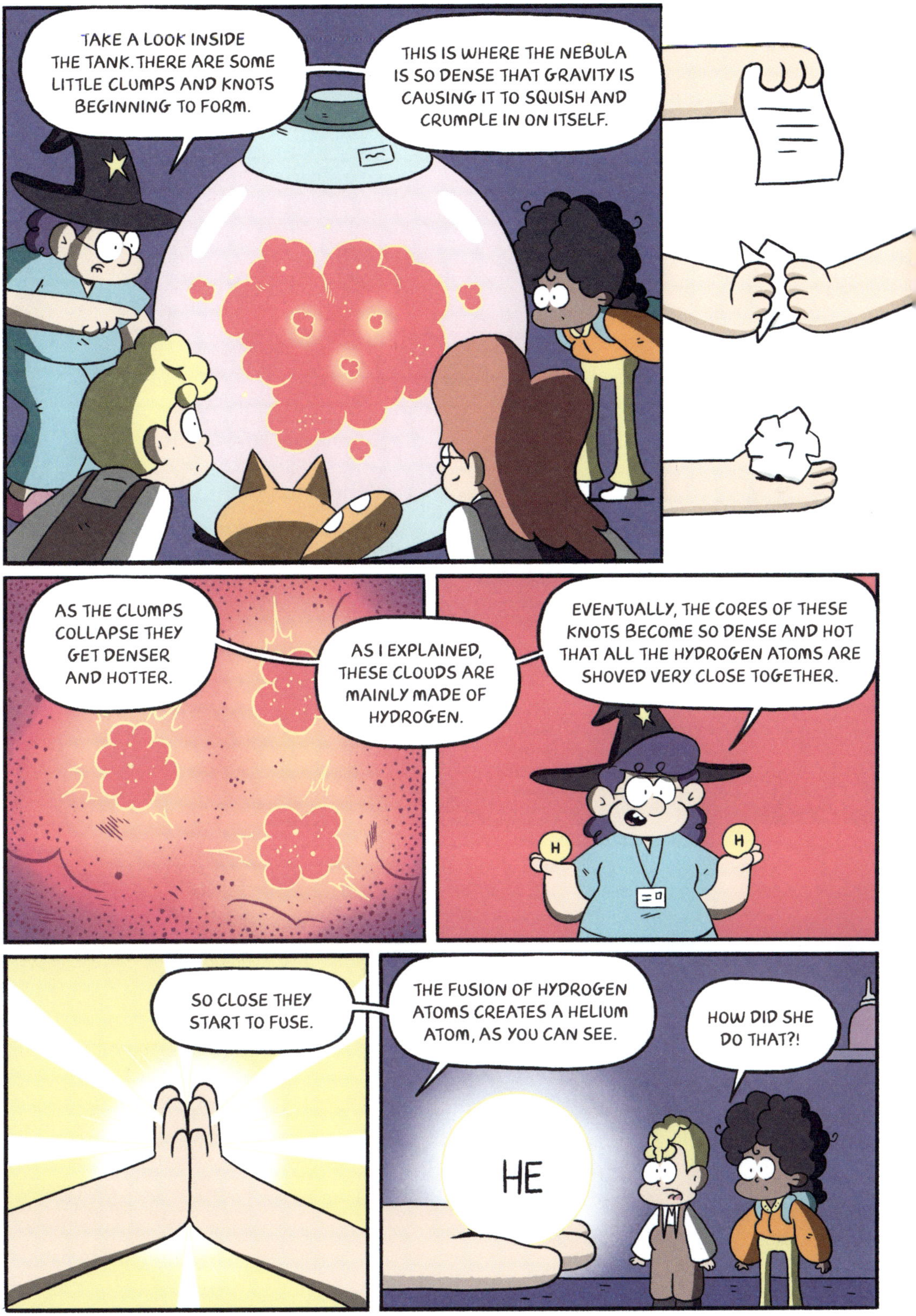
TAKE A LOOK INSIDE THE TANK. THERE ARE SOME LITTLE CLUMPS AND KNOTS BEGINNING TO FORM.
THIS IS WHERE THE NEBULA IS SO DENSE THAT GRAVITY IS CAUSING IT TO SQUISH AND CRUMPLE IN ON ITSELF.
AS THE CLUMPS COLLAPSE THEY GET DENSER AND HOTTER.
AS I EXPLAINED, THESE CLOUDS ARE MAINLY MADE OF HYDROGEN.
EVENTUALLY, THE CORES OF THESE KNOTS BECOME SO DENSE AND HOT THAT ALL THE HYDROGEN ATOMS ARE SHOVED VERY CLOSE TOGETHER.
H
H
SO CLOSE THEY START TO FUSE.
THE FUSION OF HYDROGEN ATOMS CREATES A HELIUM ATOM, AS YOU CAN SEE.
HOW DID SHE DO THAT?!
HE

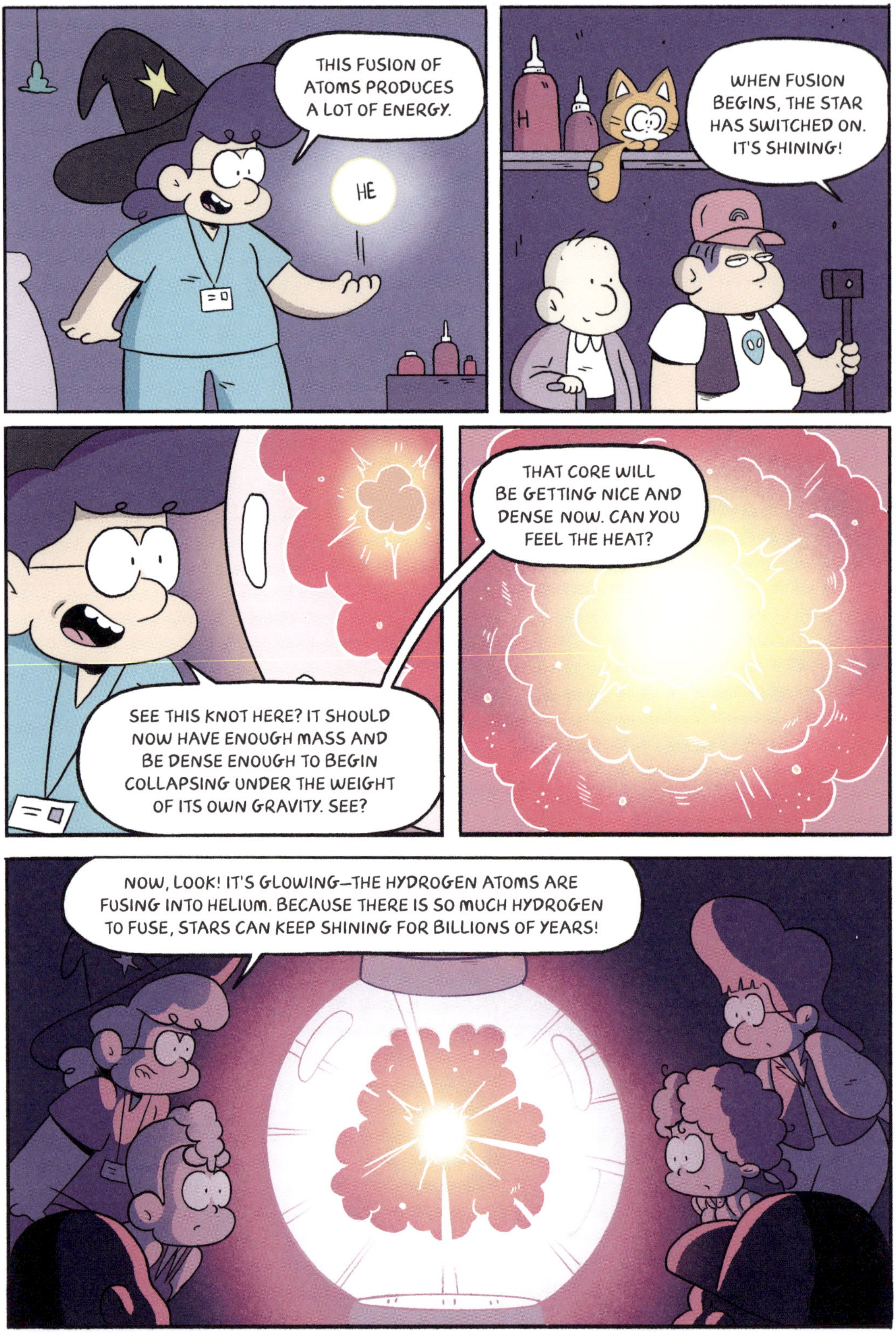
THIS FUSION OF ATOMS PRODUCES A LOT OF ENERGY.
HE
WHEN FUSION BEGINS, THE STAR HAS SWITCHED ON. IT'S SHINING!
H
SEE THIS KNOT HERE? IT SHOULD NOW HAVE ENOUGH MASS AND BE DENSE ENOUGH TO BEGIN COLLAPSING UNDER THE WEIGHT OF ITS OWN GRAVITY. SEE?
THAT CORE WILL BE GETTING NICE AND DENSE NOW. CAN YOU FEEL THE HEAT?
NOW, LOOK! IT'S GLOWING—THE HYDROGEN ATOMS ARE FUSING INTO HELIUM. BECAUSE THERE IS SO MUCH HYDROGEN TO FUSE, STARS CAN KEEP SHINING FOR BILLIONS OF YEARS!

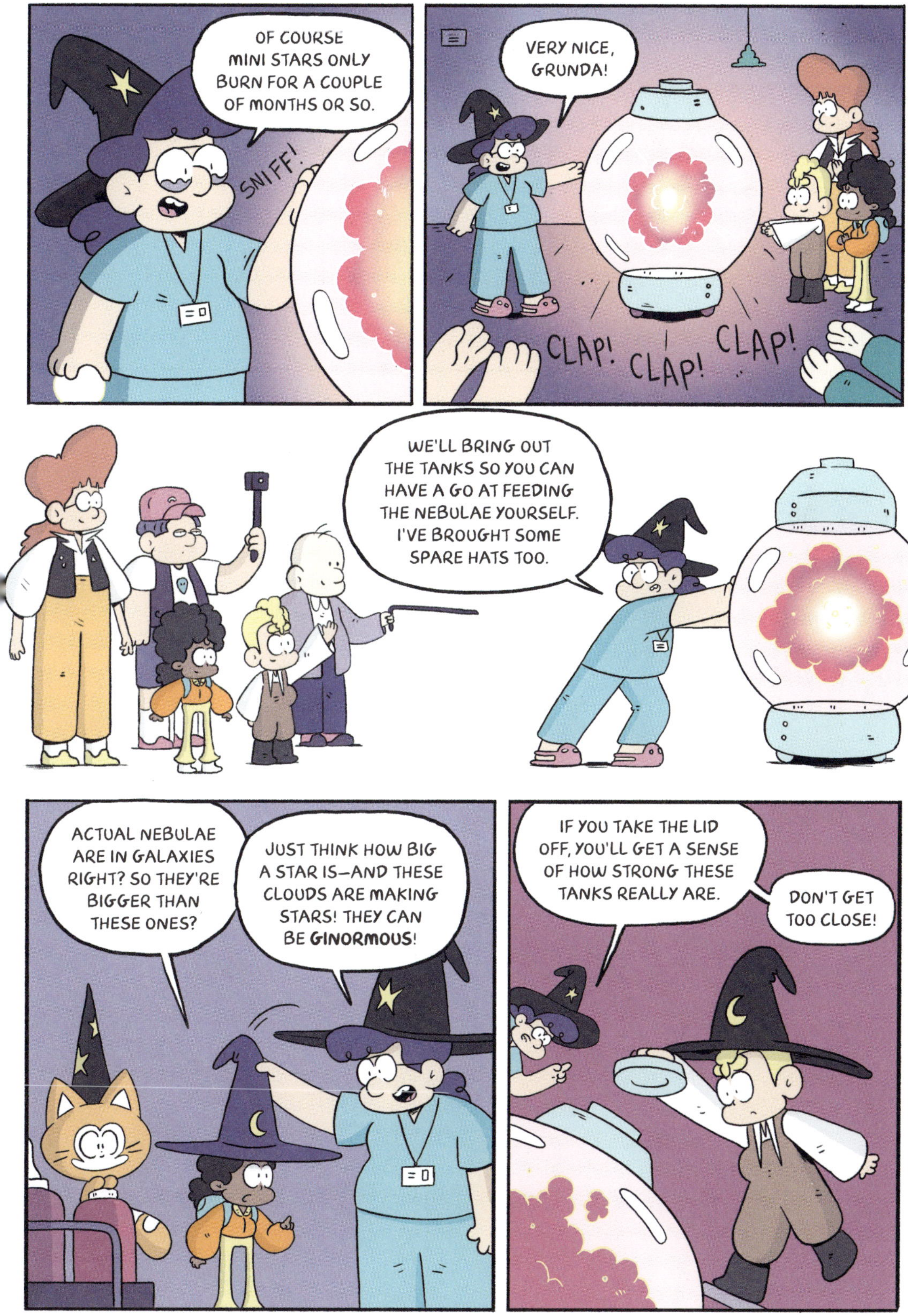
OF COURSE MINI STARS ONLY BURN FOR A COUPLE OF MONTHS OR SO.
SNIFF!
VERY NICE, GRUNDA!
CLAP! CLAP! CLAP!
WE'LL BRING OUT THE TANKS SO YOU CAN HAVE A GO AT FEEDING THE NEBULAE YOURSELF. I'VE BROUGHT SOME SPARE HATS TOO.
ACTUAL NEBULAE ARE IN GALAXIES RIGHT? SO THEY'RE BIGGER THAN THESE ONES?
JUST THINK HOW BIG A STAR IS—AND THESE CLOUDS ARE MAKING STARS! THEY CAN BE **GINORMOUS**!
IF YOU TAKE THE LID OFF, YOU'LL GET A SENSE OF HOW STRONG THESE TANKS REALLY ARE.
DON'T GET TOO CLOSE!

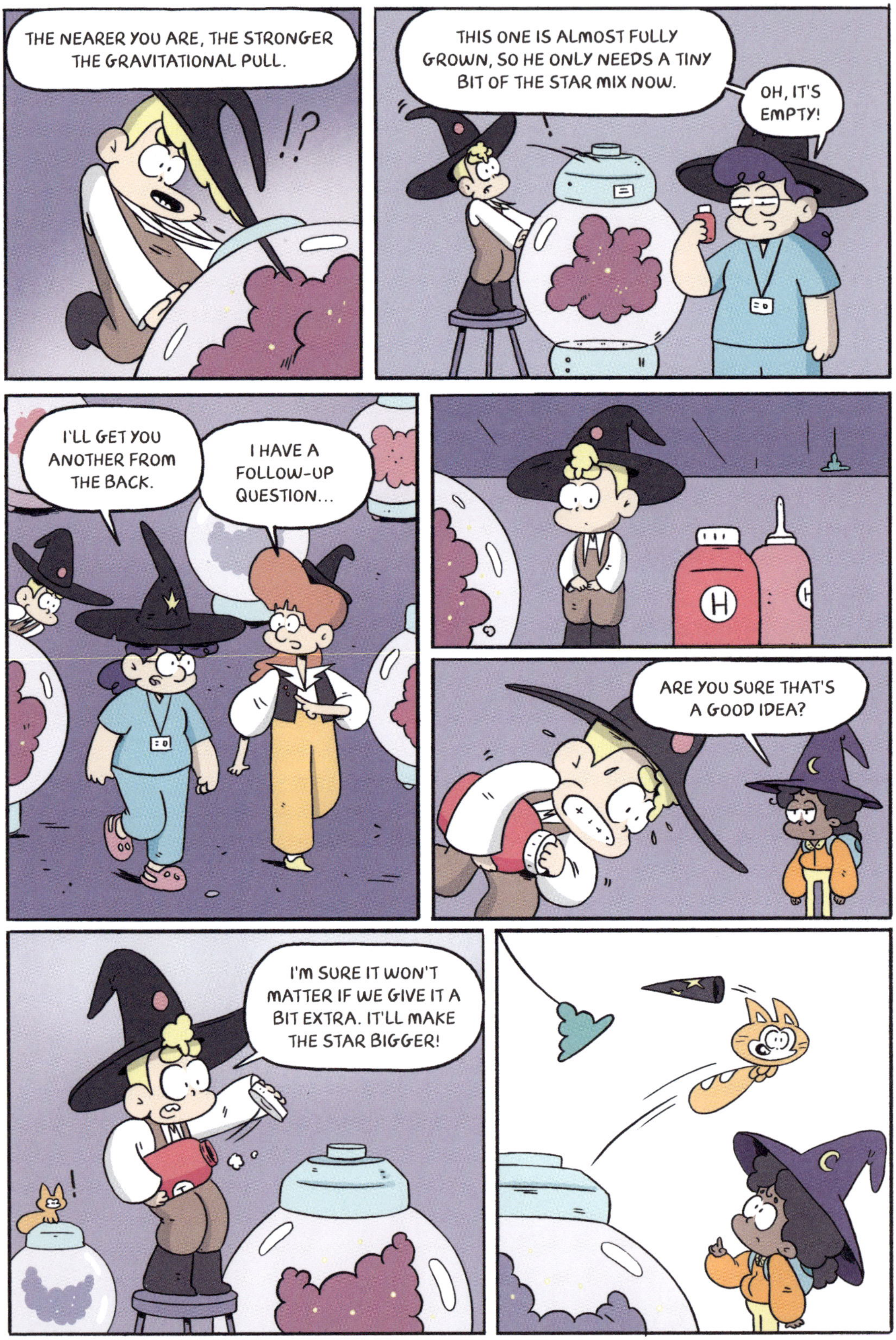
THE NEARER YOU ARE, THE STRONGER THE GRAVITATIONAL PULL.
!?
THIS ONE IS ALMOST FULLY GROWN, SO HE ONLY NEEDS A TINY BIT OF THE STAR MIX NOW.
OH, IT'S EMPTY!
I'LL GET YOU ANOTHER FROM THE BACK.
I HAVE A FOLLOW-UP QUESTION...
ARE YOU SURE THAT'S A GOOD IDEA?
I'M SURE IT WON'T MATTER IF WE GIVE IT A BIT EXTRA. IT'LL MAKE THE STAR BIGGER!
!

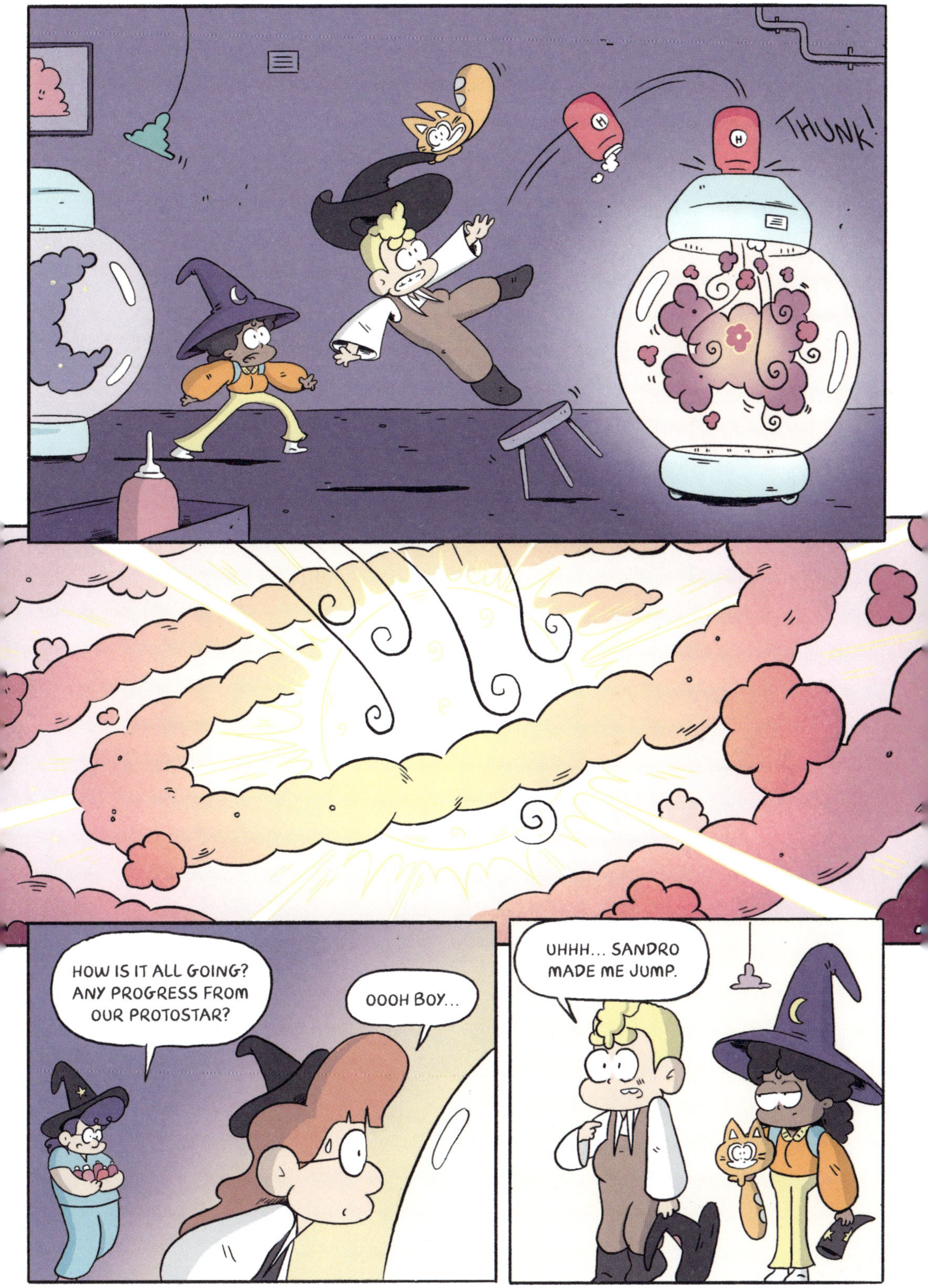
THUNK!
HOW IS IT ALL GOING? ANY PROGRESS FROM OUR PROTOSTAR?
OOOH BOY...
UHHH... SANDRO MADE ME JUMP.

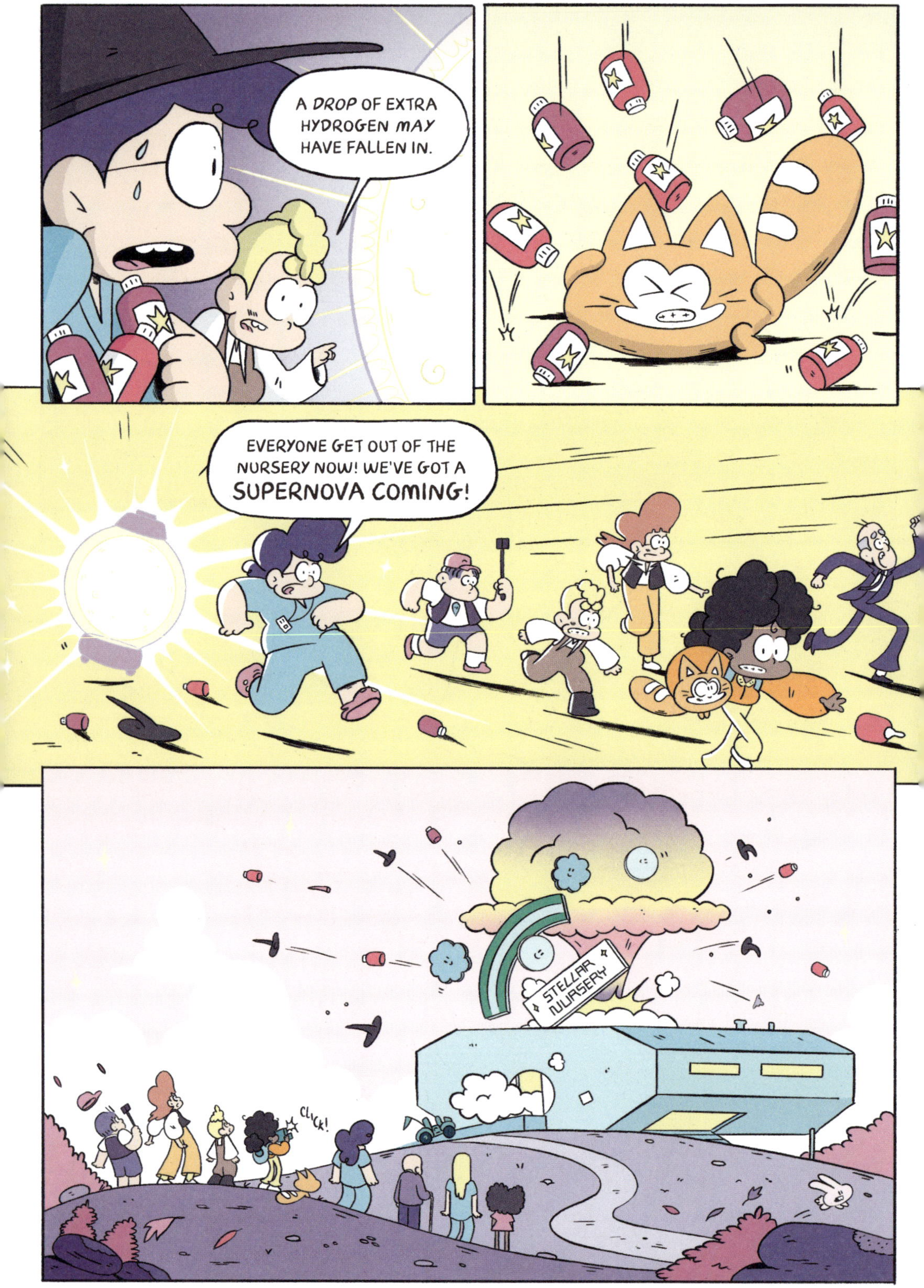
A DROP OF EXTRA HYDROGEN MAY HAVE FALLEN IN.
EVERYONE GET OUT OF THE NURSERY NOW! WE'VE GOT A SUPERNOVA COMING!
STELLAR NURSERY
CLICK!

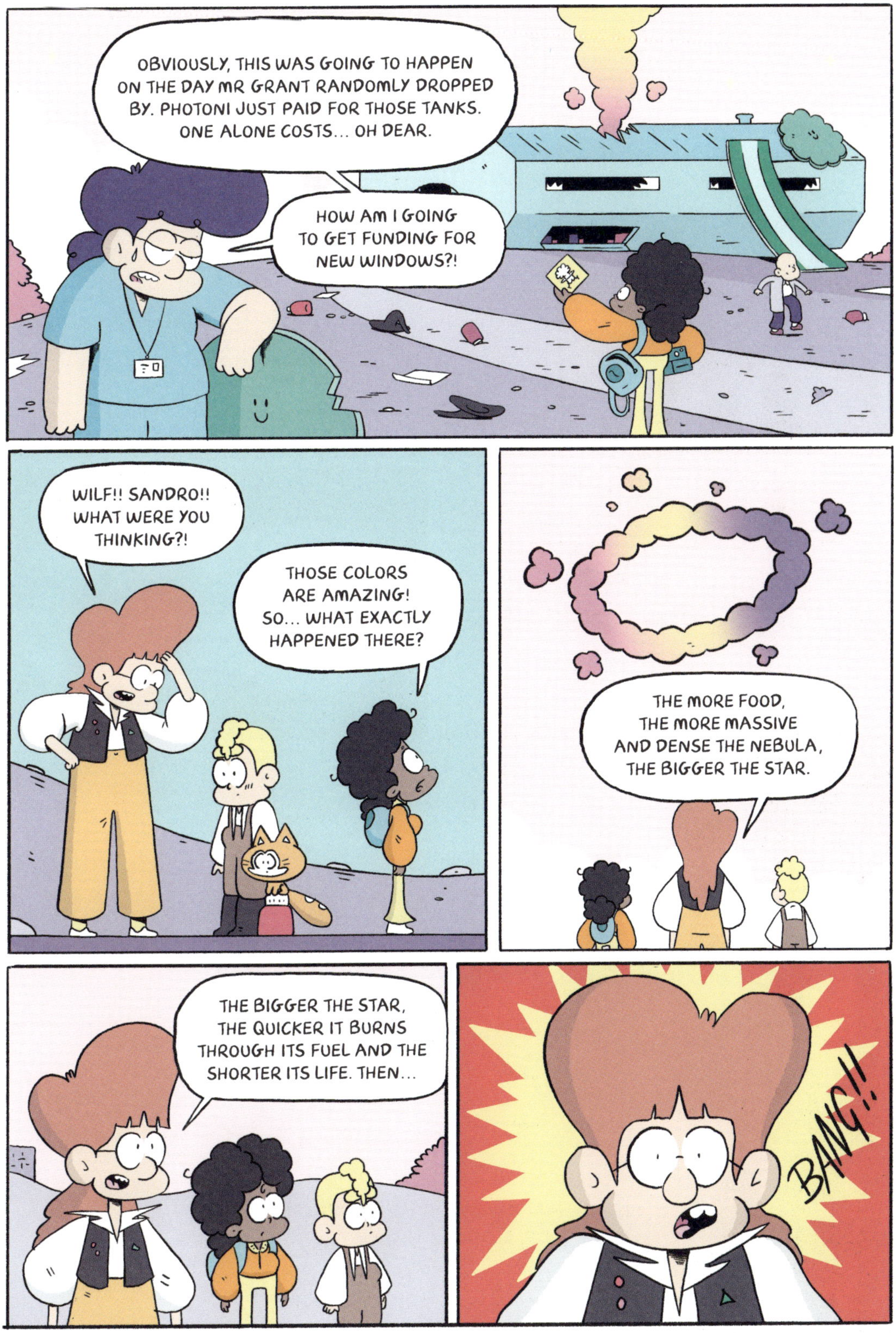
OBVIOUSLY, THIS WAS GOING TO HAPPEN ON THE DAY MR GRANT RANDOMLY DROPPED BY. PHOTONI JUST PAID FOR THOSE TANKS. ONE ALONE COSTS... OH DEAR.
HOW AM I GOING TO GET FUNDING FOR NEW WINDOWS?!
WILF!! SANDRO!! WHAT WERE YOU THINKING?!
THOSE COLORS ARE AMAZING! SO... WHAT EXACTLY HAPPENED THERE?
THE MORE FOOD, THE MORE MASSIVE AND DENSE THE NEBULA, THE BIGGER THE STAR.
THE BIGGER THE STAR, THE QUICKER IT BURNS THROUGH ITS FUEL AND THE SHORTER ITS LIFE. THEN...
BANG!!

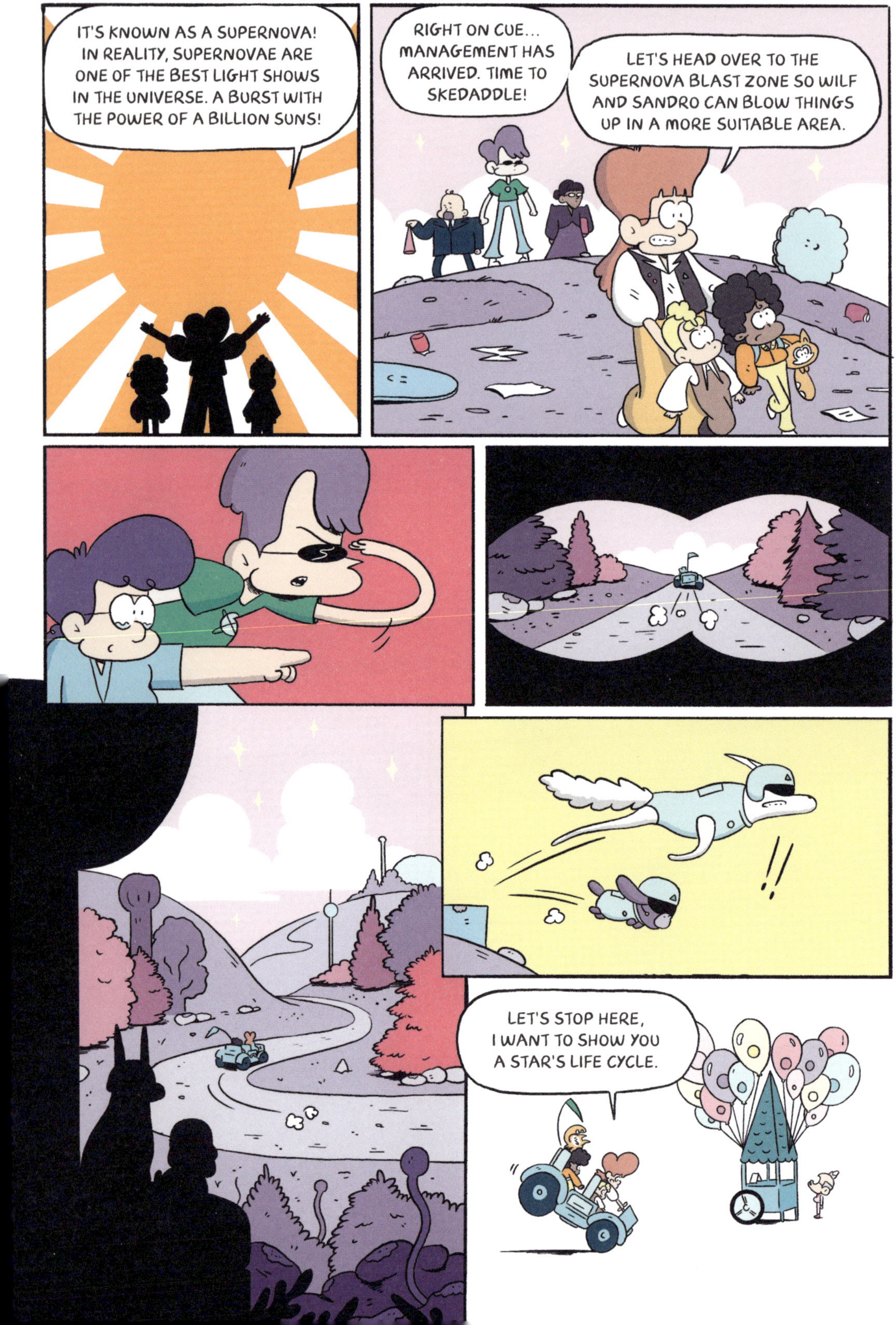
IT'S KNOWN AS A SUPERNOVA! IN REALITY, SUPERNOVAE ARE ONE OF THE BEST LIGHT SHOWS IN THE UNIVERSE. A BURST WITH THE POWER OF A BILLION SUNS!
RIGHT ON CUE... MANAGEMENT HAS ARRIVED. TIME TO SKEDADDLE!
LET'S HEAD OVER TO THE SUPERNOVA BLAST ZONE SO WILF AND SANDRO CAN BLOW THINGS UP IN A MORE SUITABLE AREA.
!!
LET'S STOP HERE, I WANT TO SHOW YOU A STAR'S LIFE CYCLE.

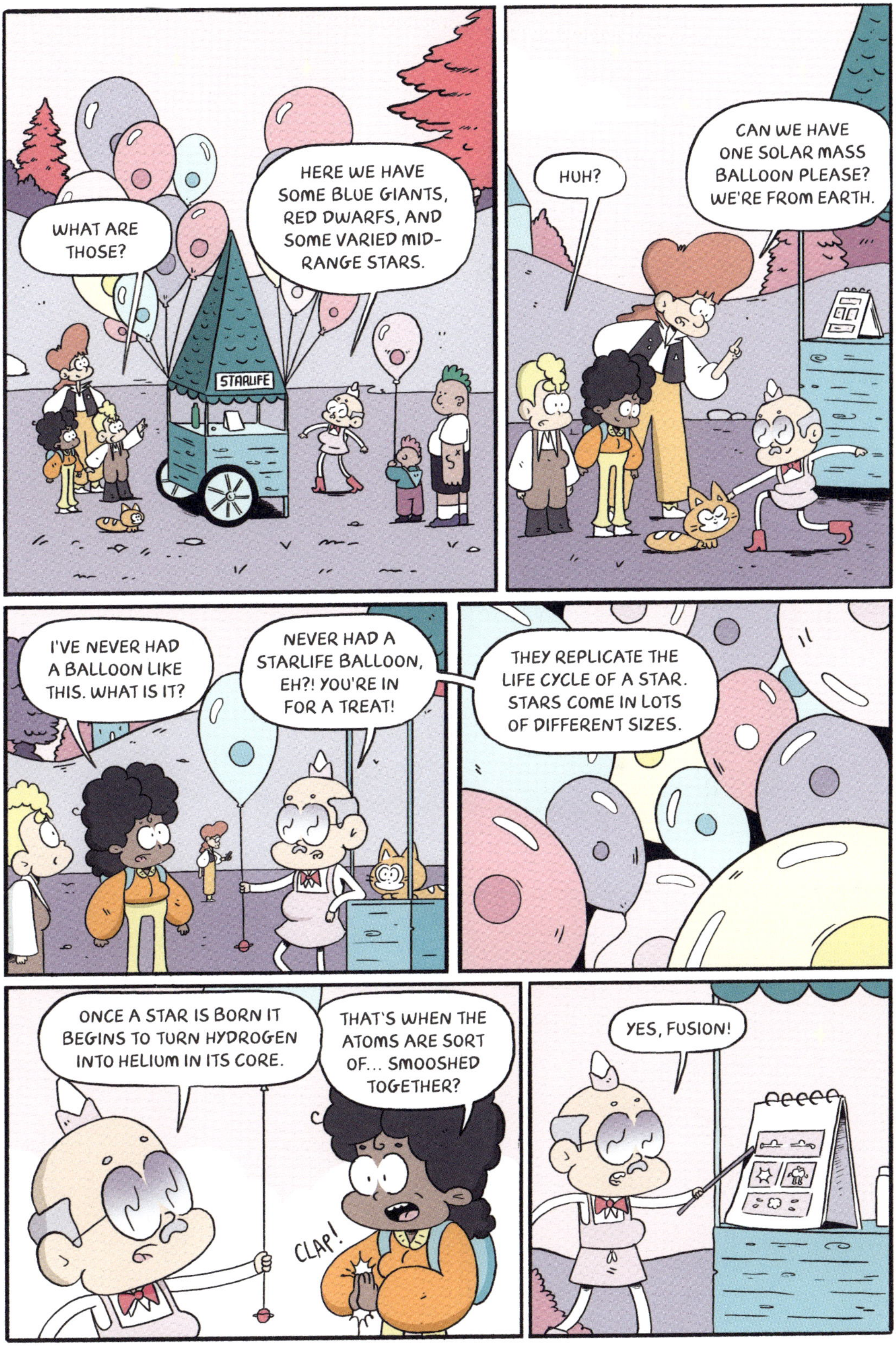
WHAT ARE THOSE?
HERE WE HAVE SOME BLUE GIANTS, RED DWARFS, AND SOME VARIED MID-RANGE STARS.
STARLIFE
HUH?
CAN WE HAVE ONE SOLAR MASS BALLOON PLEASE? WE'RE FROM EARTH.
I'VE NEVER HAD A BALLOON LIKE THIS. WHAT IS IT?
NEVER HAD A STARLIFE BALLOON, EH?! YOU'RE IN FOR A TREAT!
THEY REPLICATE THE LIFE CYCLE OF A STAR. STARS COME IN LOTS OF DIFFERENT SIZES.
ONCE A STAR IS BORN IT BEGINS TO TURN HYDROGEN INTO HELIUM IN ITS CORE.
THAT'S WHEN THE ATOMS ARE SORT OF... SMOOSHED TOGETHER?
CLAP!
YES, FUSION!

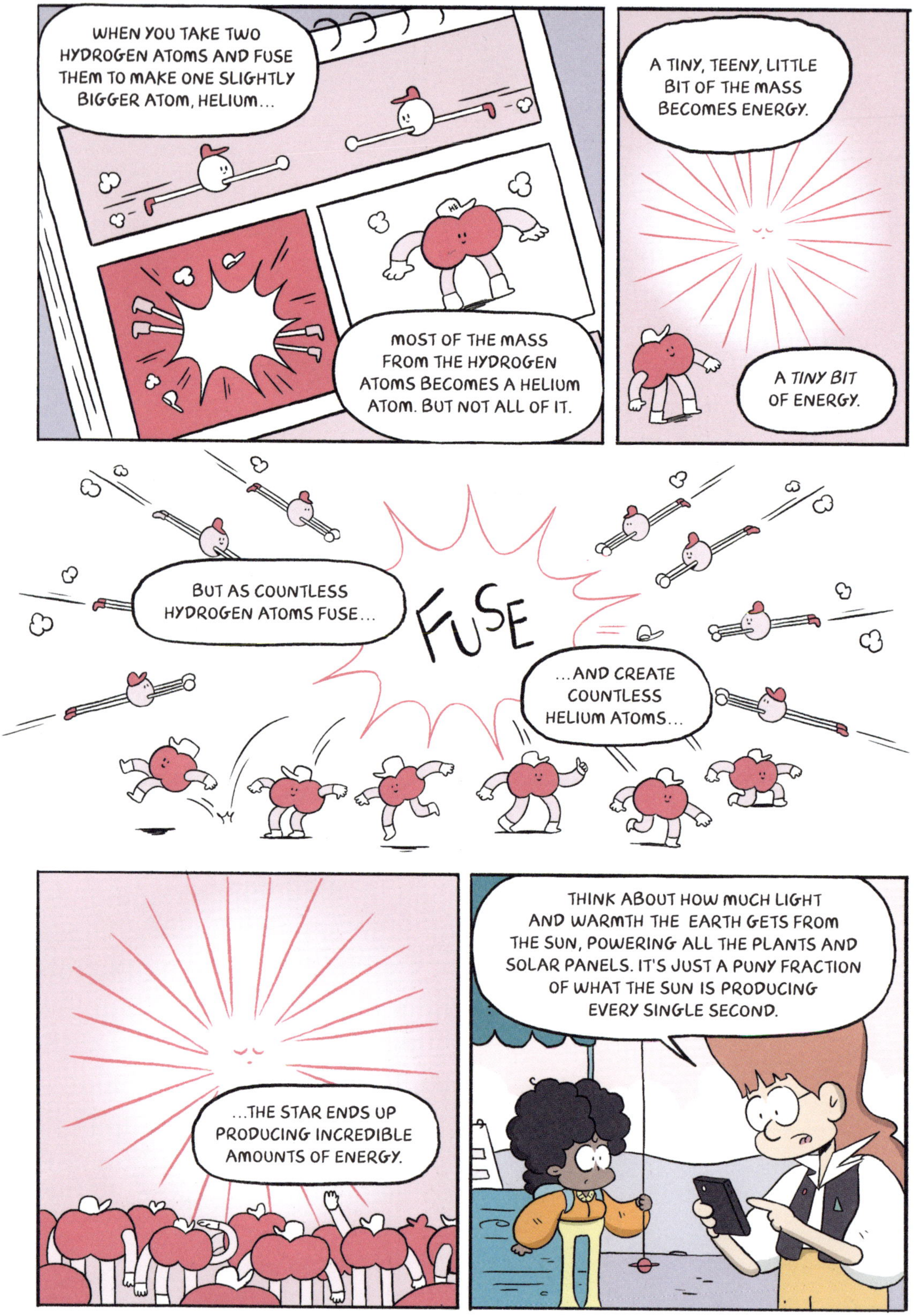
WHEN YOU TAKE TWO HYDROGEN ATOMS AND FUSE THEM TO MAKE ONE SLIGHTLY BIGGER ATOM, HELIUM...
HE
MOST OF THE MASS FROM THE HYDROGEN ATOMS BECOMES A HELIUM ATOM. BUT NOT ALL OF IT.
A TINY, TEENY, LITTLE BIT OF THE MASS BECOMES ENERGY.
A *TINY* BIT OF ENERGY.
BUT AS COUNTLESS HYDROGEN ATOMS FUSE...
FUSE
...AND CREATE COUNTLESS HELIUM ATOMS...
...THE STAR ENDS UP PRODUCING INCREDIBLE AMOUNTS OF ENERGY.
THINK ABOUT HOW MUCH LIGHT AND WARMTH THE EARTH GETS FROM THE SUN, POWERING ALL THE PLANTS AND SOLAR PANELS. IT'S JUST A PUNY FRACTION OF WHAT THE SUN IS PRODUCING EVERY SINGLE SECOND.

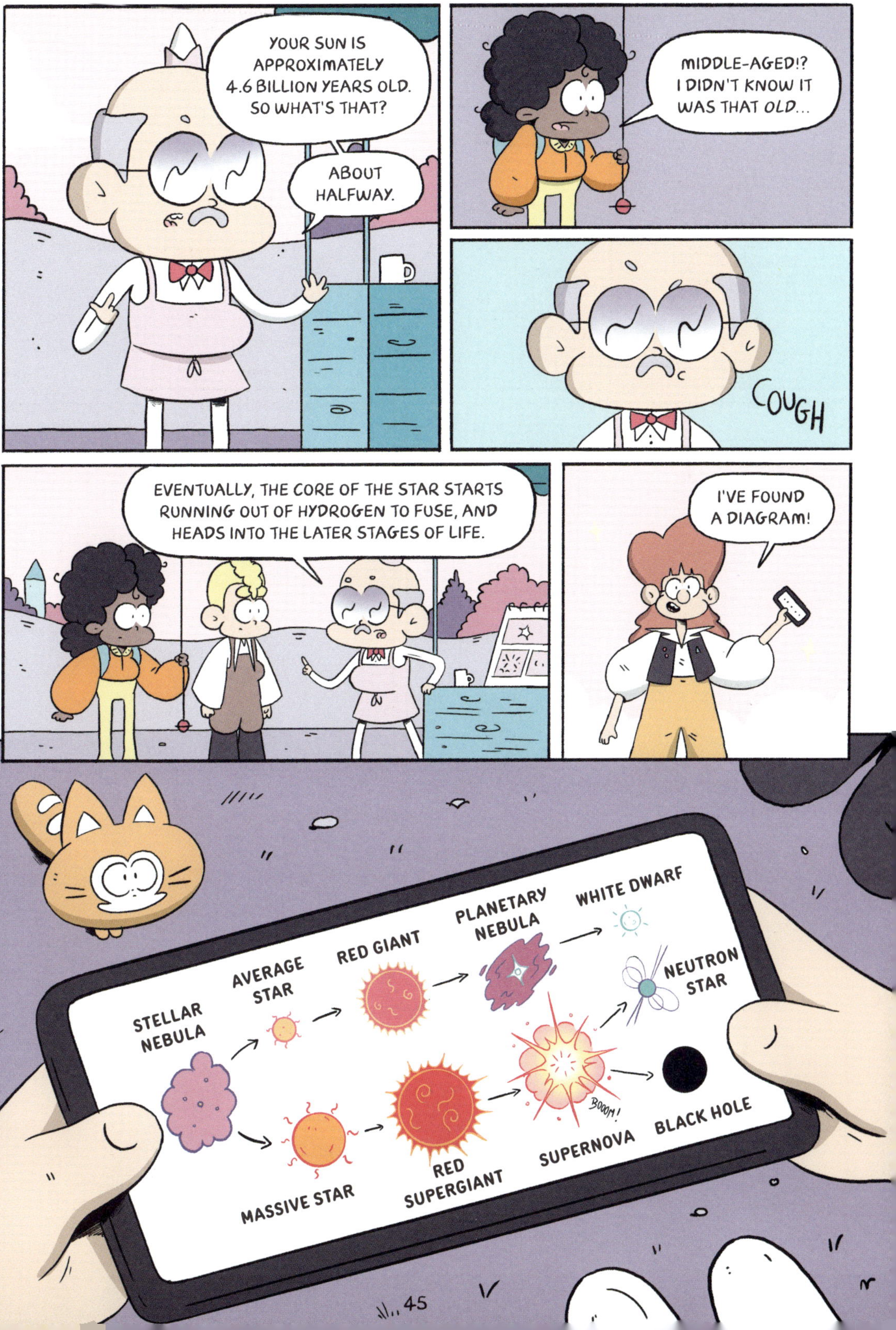

YOUR SUN IS APPROXIMATELY 4.6 BILLION YEARS OLD. SO WHAT'S THAT?
ABOUT HALFWAY.
MIDDLE-AGED!? I DIDN'T KNOW IT WAS THAT OLD...
COUGH
EVENTUALLY, THE CORE OF THE STAR STARTS RUNNING OUT OF HYDROGEN TO FUSE, AND HEADS INTO THE LATER STAGES OF LIFE.
I'VE FOUND A DIAGRAM!
STELLAR NEBULA
AVERAGE STAR
RED GIANT
PLANETARY NEBULA
WHITE DWARF
NEUTRON STAR
MASSIVE STAR
RED SUPERGIANT
SUPERNOVA
BOOOM!
BLACK HOLE

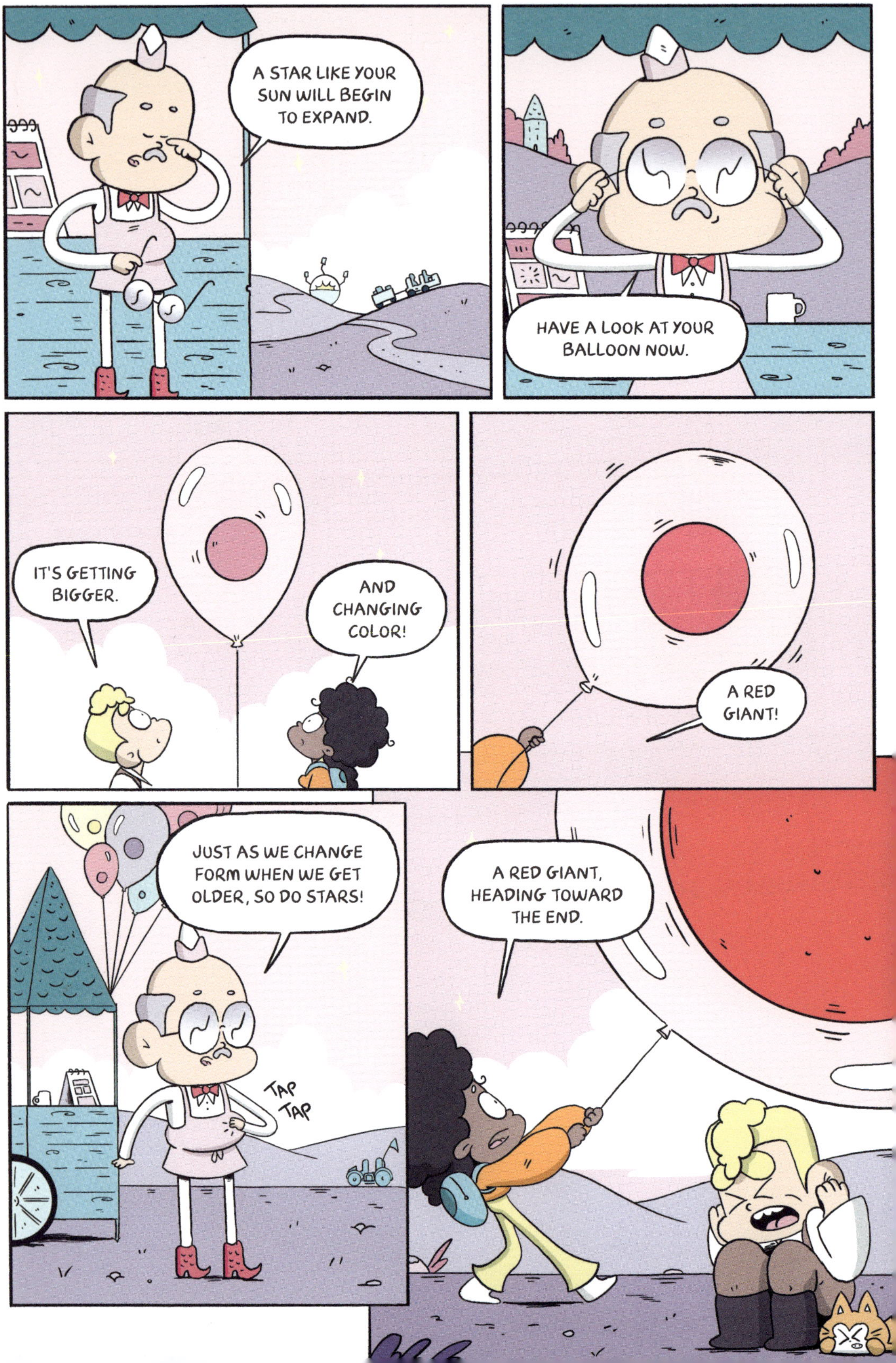
A STAR LIKE YOUR SUN WILL BEGIN TO EXPAND.
HAVE A LOOK AT YOUR BALLOON NOW.
IT'S GETTING BIGGER.
AND CHANGING COLOR!
A RED GIANT!
JUST AS WE CHANGE FORM WHEN WE GET OLDER, SO DO STARS!
TAP TAP
A RED GIANT, HEADING TOWARD THE END.

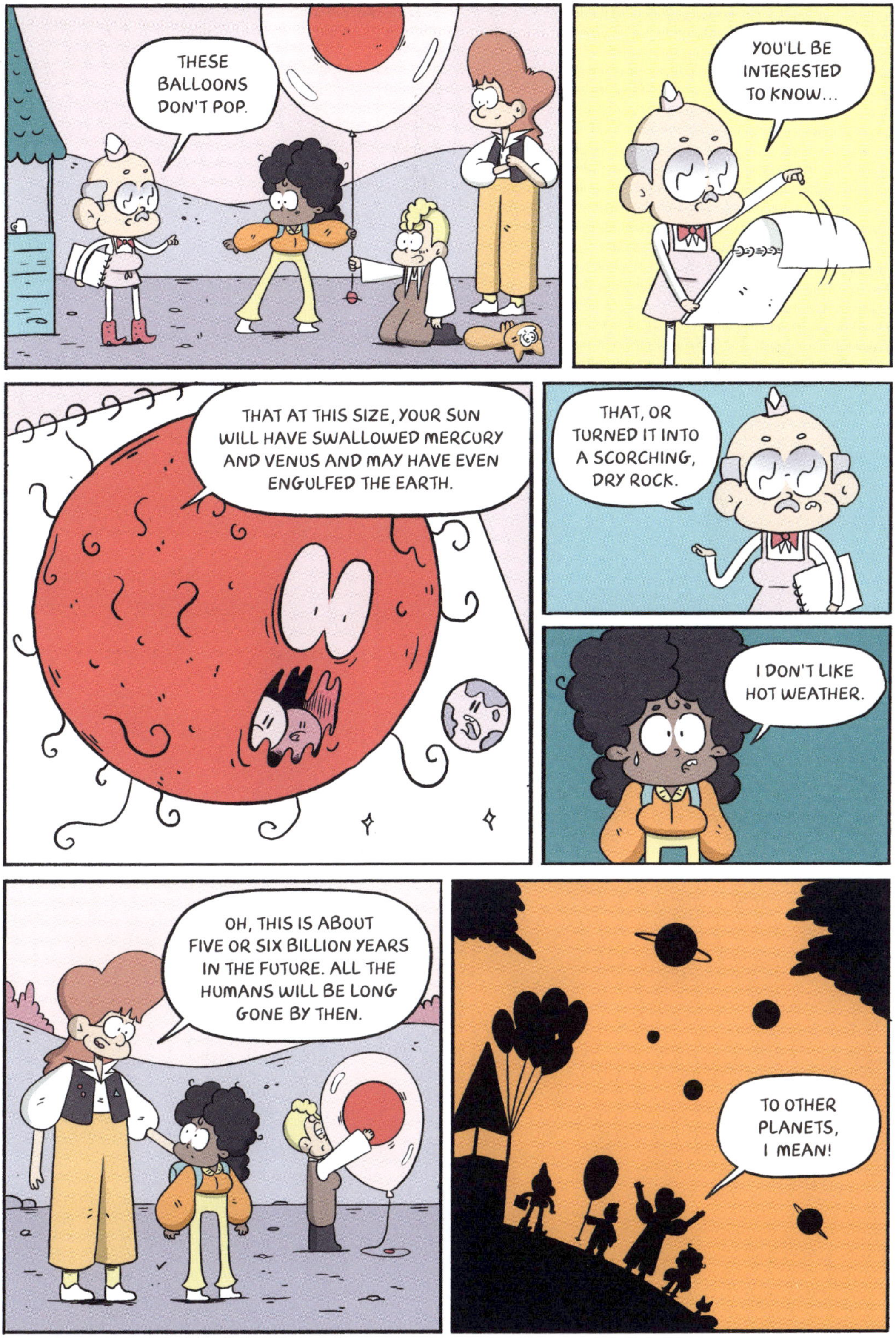
THESE BALLOONS DON'T POP.
YOU'LL BE INTERESTED TO KNOW...
THAT AT THIS SIZE, YOUR SUN WILL HAVE SWALLOWED MERCURY AND VENUS AND MAY HAVE EVEN ENGULFED THE EARTH.
THAT, OR TURNED IT INTO A SCORCHING, DRY ROCK.
I DON'T LIKE HOT WEATHER.
OH, THIS IS ABOUT FIVE OR SIX BILLION YEARS IN THE FUTURE. ALL THE HUMANS WILL BE LONG GONE BY THEN.
TO OTHER PLANETS, I MEAN!

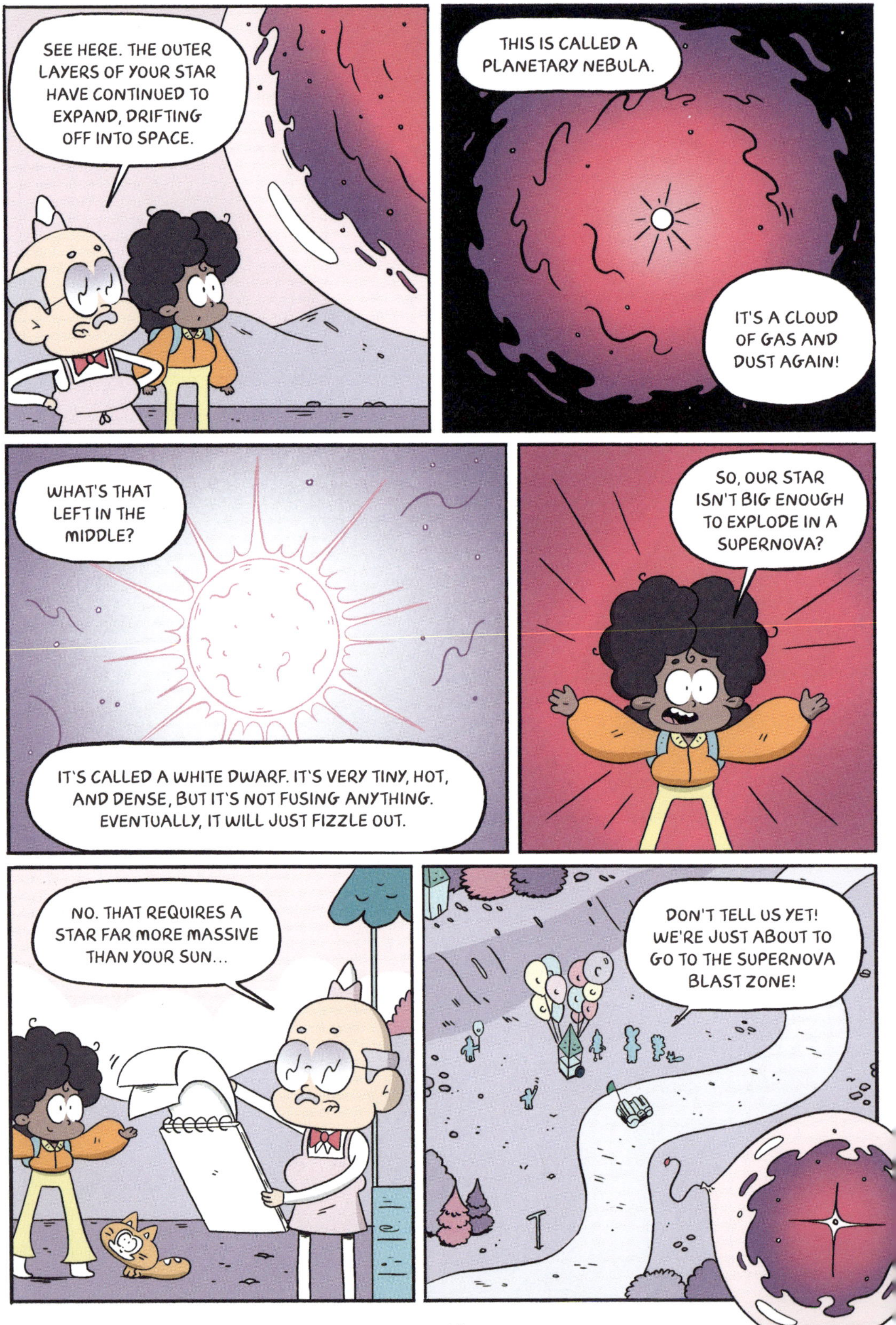
SEE HERE. THE OUTER LAYERS OF YOUR STAR HAVE CONTINUED TO EXPAND, DRIFTING OFF INTO SPACE.
THIS IS CALLED A PLANETARY NEBULA.
IT'S A CLOUD OF GAS AND DUST AGAIN!
WHAT'S THAT LEFT IN THE MIDDLE?
IT'S CALLED A WHITE DWARF. IT'S VERY TINY, HOT, AND DENSE, BUT IT'S NOT FUSING ANYTHING. EVENTUALLY, IT WILL JUST FIZZLE OUT.
SO, OUR STAR ISN'T BIG ENOUGH TO EXPLODE IN A SUPERNOVA?
NO. THAT REQUIRES A STAR FAR MORE MASSIVE THAN YOUR SUN...
DON'T TELL US YET! WE'RE JUST ABOUT TO GO TO THE SUPERNOVA BLAST ZONE!

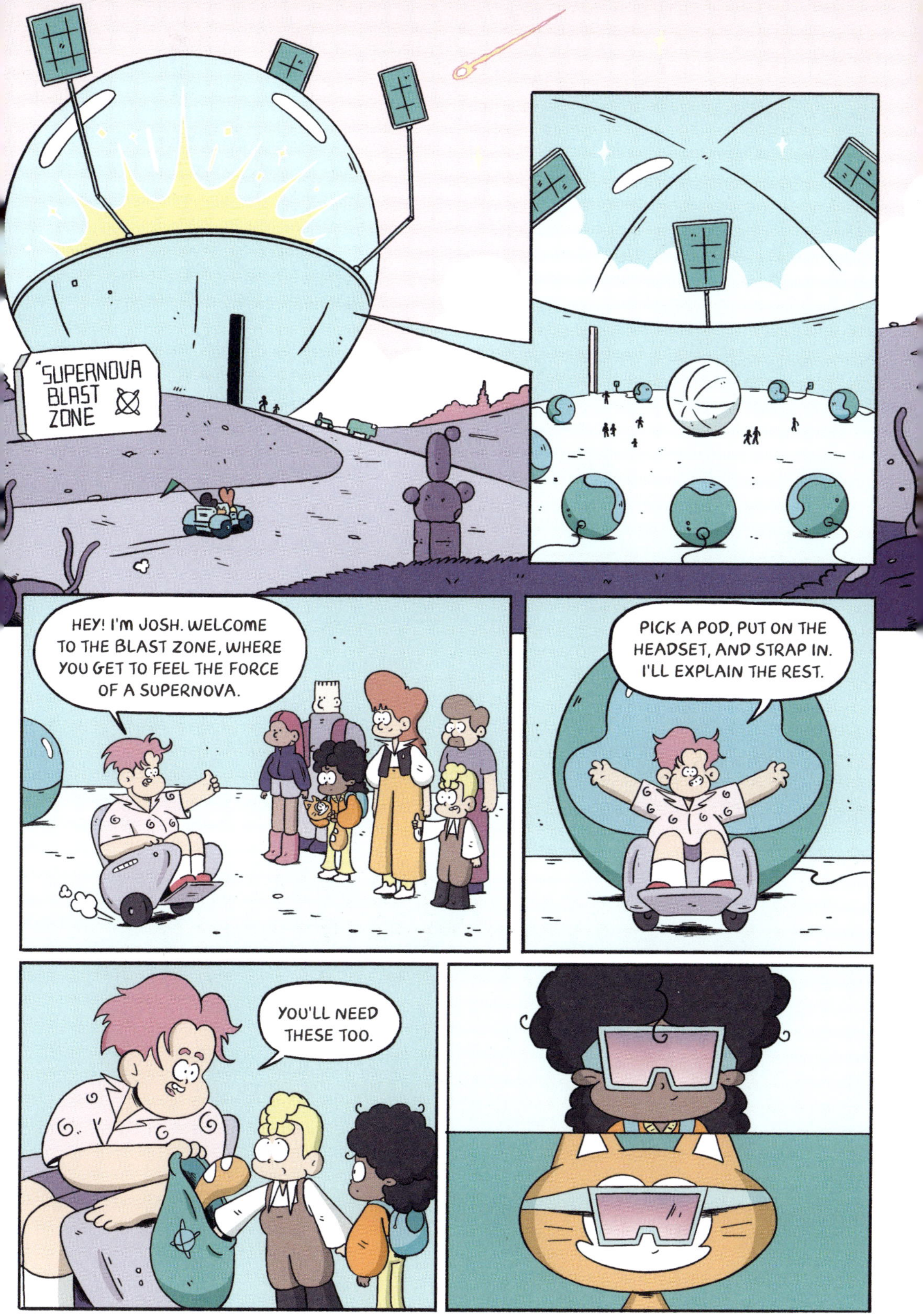
SUPERNOVA
BLAST
ZONE
HEY! I'M JOSH. WELCOME TO THE BLAST ZONE, WHERE YOU GET TO FEEL THE FORCE OF A SUPERNOVA.
PICK A POD, PUT ON THE HEADSET, AND STRAP IN. I'LL EXPLAIN THE REST.
YOU'LL NEED THESE TOO.

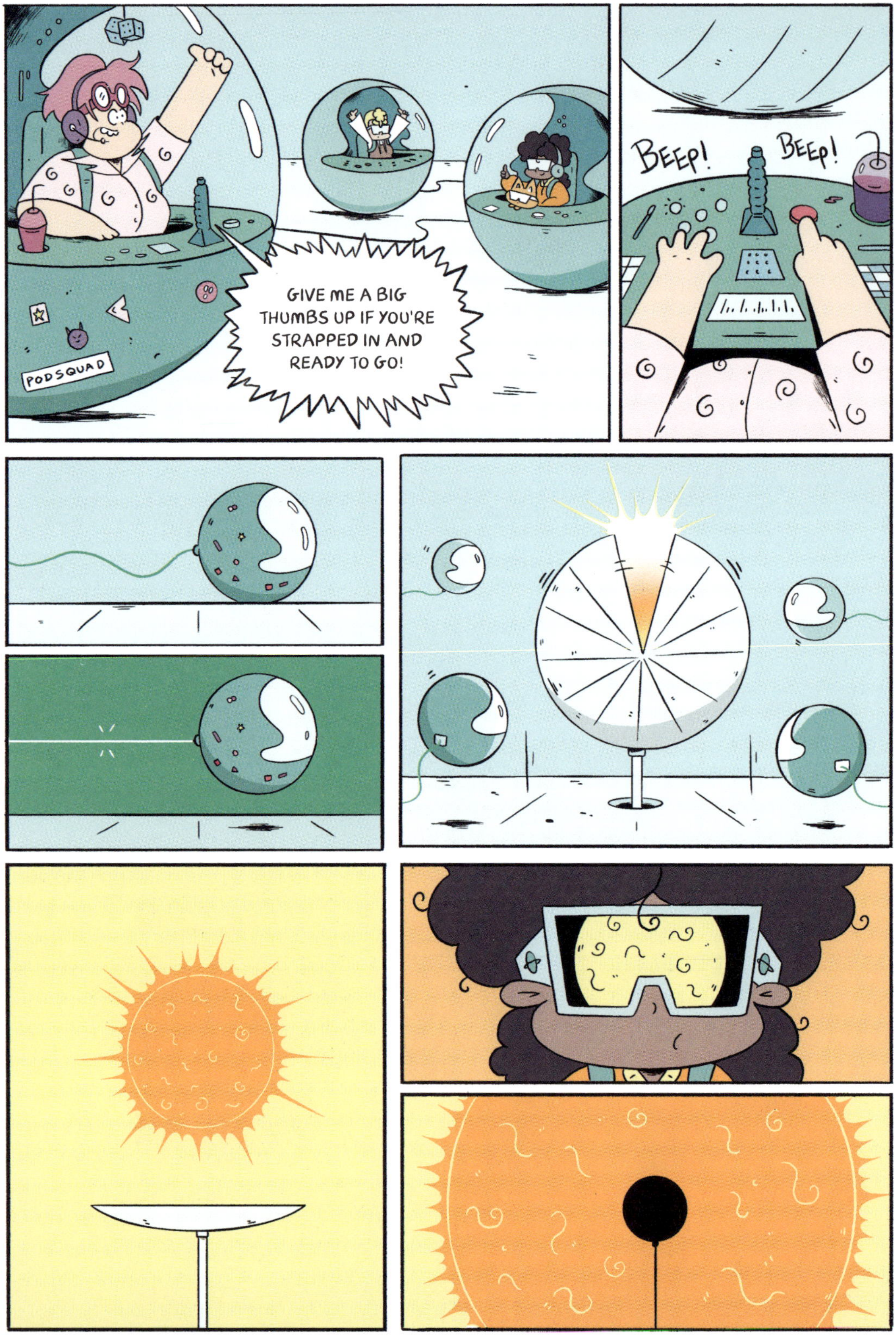
PODSQUAD
GIVE ME A BIG THUMBS UP IF YOU'RE STRAPPED IN AND READY TO GO!
BEEP! BEEP!

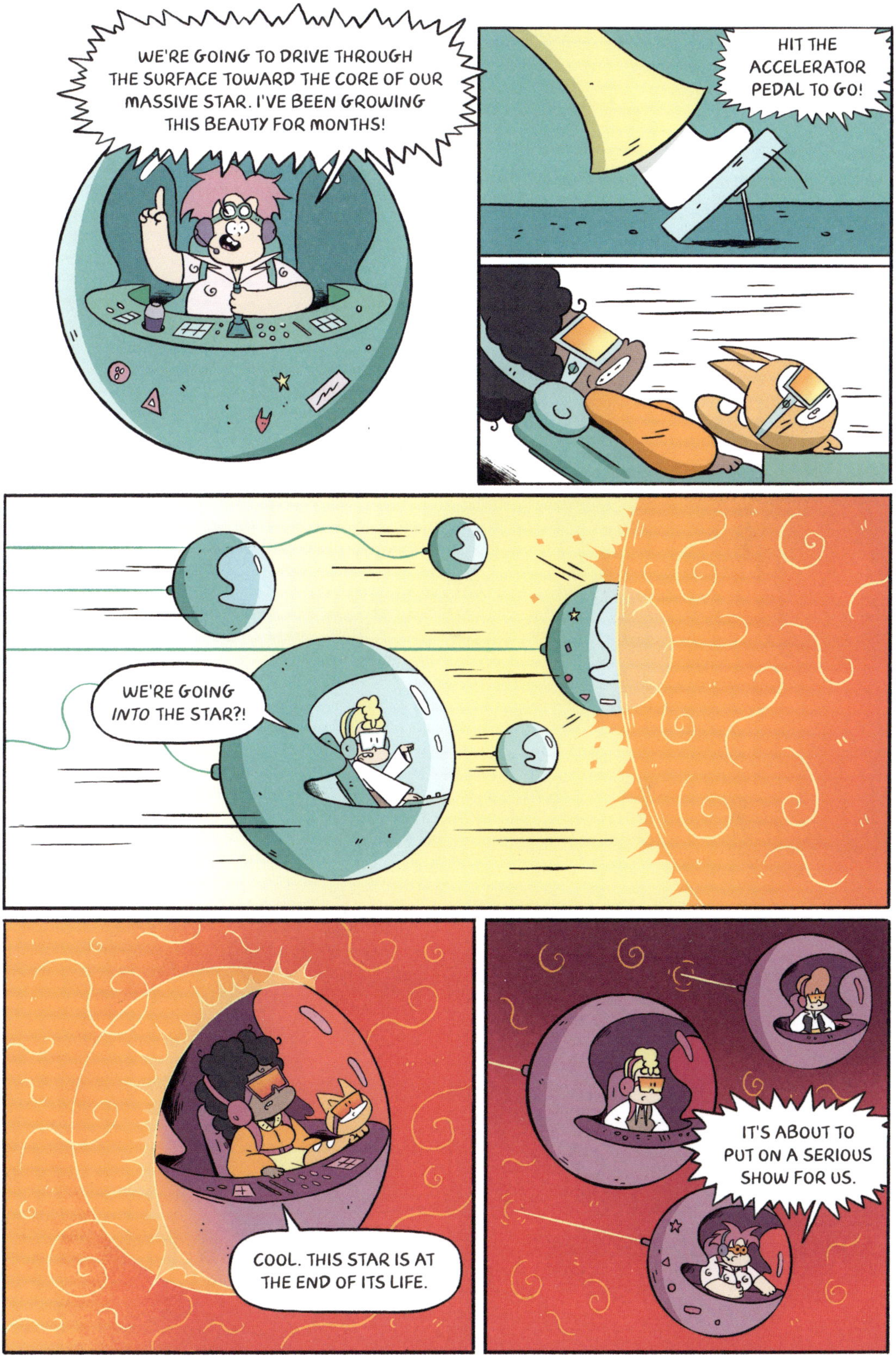
WE'RE GOING TO DRIVE THROUGH THE SURFACE TOWARD THE CORE OF OUR MASSIVE STAR. I'VE BEEN GROWING THIS BEAUTY FOR MONTHS!
HIT THE ACCELERATOR PEDAL TO GO!
WE'RE GOING *INTO* THE STAR?!
COOL. THIS STAR IS AT THE END OF ITS LIFE.
IT'S ABOUT TO PUT ON A SERIOUS SHOW FOR US.

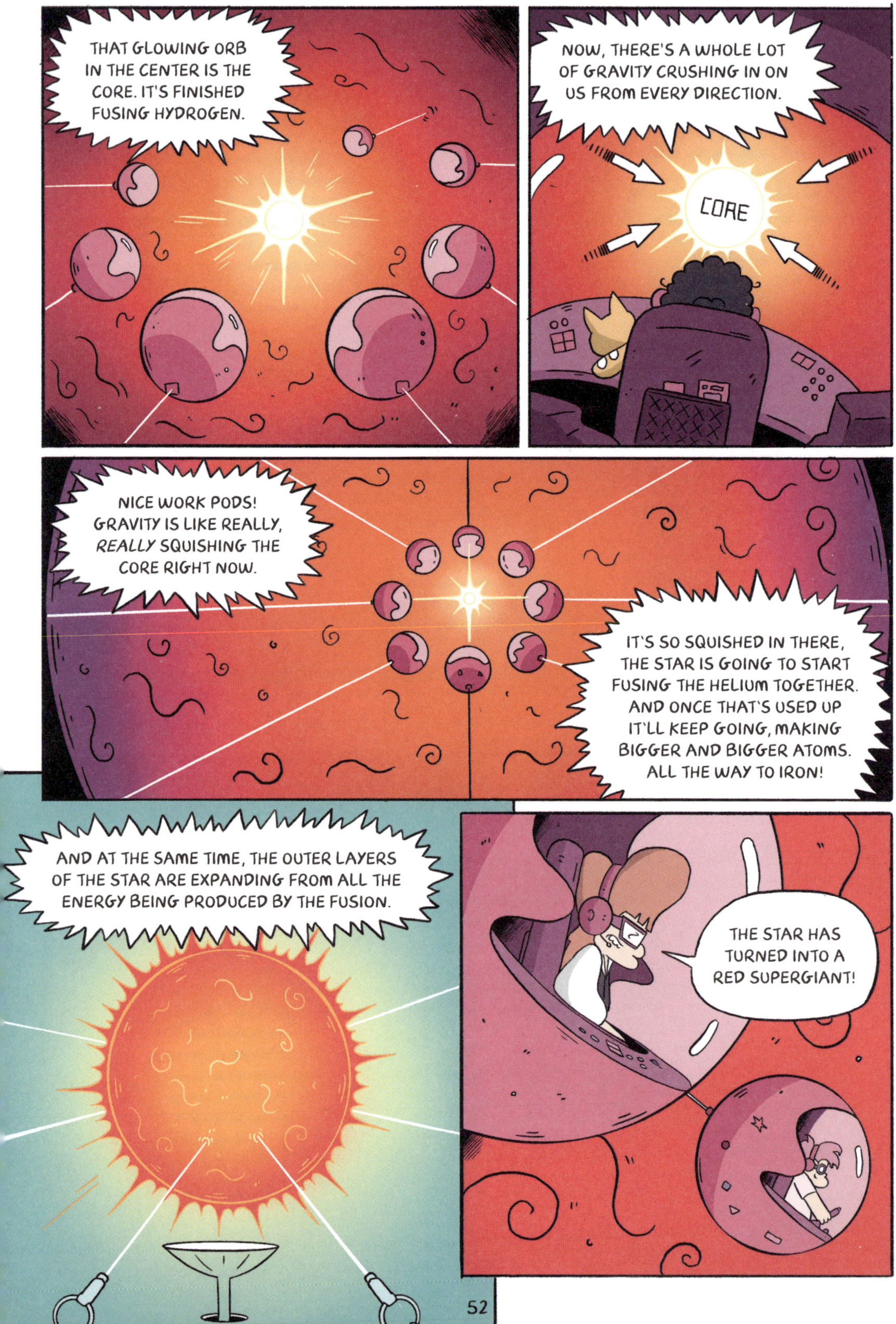
THAT GLOWING ORB IN THE CENTER IS THE CORE. IT'S FINISHED FUSING HYDROGEN.
NOW, THERE'S A WHOLE LOT OF GRAVITY CRUSHING IN ON US FROM EVERY DIRECTION.
CORE
NICE WORK PODS! GRAVITY IS LIKE REALLY, *REALLY* SQUISHING THE CORE RIGHT NOW.
IT'S SO SQUISHED IN THERE, THE STAR IS GOING TO START FUSING THE HELIUM TOGETHER. AND ONCE THAT'S USED UP IT'LL KEEP GOING, MAKING BIGGER AND BIGGER ATOMS. ALL THE WAY TO IRON!
AND AT THE SAME TIME, THE OUTER LAYERS OF THE STAR ARE EXPANDING FROM ALL THE ENERGY BEING PRODUCED BY THE FUSION.
THE STAR HAS TURNED INTO A RED SUPERGIANT!

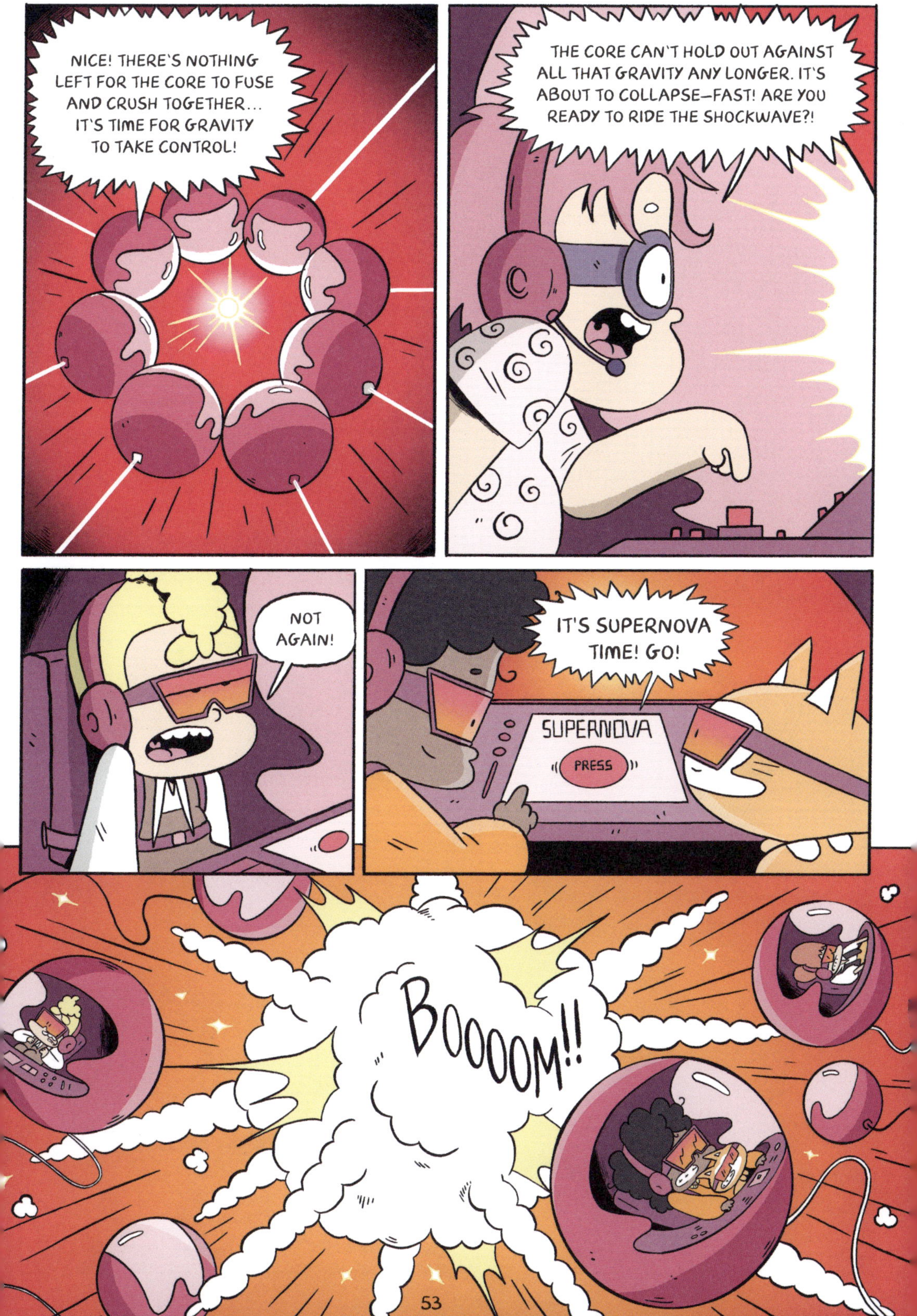
NICE! THERE'S NOTHING LEFT FOR THE CORE TO FUSE AND CRUSH TOGETHER... IT'S TIME FOR GRAVITY TO TAKE CONTROL!
THE CORE CAN'T HOLD OUT AGAINST ALL THAT GRAVITY ANY LONGER. IT'S ABOUT TO COLLAPSE—FAST! ARE YOU READY TO RIDE THE SHOCKWAVE?!
NOT AGAIN!
IT'S SUPERNOVA TIME! GO!
SUPERNOVA
PRESS
BOOOOM!!

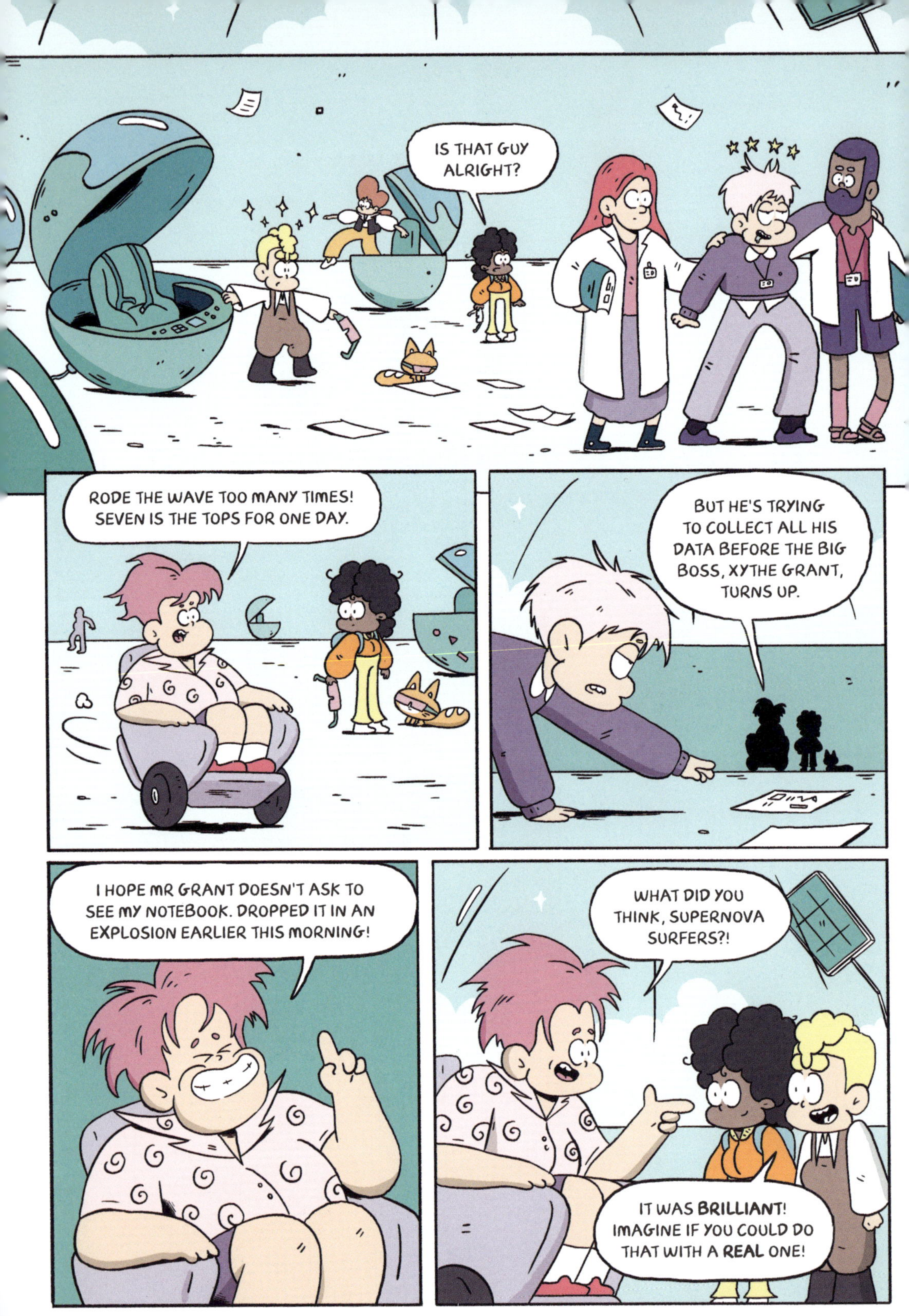
IS THAT GUY ALRIGHT?
RODE THE WAVE TOO MANY TIMES! SEVEN IS THE TOPS FOR ONE DAY.
BUT HE'S TRYING TO COLLECT ALL HIS DATA BEFORE THE BIG BOSS, XYTHE GRANT, TURNS UP.
I HOPE MR GRANT DOESN'T ASK TO SEE MY NOTEBOOK. DROPPED IT IN AN EXPLOSION EARLIER THIS MORNING!
WHAT DID YOU THINK, SUPERNOVA SURFERS?!
IT WAS **BRILLIANT**! IMAGINE IF YOU COULD DO THAT WITH A **REAL** ONE!

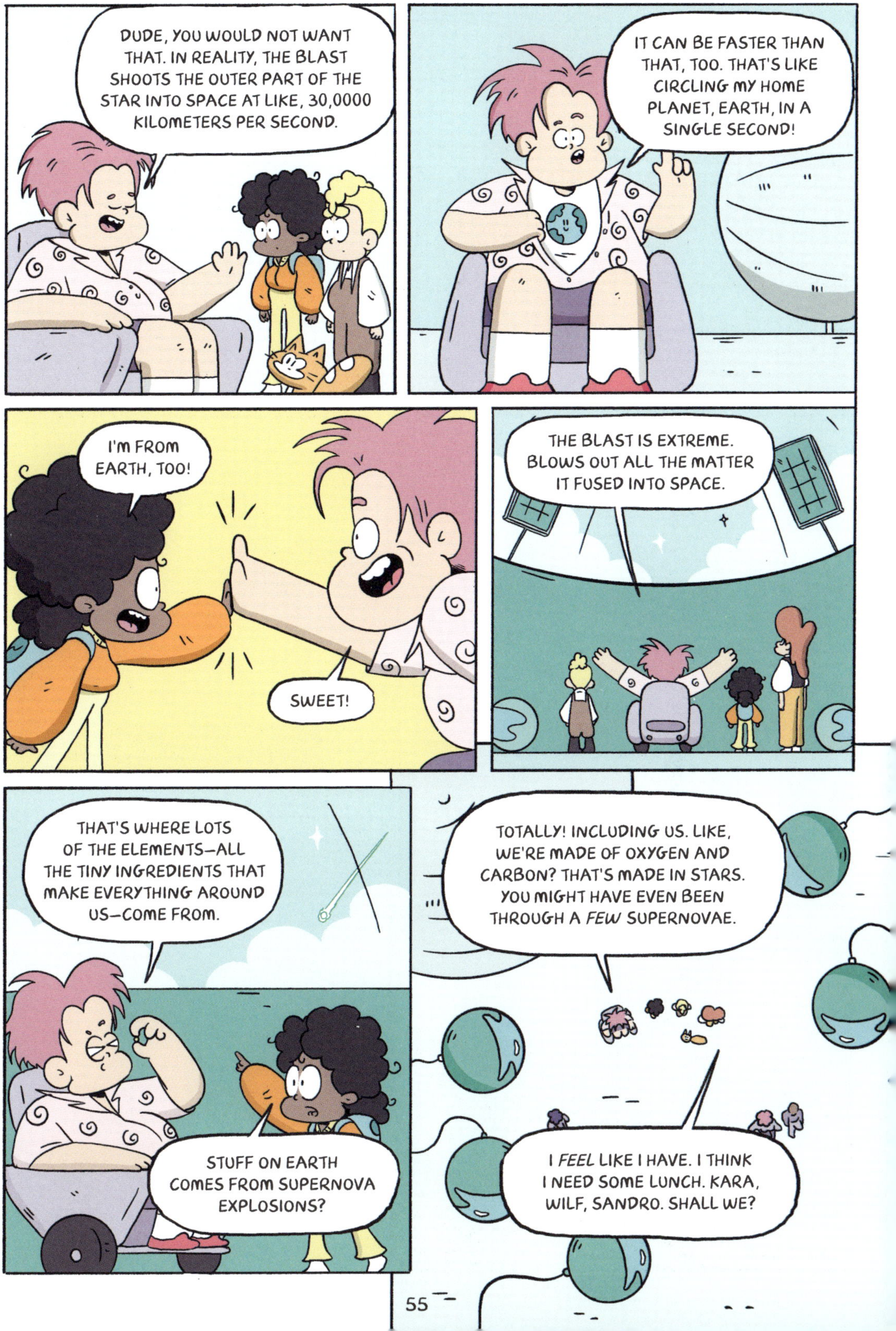
DUDE, YOU WOULD NOT WANT THAT. IN REALITY, THE BLAST SHOOTS THE OUTER PART OF THE STAR INTO SPACE AT LIKE, 30,0000 KILOMETERS PER SECOND.
IT CAN BE FASTER THAN THAT, TOO. THAT'S LIKE CIRCLING MY HOME PLANET, EARTH, IN A SINGLE SECOND!
I'M FROM EARTH, TOO!
SWEET!
THE BLAST IS EXTREME. BLOWS OUT ALL THE MATTER IT FUSED INTO SPACE.
THAT'S WHERE LOTS OF THE ELEMENTS—ALL THE TINY INGREDIENTS THAT MAKE EVERYTHING AROUND US—COME FROM.
STUFF ON EARTH COMES FROM SUPERNOVA EXPLOSIONS?
TOTALLY! INCLUDING US. LIKE, WE'RE MADE OF OXYGEN AND CARBON? THAT'S MADE IN STARS. YOU MIGHT HAVE EVEN BEEN THROUGH A *FEW* SUPERNOVAE.
I *FEEL* LIKE I HAVE. I THINK I NEED SOME LUNCH. KARA, WILF, SANDRO. SHALL WE?

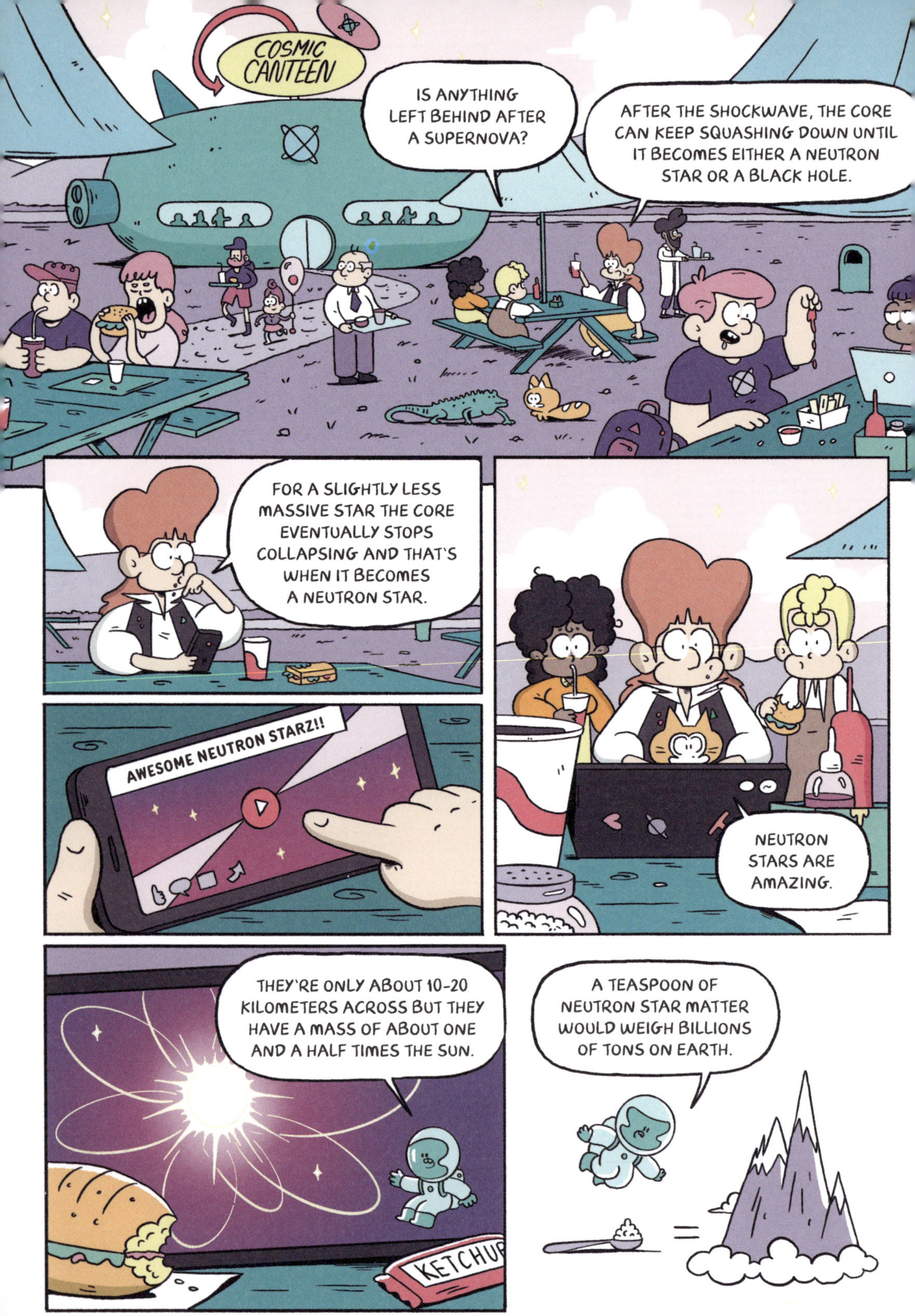
COSMIC CANTEEN
IS ANYTHING LEFT BEHIND AFTER A SUPERNOVA?
AFTER THE SHOCKWAVE, THE CORE CAN KEEP SQUASHING DOWN UNTIL IT BECOMES EITHER A NEUTRON STAR OR A BLACK HOLE.
FOR A SLIGHTLY LESS MASSIVE STAR THE CORE EVENTUALLY STOPS COLLAPSING AND THAT'S WHEN IT BECOMES A NEUTRON STAR.
AWESOME NEUTRON STARZ!!
NEUTRON STARS ARE AMAZING.
THEY'RE ONLY ABOUT 10-20 KILOMETERS ACROSS BUT THEY HAVE A MASS OF ABOUT ONE AND A HALF TIMES THE SUN.
KETCHUP
A TEASPOON OF NEUTRON STAR MATTER WOULD WEIGH BILLIONS OF TONS ON EARTH.

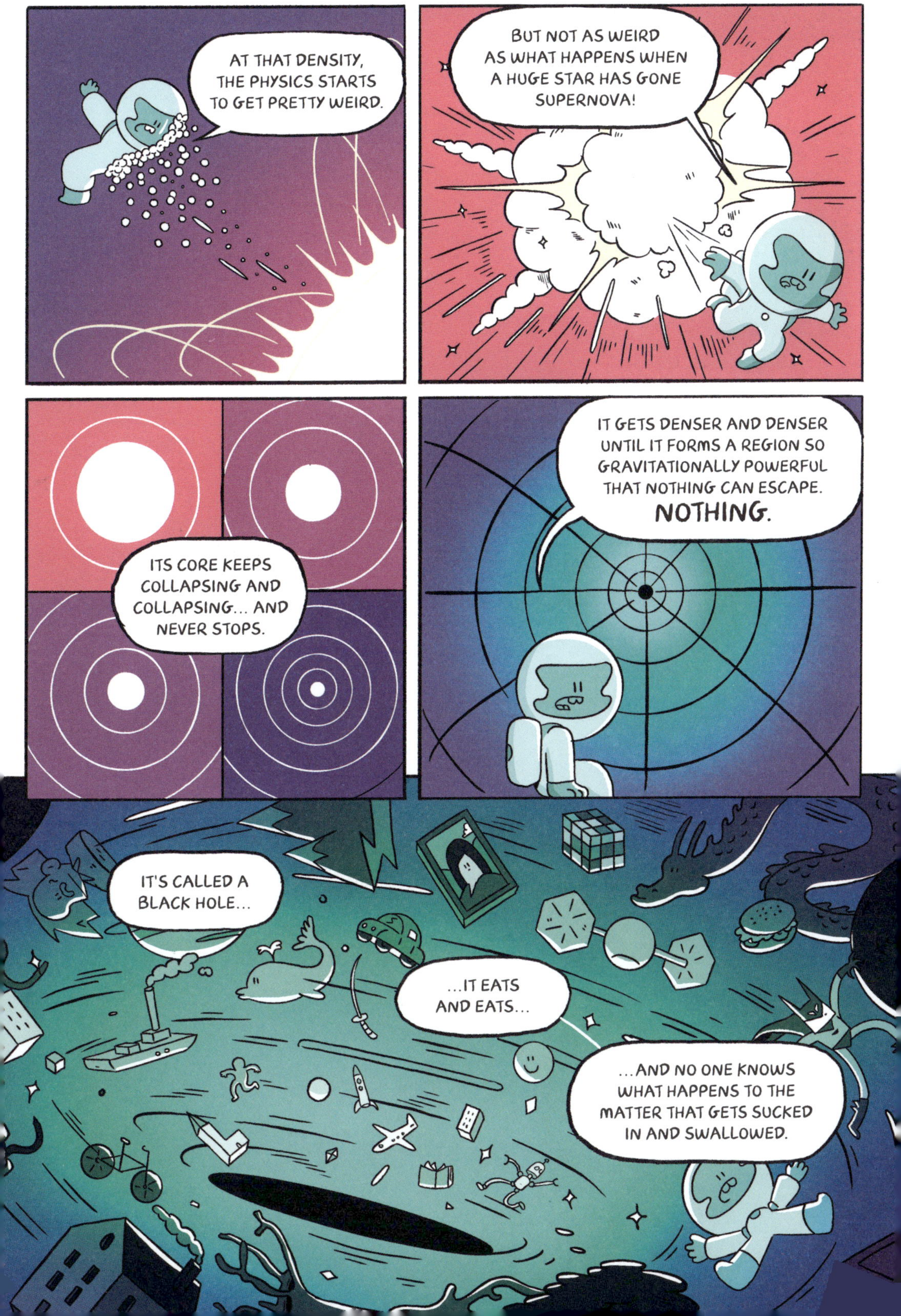
AT THAT DENSITY, THE PHYSICS STARTS TO GET PRETTY WEIRD.
BUT NOT AS WEIRD AS WHAT HAPPENS WHEN A HUGE STAR HAS GONE SUPERNOVA!
ITS CORE KEEPS COLLAPSING AND COLLAPSING... AND NEVER STOPS.
IT GETS DENSER AND DENSER UNTIL IT FORMS A REGION SO GRAVITATIONALLY POWERFUL THAT NOTHING CAN ESCAPE. NOTHING.
IT'S CALLED A BLACK HOLE...
...IT EATS AND EATS...
...AND NO ONE KNOWS WHAT HAPPENS TO THE MATTER THAT GETS SUCKED IN AND SWALLOWED.

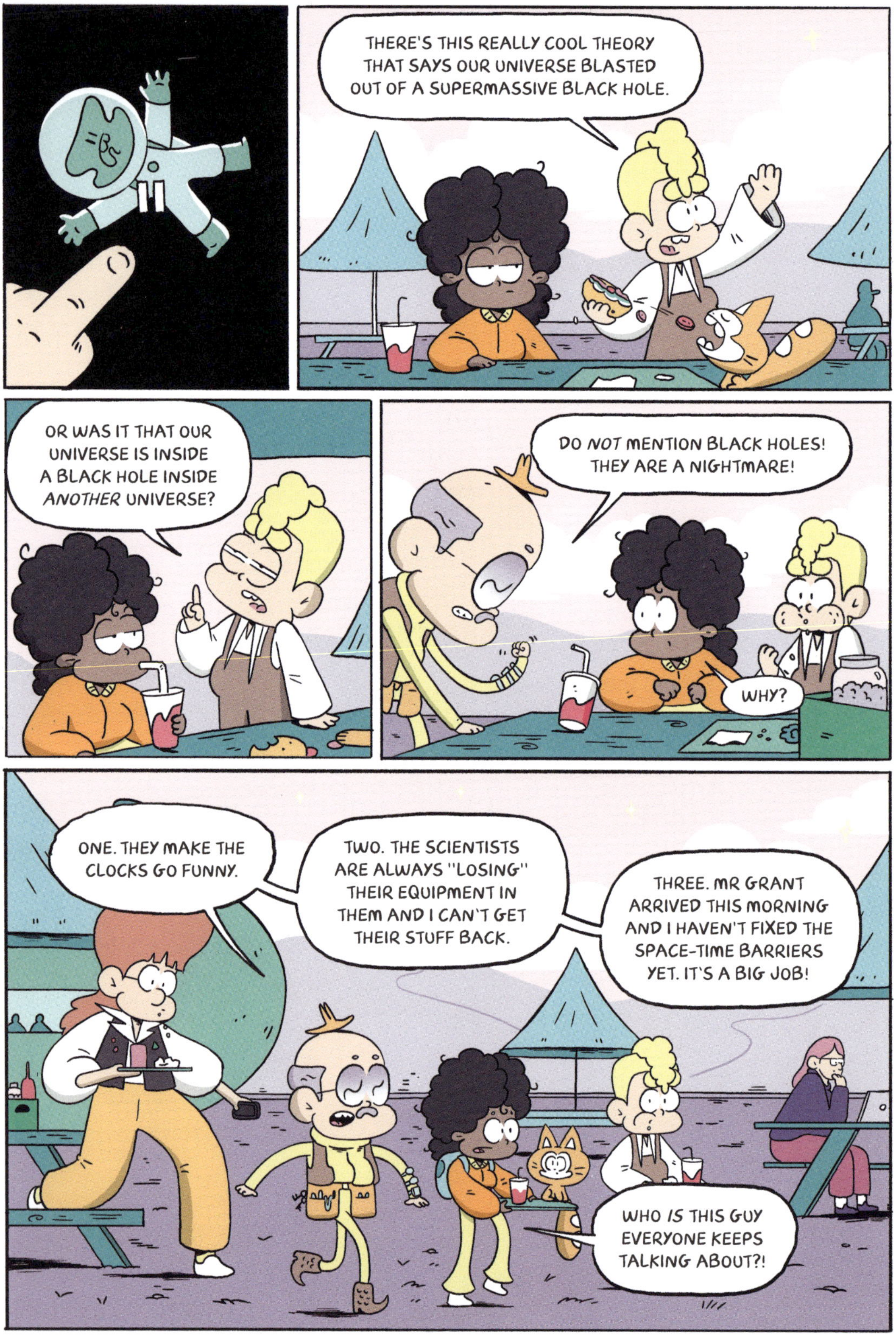
THERE'S THIS REALLY COOL THEORY THAT SAYS OUR UNIVERSE BLASTED OUT OF A SUPERMASSIVE BLACK HOLE.
OR WAS IT THAT OUR UNIVERSE IS INSIDE A BLACK HOLE INSIDE *ANOTHER* UNIVERSE?
DO *NOT* MENTION BLACK HOLES! THEY ARE A NIGHTMARE!
WHY?
ONE. THEY MAKE THE CLOCKS GO FUNNY.
TWO. THE SCIENTISTS ARE ALWAYS "LOSING" THEIR EQUIPMENT IN THEM AND I CAN'T GET THEIR STUFF BACK.
THREE. MR GRANT ARRIVED THIS MORNING AND I HAVEN'T FIXED THE SPACE-TIME BARRIERS YET. IT'S A BIG JOB!
WHO *IS* THIS GUY EVERYONE KEEPS TALKING ABOUT?!

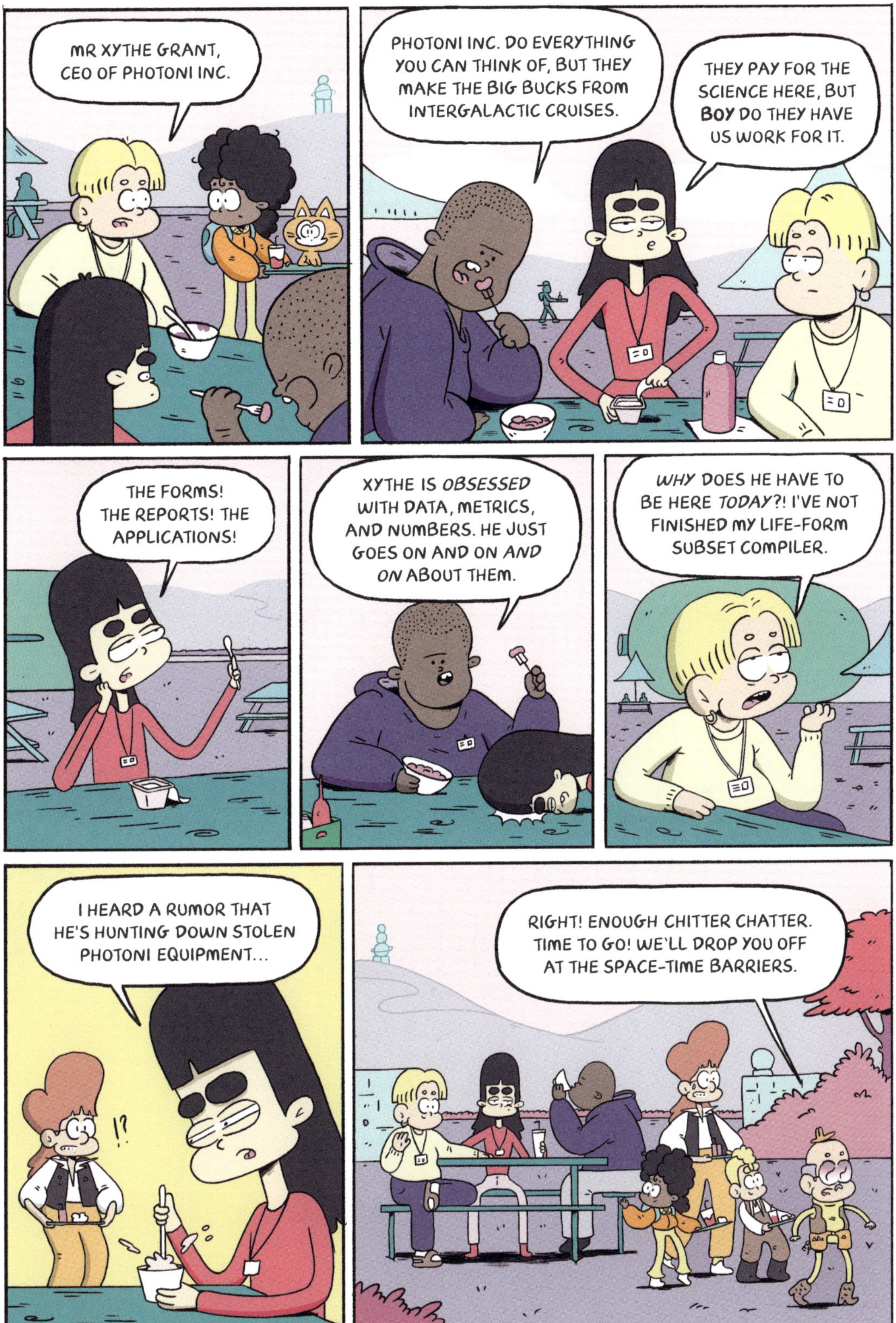
MR XYTHE GRANT, CEO OF PHOTONI INC.
PHOTONI INC. DO EVERYTHING YOU CAN THINK OF, BUT THEY MAKE THE BIG BUCKS FROM INTERGALACTIC CRUISES.
THEY PAY FOR THE SCIENCE HERE, BUT **BOY** DO THEY HAVE US WORK FOR IT.
THE FORMS! THE REPORTS! THE APPLICATIONS!
XYTHE IS *OBSESSED* WITH DATA, METRICS, AND NUMBERS. HE JUST GOES ON AND ON *AND ON* ABOUT THEM.
WHY DOES HE HAVE TO BE HERE *TODAY*?! I'VE NOT FINISHED MY LIFE-FORM SUBSET COMPILER.
I HEARD A RUMOR THAT HE'S HUNTING DOWN STOLEN PHOTONI EQUIPMENT...
!?
RIGHT! ENOUGH CHITTER CHATTER. TIME TO GO! WE'LL DROP YOU OFF AT THE SPACE-TIME BARRIERS.

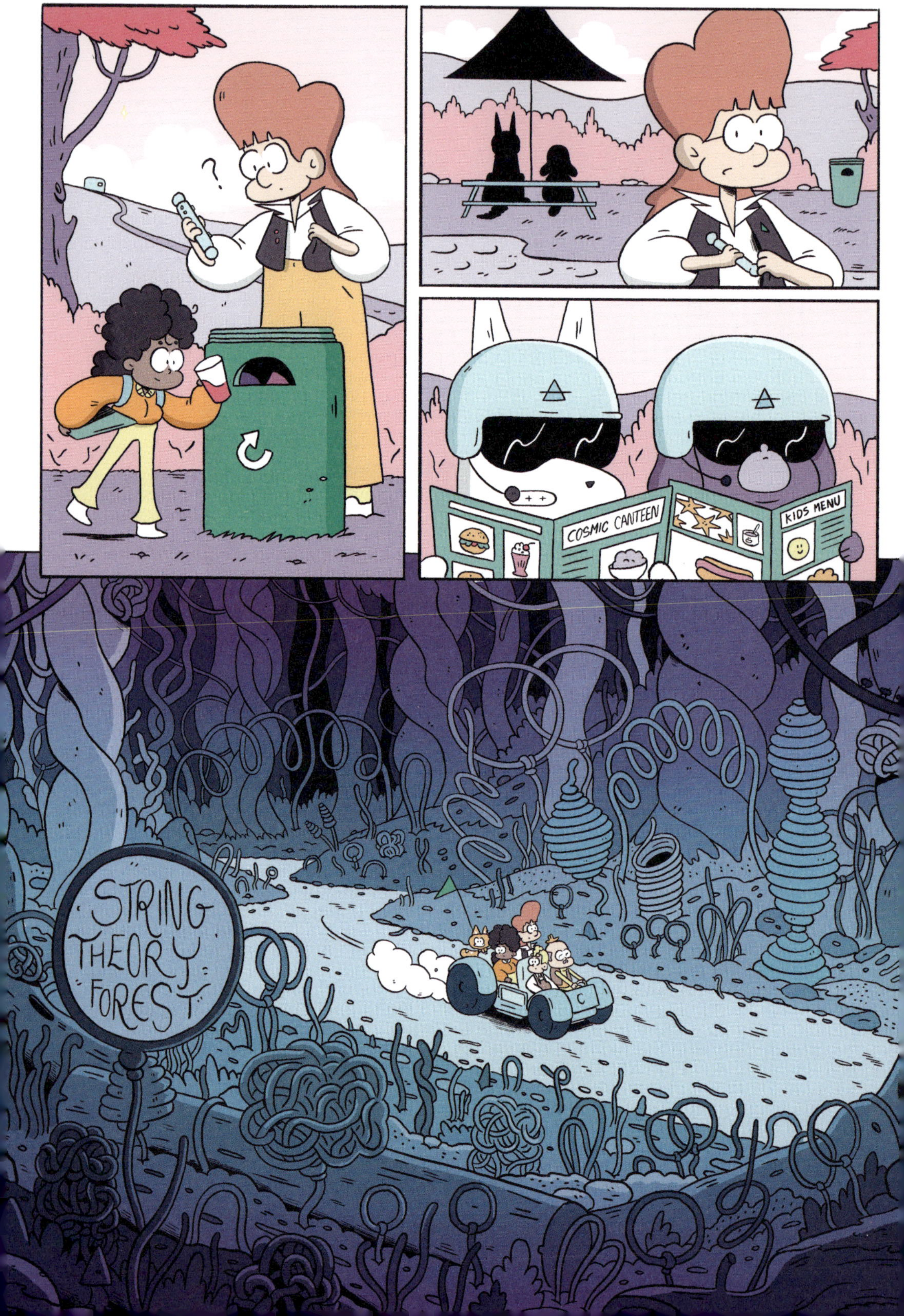
?
COSMIC CANTEEN
KIDS MENU
STRING THEORY FOREST

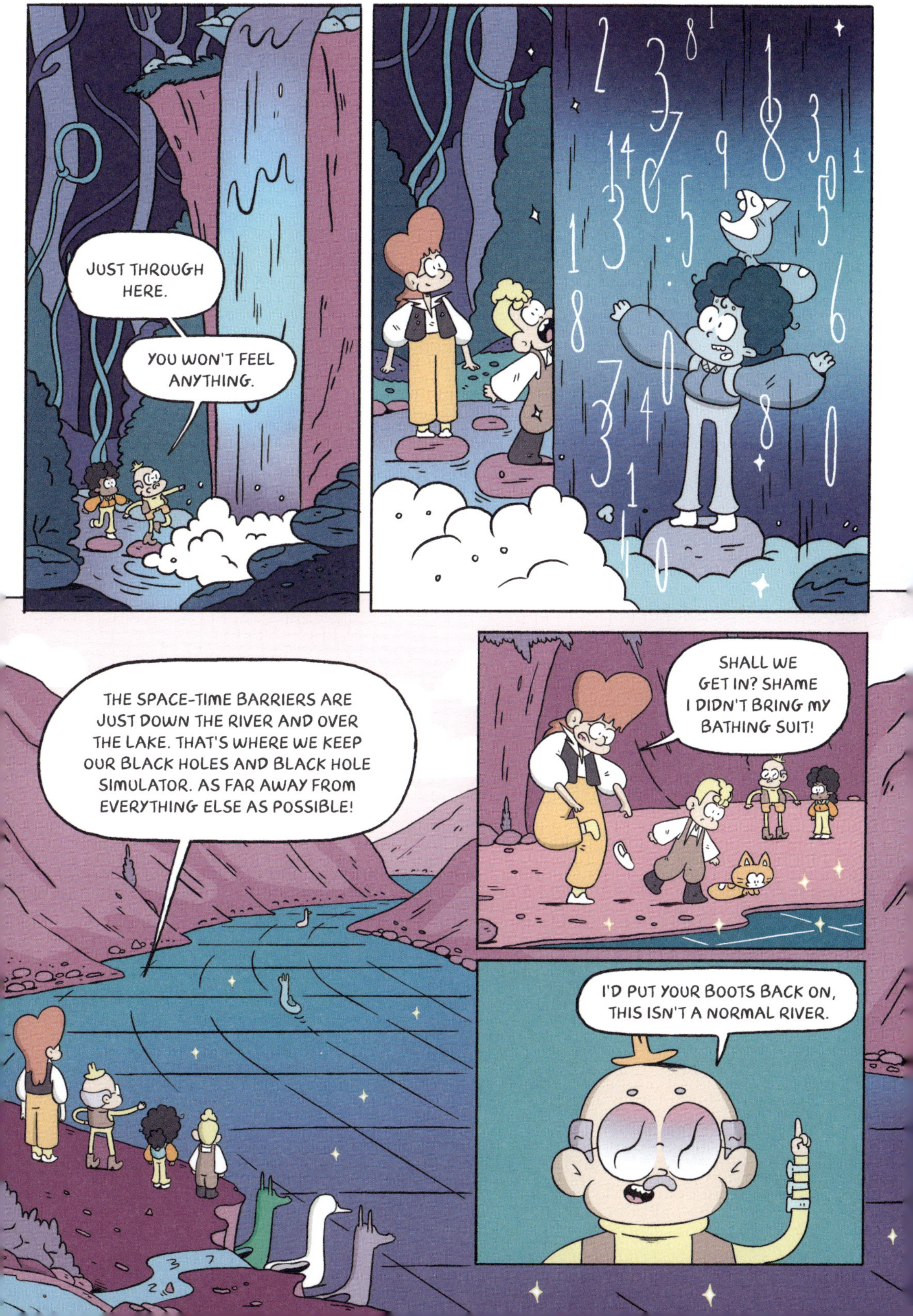

JUST THROUGH HERE.
YOU WON'T FEEL ANYTHING.
THE SPACE-TIME BARRIERS ARE JUST DOWN THE RIVER AND OVER THE LAKE. THAT'S WHERE WE KEEP OUR BLACK HOLES AND BLACK HOLE SIMULATOR. AS FAR AWAY FROM EVERYTHING ELSE AS POSSIBLE!
SHALL WE GET IN? SHAME I DIDN'T BRING MY BATHING SUIT!
I'D PUT YOUR BOOTS BACK ON, THIS ISN'T A NORMAL RIVER.

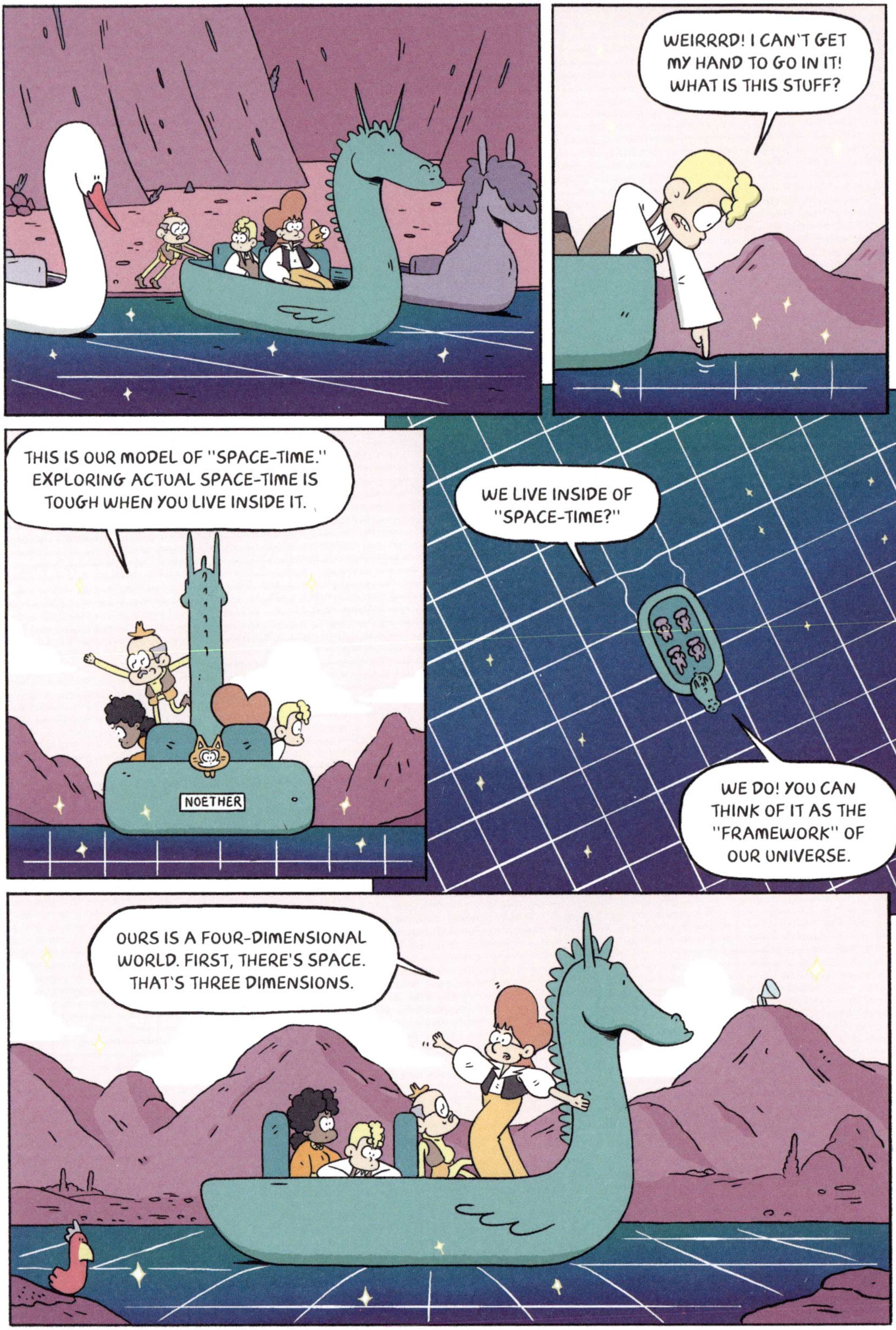
WEIRRRD! I CAN'T GET MY HAND TO GO IN IT! WHAT IS THIS STUFF?
THIS IS OUR MODEL OF "SPACE-TIME." EXPLORING ACTUAL SPACE-TIME IS TOUGH WHEN YOU LIVE INSIDE IT.
NOETHER
WE LIVE INSIDE OF "SPACE-TIME?"
WE DO! YOU CAN THINK OF IT AS THE "FRAMEWORK" OF OUR UNIVERSE.
OURS IS A FOUR-DIMENSIONAL WORLD. FIRST, THERE'S SPACE. THAT'S THREE DIMENSIONS.

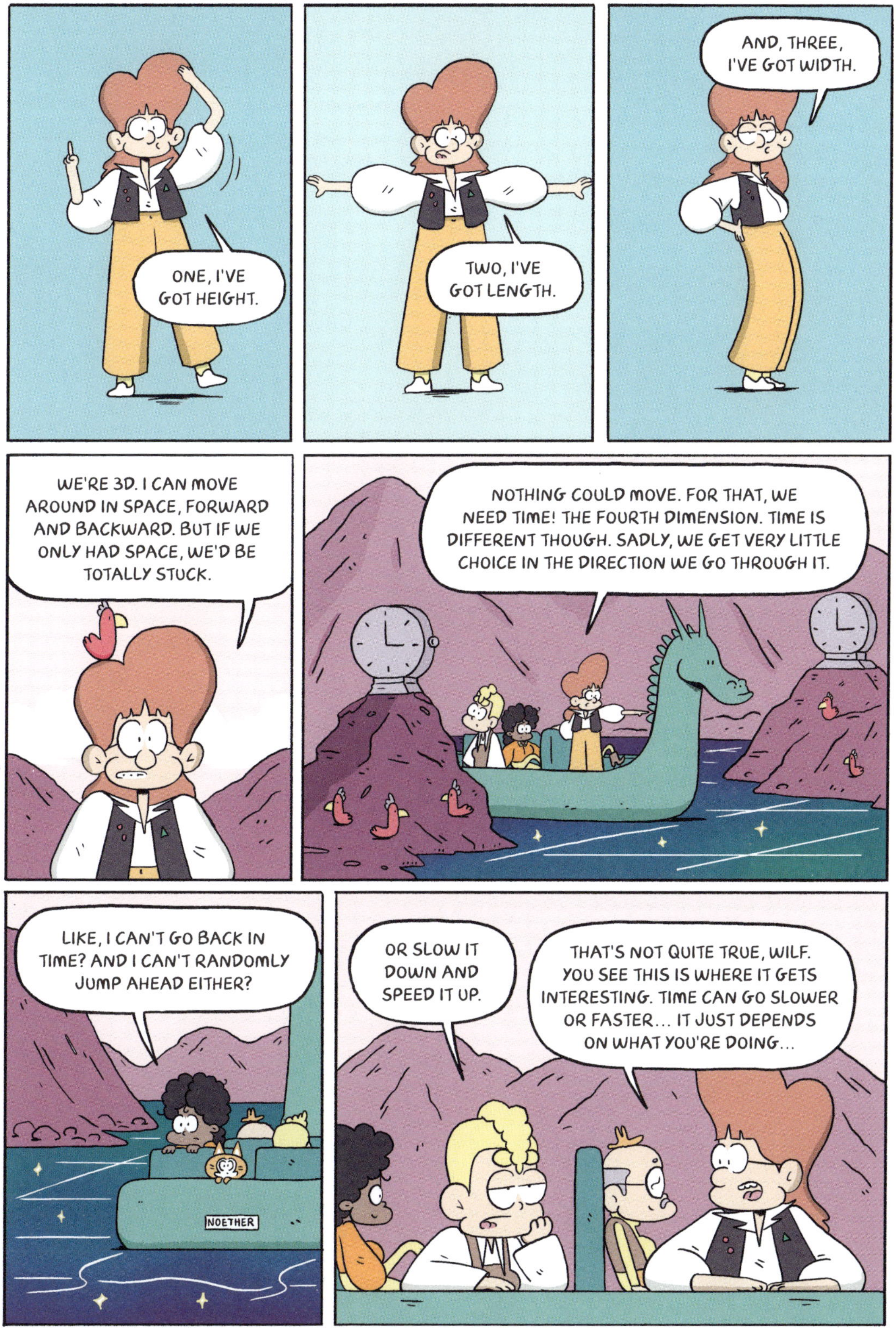
ONE, I'VE GOT HEIGHT.
TWO, I'VE GOT LENGTH.
AND, THREE, I'VE GOT WIDTH.
WE'RE 3D. I CAN MOVE AROUND IN SPACE, FORWARD AND BACKWARD. BUT IF WE ONLY HAD SPACE, WE'D BE TOTALLY STUCK.
NOTHING COULD MOVE. FOR THAT, WE NEED TIME! THE FOURTH DIMENSION. TIME IS DIFFERENT THOUGH. SADLY, WE GET VERY LITTLE CHOICE IN THE DIRECTION WE GO THROUGH IT.
LIKE, I CAN'T GO BACK IN TIME? AND I CAN'T RANDOMLY JUMP AHEAD EITHER?
NOETHER
OR SLOW IT DOWN AND SPEED IT UP.
THAT'S NOT QUITE TRUE, WILF. YOU SEE THIS IS WHERE IT GETS INTERESTING. TIME CAN GO SLOWER OR FASTER... IT JUST DEPENDS ON WHAT YOU'RE DOING...

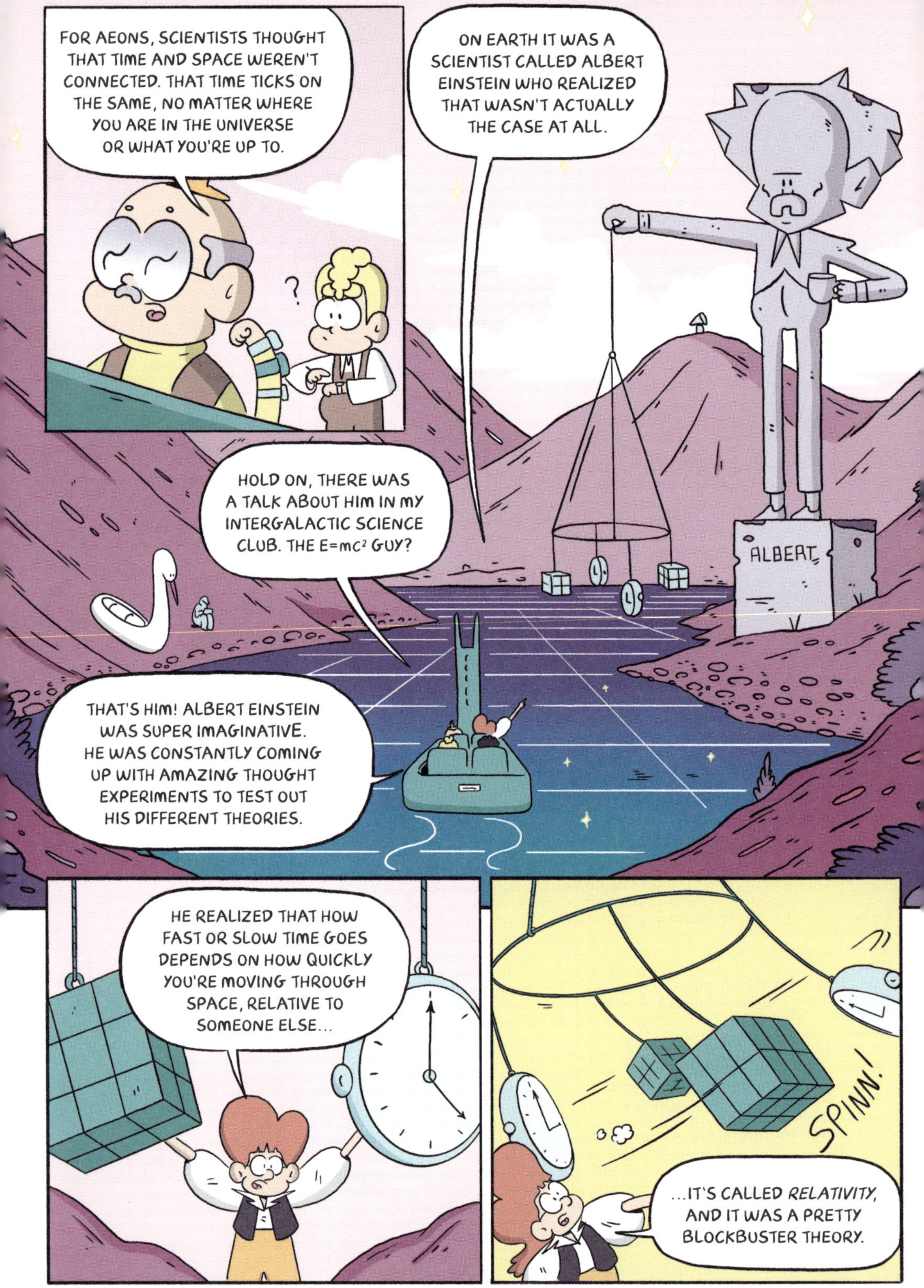
FOR AEONS, SCIENTISTS THOUGHT THAT TIME AND SPACE WEREN'T CONNECTED. THAT TIME TICKS ON THE SAME, NO MATTER WHERE YOU ARE IN THE UNIVERSE OR WHAT YOU'RE UP TO.
?
ON EARTH IT WAS A SCIENTIST CALLED ALBERT EINSTEIN WHO REALIZED THAT WASN'T ACTUALLY THE CASE AT ALL.
ALBERT
HOLD ON, THERE WAS A TALK ABOUT HIM IN MY INTERGALACTIC SCIENCE CLUB. THE $E=mc^2$ GUY?
THAT'S HIM! ALBERT EINSTEIN WAS SUPER IMAGINATIVE. HE WAS CONSTANTLY COMING UP WITH AMAZING THOUGHT EXPERIMENTS TO TEST OUT HIS DIFFERENT THEORIES.
HE REALIZED THAT HOW FAST OR SLOW TIME GOES DEPENDS ON HOW QUICKLY YOU'RE MOVING THROUGH SPACE, RELATIVE TO SOMEONE ELSE...
SPINN!
...IT'S CALLED *RELATIVITY*, AND IT WAS A PRETTY BLOCKBUSTER THEORY.

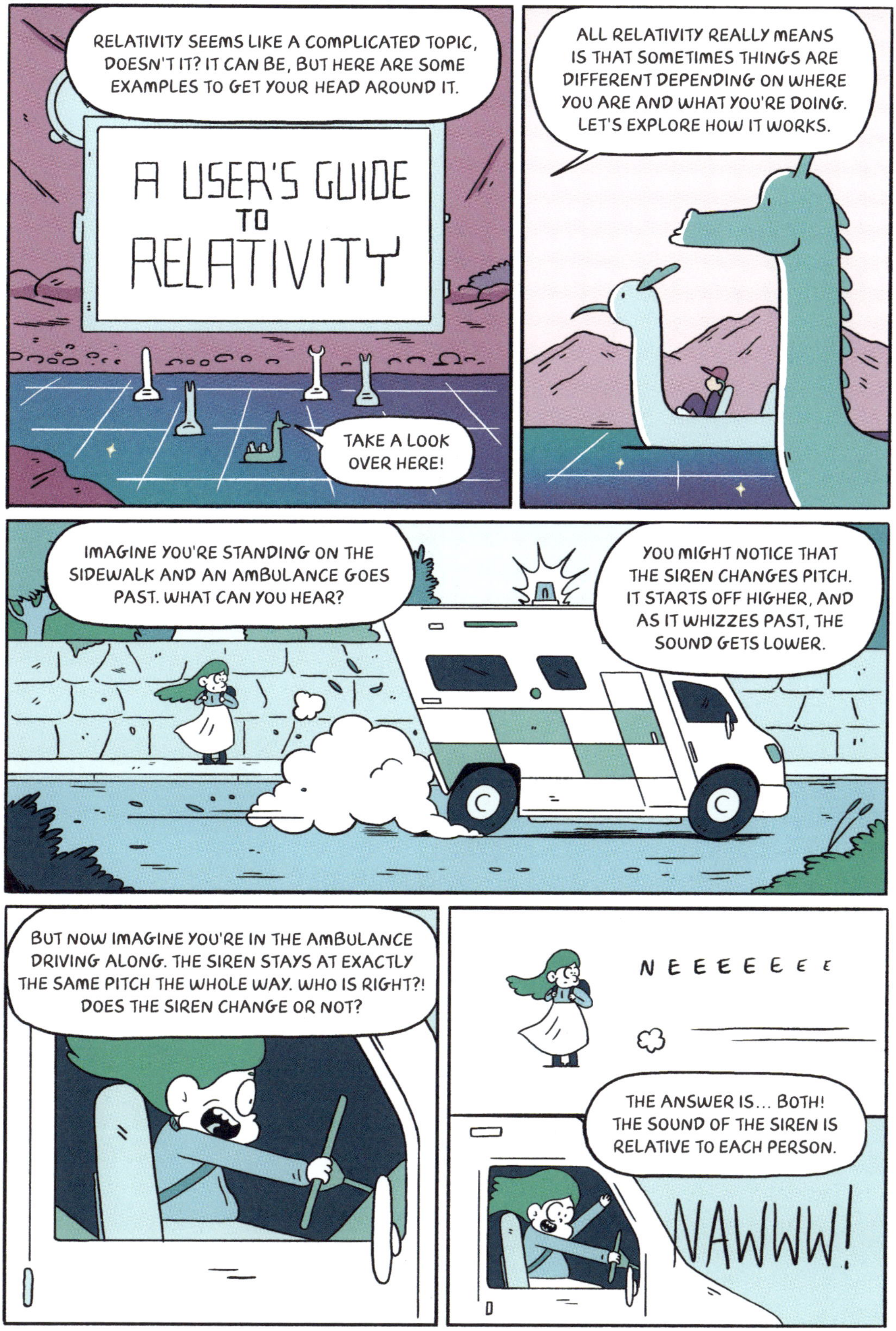
RELATIVITY SEEMS LIKE A COMPLICATED TOPIC, DOESN'T IT? IT CAN BE, BUT HERE ARE SOME EXAMPLES TO GET YOUR HEAD AROUND IT.
A USER'S GUIDE TO RELATIVITY
TAKE A LOOK OVER HERE!
ALL RELATIVITY REALLY MEANS IS THAT SOMETIMES THINGS ARE DIFFERENT DEPENDING ON WHERE YOU ARE AND WHAT YOU'RE DOING. LET'S EXPLORE HOW IT WORKS.
IMAGINE YOU'RE STANDING ON THE SIDEWALK AND AN AMBULANCE GOES PAST. WHAT CAN YOU HEAR?
YOU MIGHT NOTICE THAT THE SIREN CHANGES PITCH. IT STARTS OFF HIGHER, AND AS IT WHIZZES PAST, THE SOUND GETS LOWER.
BUT NOW IMAGINE YOU'RE IN THE AMBULANCE DRIVING ALONG. THE SIREN STAYS AT EXACTLY THE SAME PITCH THE WHOLE WAY. WHO IS RIGHT?! DOES THE SIREN CHANGE OR NOT?
NEEEEEEEE
THE ANSWER IS... BOTH! THE SOUND OF THE SIREN IS RELATIVE TO EACH PERSON.
NAWWW!

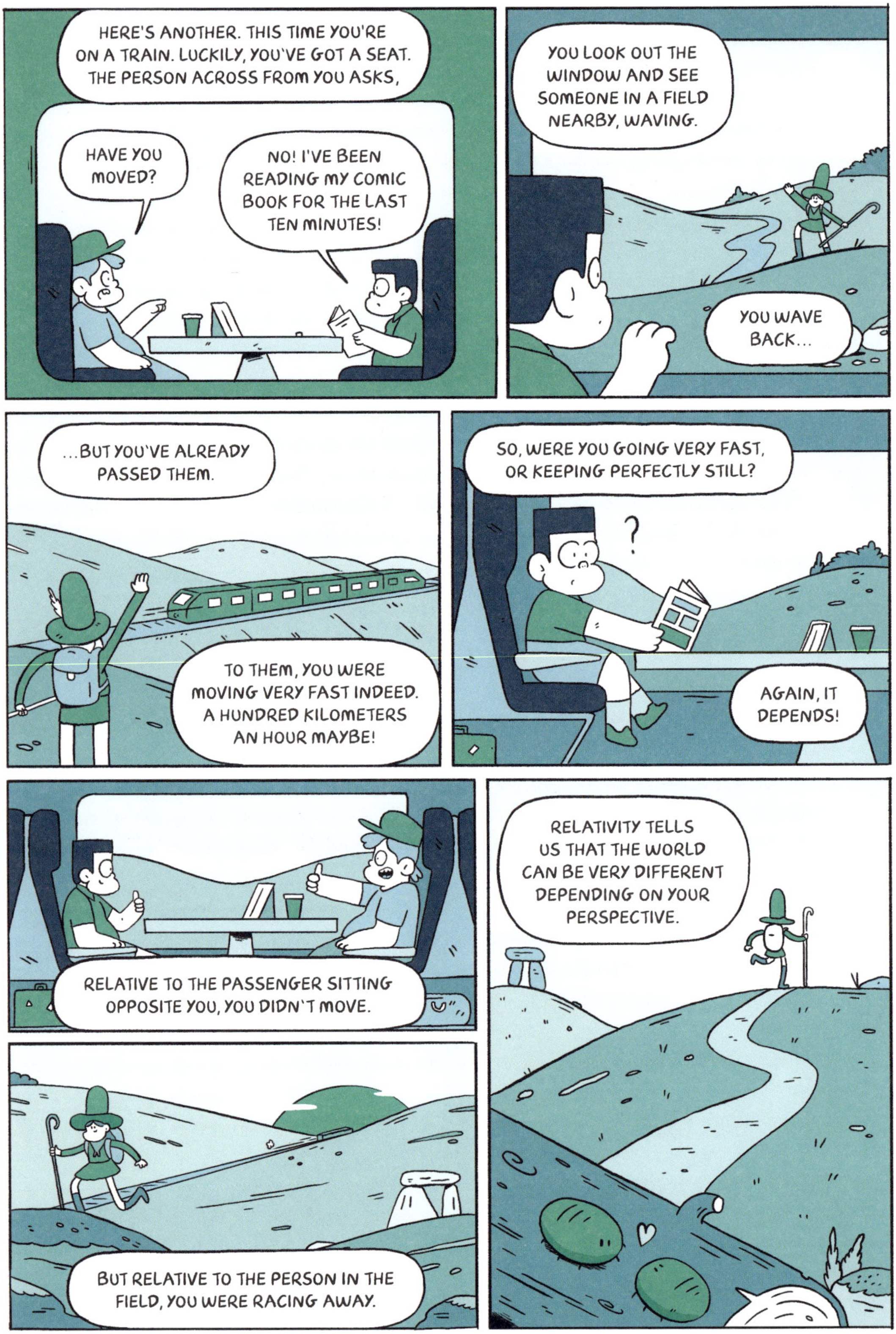
HERE'S ANOTHER. THIS TIME YOU'RE ON A TRAIN. LUCKILY, YOU'VE GOT A SEAT. THE PERSON ACROSS FROM YOU ASKS,
HAVE YOU MOVED?
NO! I'VE BEEN READING MY COMIC BOOK FOR THE LAST TEN MINUTES!
YOU LOOK OUT THE WINDOW AND SEE SOMEONE IN A FIELD NEARBY, WAVING.
YOU WAVE BACK...
...BUT YOU'VE ALREADY PASSED THEM.
TO THEM, YOU WERE MOVING VERY FAST INDEED. A HUNDRED KILOMETERS AN HOUR MAYBE!
SO, WERE YOU GOING VERY FAST, OR KEEPING PERFECTLY STILL?
?
AGAIN, IT DEPENDS!
RELATIVE TO THE PASSENGER SITTING OPPOSITE YOU, YOU DIDN'T MOVE.
BUT RELATIVE TO THE PERSON IN THE FIELD, YOU WERE RACING AWAY.
RELATIVITY TELLS US THAT THE WORLD CAN BE VERY DIFFERENT DEPENDING ON YOUR PERSPECTIVE.

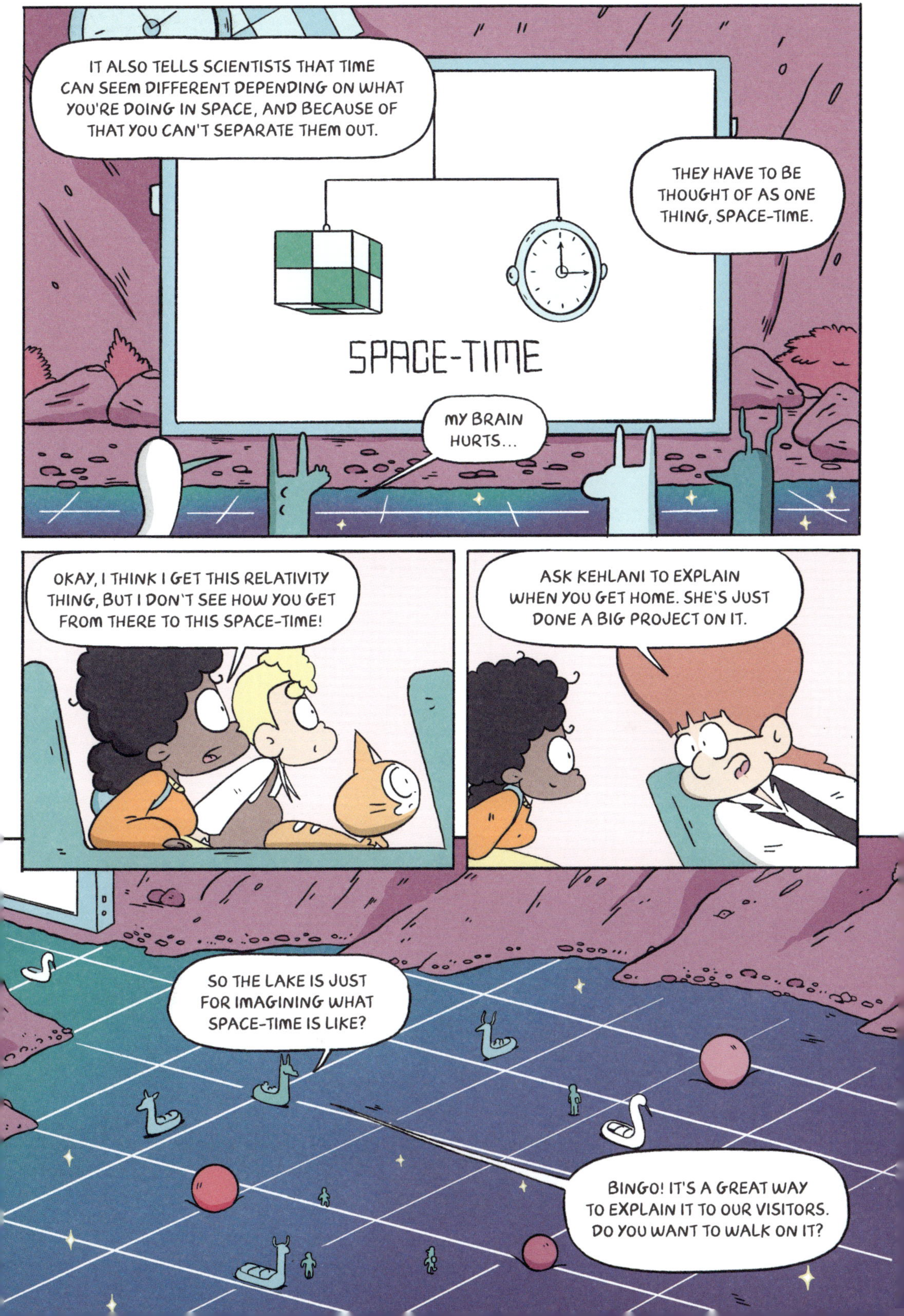
IT ALSO TELLS SCIENTISTS THAT TIME CAN SEEM DIFFERENT DEPENDING ON WHAT YOU'RE DOING IN SPACE, AND BECAUSE OF THAT YOU CAN'T SEPARATE THEM OUT.
THEY HAVE TO BE THOUGHT OF AS ONE THING, SPACE-TIME.
SPACE-TIME
MY BRAIN HURTS...
OKAY, I THINK I GET THIS RELATIVITY THING, BUT I DON'T SEE HOW YOU GET FROM THERE TO THIS SPACE-TIME!
ASK KEHLANI TO EXPLAIN WHEN YOU GET HOME. SHE'S JUST DONE A BIG PROJECT ON IT.
SO THE LAKE IS JUST FOR IMAGINING WHAT SPACE-TIME IS LIKE?
BINGO! IT'S A GREAT WAY TO EXPLAIN IT TO OUR VISITORS. DO YOU WANT TO WALK ON IT?

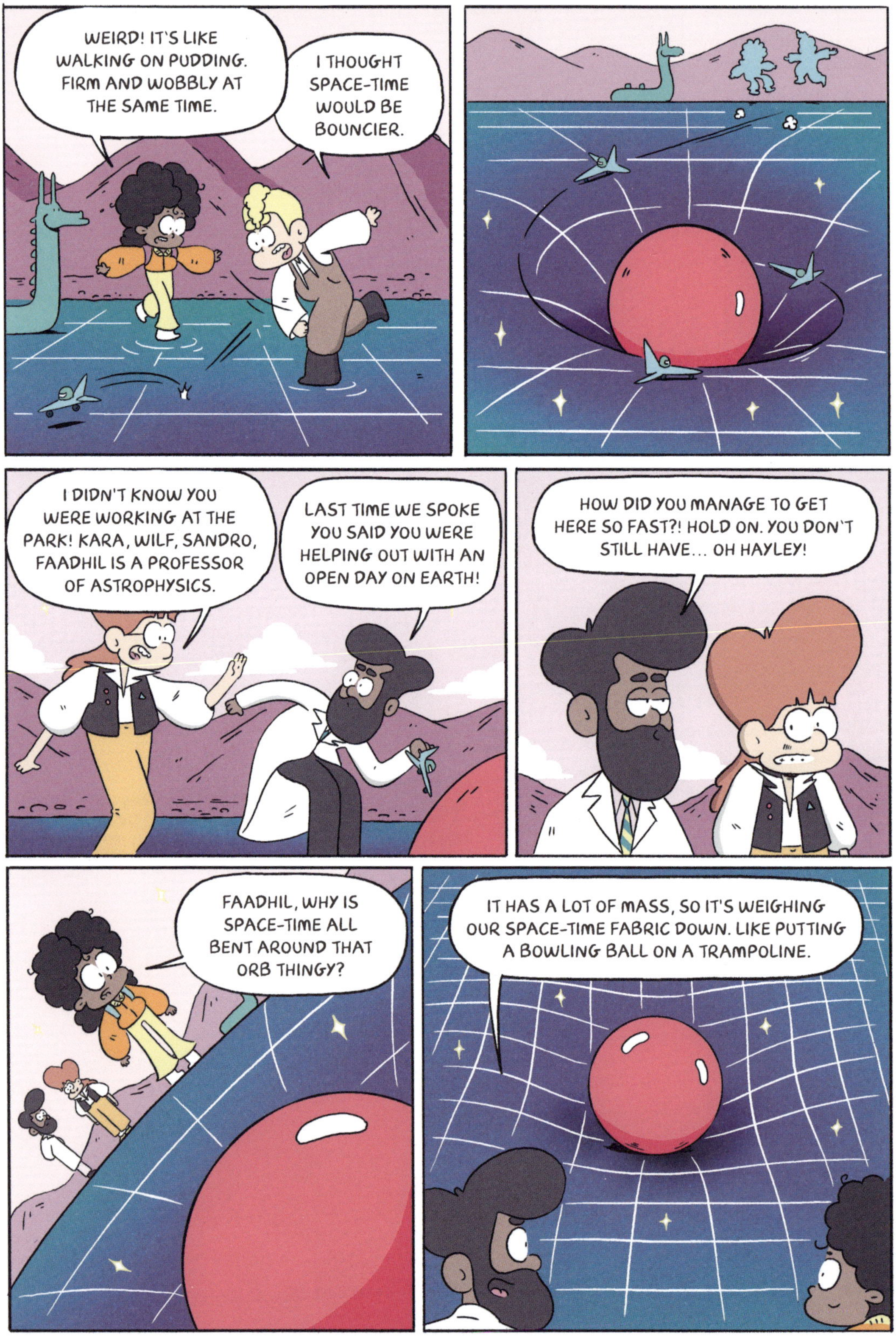
WEIRD! IT'S LIKE WALKING ON PUDDING. FIRM AND WOBBLY AT THE SAME TIME.
I THOUGHT SPACE-TIME WOULD BE BOUNCIER.
I DIDN'T KNOW YOU WERE WORKING AT THE PARK! KARA, WILF, SANDRO, FAADHIL IS A PROFESSOR OF ASTROPHYSICS.
LAST TIME WE SPOKE YOU SAID YOU WERE HELPING OUT WITH AN OPEN DAY ON EARTH!
HOW DID YOU MANAGE TO GET HERE SO FAST?! HOLD ON. YOU DON'T STILL HAVE... OH HAYLEY!
FAADHIL, WHY IS SPACE-TIME ALL BENT AROUND THAT ORB THINGY?
IT HAS A LOT OF MASS, SO IT'S WEIGHING OUR SPACE-TIME FABRIC DOWN. LIKE PUTTING A BOWLING BALL ON A TRAMPOLINE.

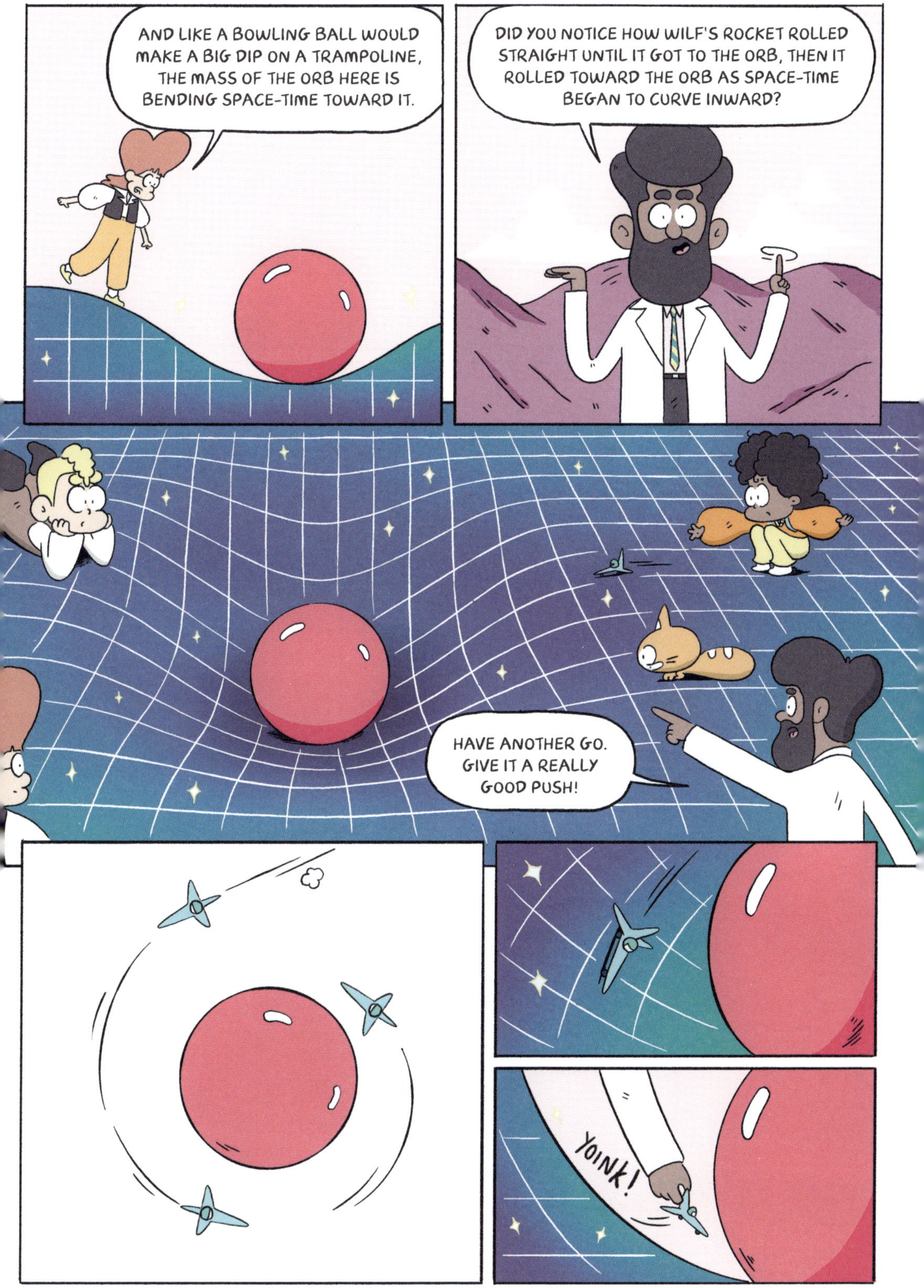
AND LIKE A BOWLING BALL WOULD MAKE A BIG DIP ON A TRAMPOLINE, THE MASS OF THE ORB HERE IS BENDING SPACE-TIME TOWARD IT.
DID YOU NOTICE HOW WILF'S ROCKET ROLLED STRAIGHT UNTIL IT GOT TO THE ORB, THEN IT ROLLED TOWARD THE ORB AS SPACE-TIME BEGAN TO CURVE INWARD?
HAVE ANOTHER GO. GIVE IT A REALLY GOOD PUSH!
YOINK!

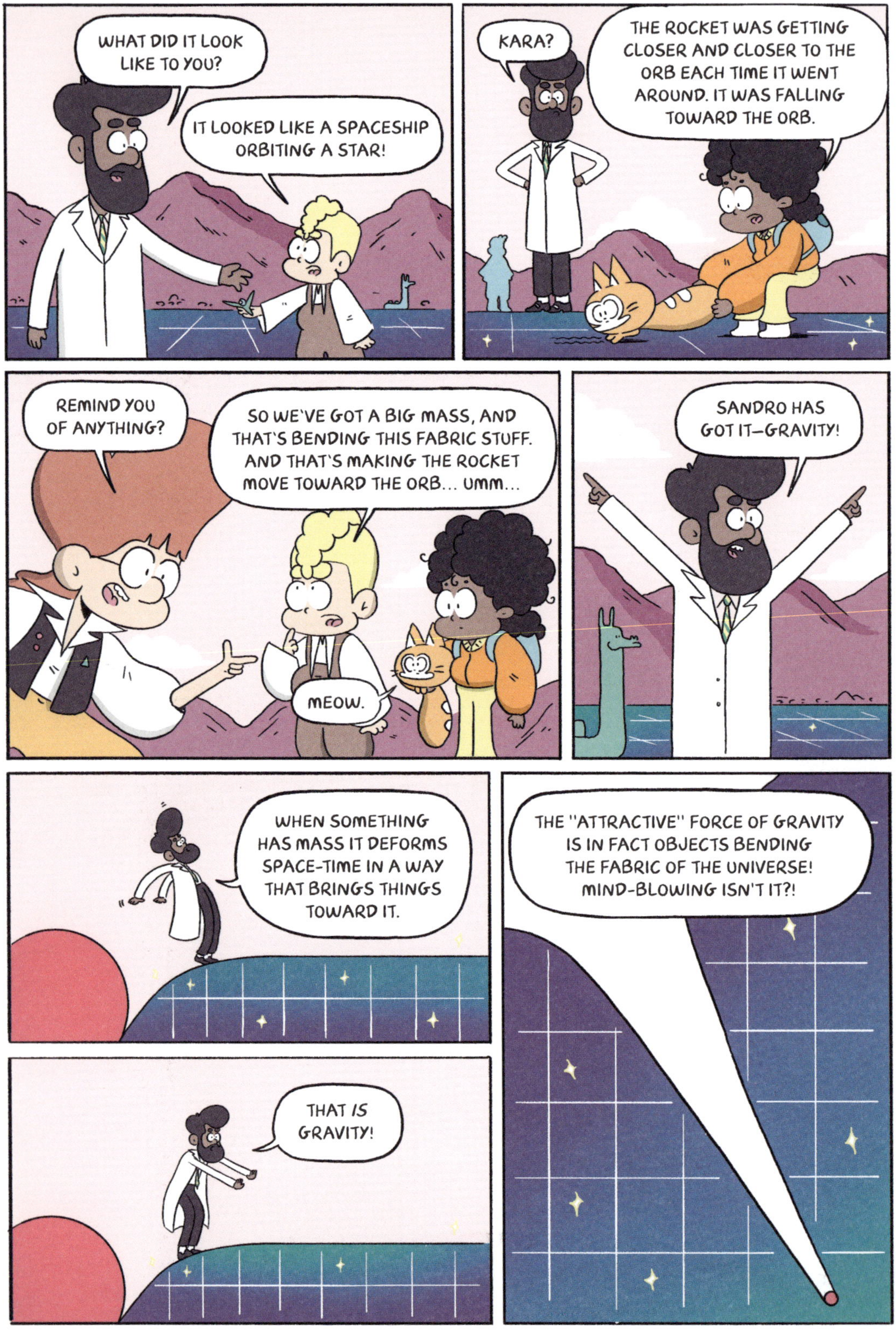
WHAT DID IT LOOK LIKE TO YOU?
IT LOOKED LIKE A SPACESHIP ORBITING A STAR!
KARA?
THE ROCKET WAS GETTING CLOSER AND CLOSER TO THE ORB EACH TIME IT WENT AROUND. IT WAS FALLING TOWARD THE ORB.
REMIND YOU OF ANYTHING?
SO WE'VE GOT A BIG MASS, AND THAT'S BENDING THIS FABRIC STUFF. AND THAT'S MAKING THE ROCKET MOVE TOWARD THE ORB... UMM...
MEOW.
SANDRO HAS GOT IT—GRAVITY!
WHEN SOMETHING HAS MASS IT DEFORMS SPACE-TIME IN A WAY THAT BRINGS THINGS TOWARD IT.
THAT *IS* GRAVITY!
THE "ATTRACTIVE" FORCE OF GRAVITY IS IN FACT OBJECTS BENDING THE FABRIC OF THE UNIVERSE! MIND-BLOWING ISN'T IT?!

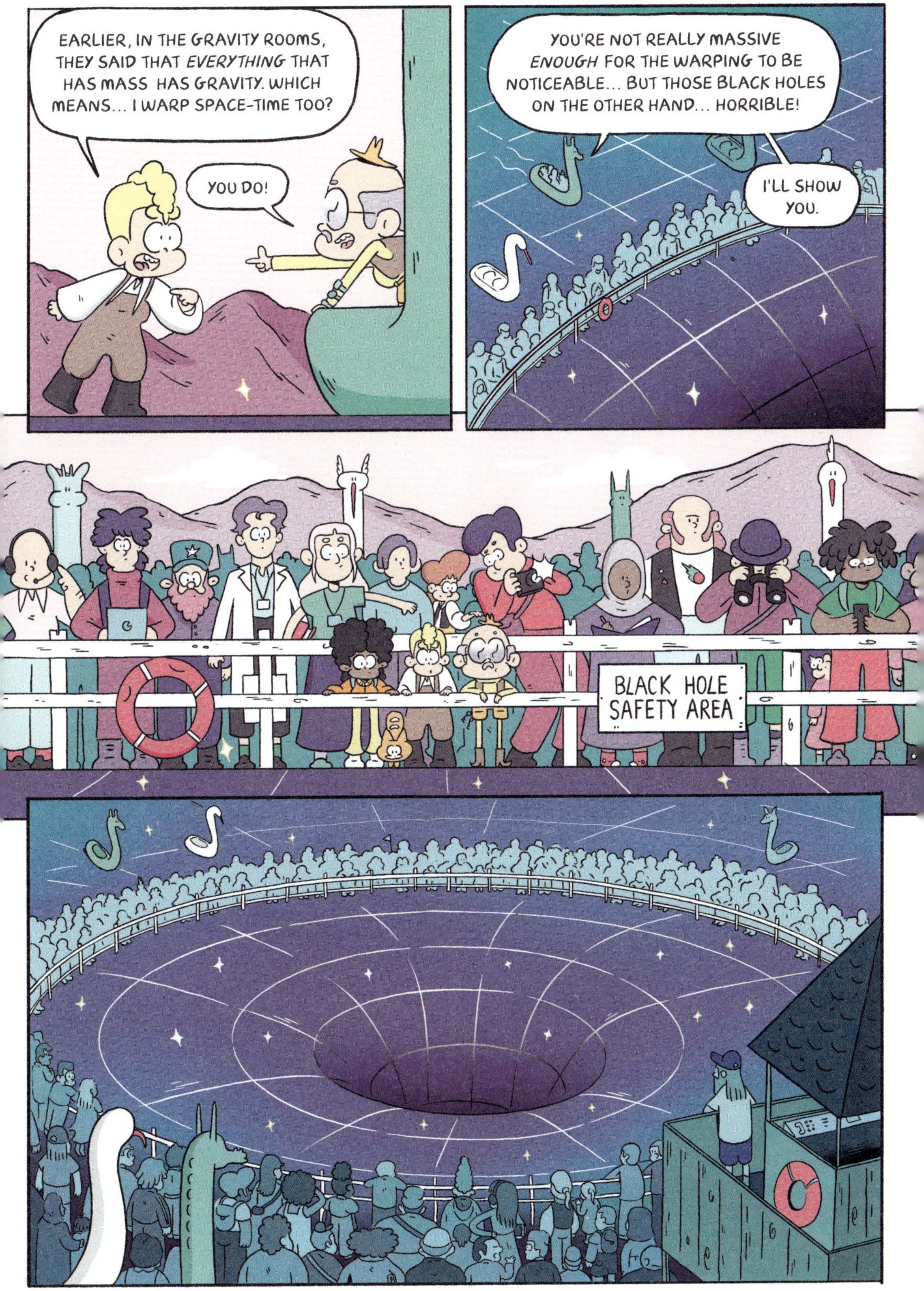
EARLIER, IN THE GRAVITY ROOMS, THEY SAID THAT *EVERYTHING* THAT HAS MASS HAS GRAVITY. WHICH MEANS... I WARP SPACE-TIME TOO?
YOU DO!
YOU'RE NOT REALLY MASSIVE *ENOUGH* FOR THE WARPING TO BE NOTICEABLE... BUT THOSE BLACK HOLES ON THE OTHER HAND... HORRIBLE!
I'LL SHOW YOU.
BLACK HOLE SAFETY AREA

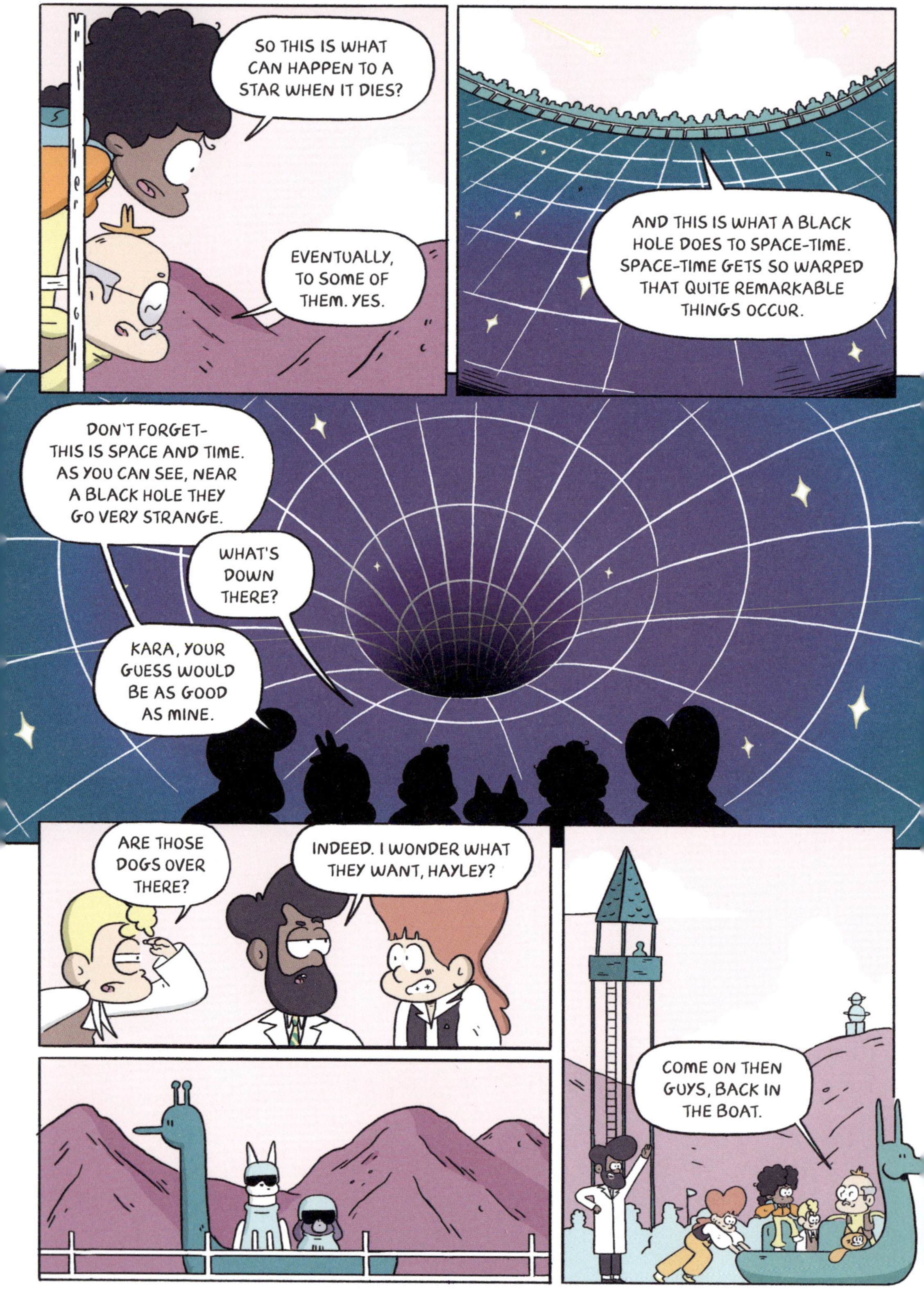
SO THIS IS WHAT CAN HAPPEN TO A STAR WHEN IT DIES?
EVENTUALLY, TO SOME OF THEM. YES.
AND THIS IS WHAT A BLACK HOLE DOES TO SPACE-TIME. SPACE-TIME GETS SO WARPED THAT QUITE REMARKABLE THINGS OCCUR.
DON'T FORGET- THIS IS SPACE AND TIME. AS YOU CAN SEE, NEAR A BLACK HOLE THEY GO VERY STRANGE.
WHAT'S DOWN THERE?
KARA, YOUR GUESS WOULD BE AS GOOD AS MINE.
ARE THOSE DOGS OVER THERE?
INDEED. I WONDER WHAT THEY WANT, HAYLEY?
COME ON THEN GUYS, BACK IN THE BOAT.

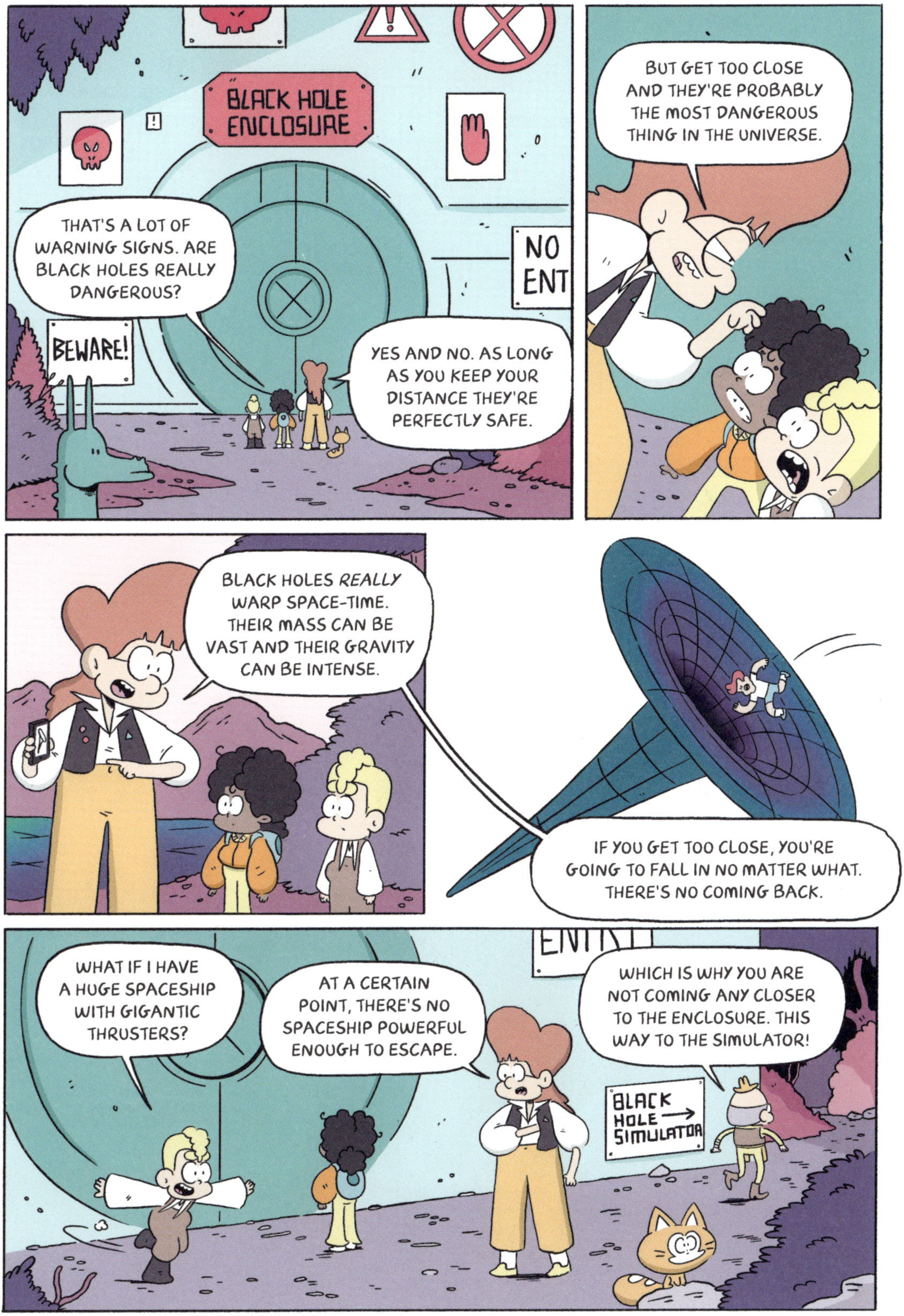
BLACK HOLE ENCLOSURE
THAT'S A LOT OF WARNING SIGNS. ARE BLACK HOLES REALLY DANGEROUS?
BEWARE!
NO ENT
YES AND NO. AS LONG AS YOU KEEP YOUR DISTANCE THEY'RE PERFECTLY SAFE.
BUT GET TOO CLOSE AND THEY'RE PROBABLY THE MOST DANGEROUS THING IN THE UNIVERSE.
BLACK HOLES *REALLY* WARP SPACE-TIME. THEIR MASS CAN BE VAST AND THEIR GRAVITY CAN BE INTENSE.
IF YOU GET TOO CLOSE, YOU'RE GOING TO FALL IN NO MATTER WHAT. THERE'S NO COMING BACK.
WHAT IF I HAVE A HUGE SPACESHIP WITH GIGANTIC THRUSTERS?
AT A CERTAIN POINT, THERE'S NO SPACESHIP POWERFUL ENOUGH TO ESCAPE.
WHICH IS WHY YOU ARE NOT COMING ANY CLOSER TO THE ENCLOSURE. THIS WAY TO THE SIMULATOR!
BLACK HOLE SIMULATOR

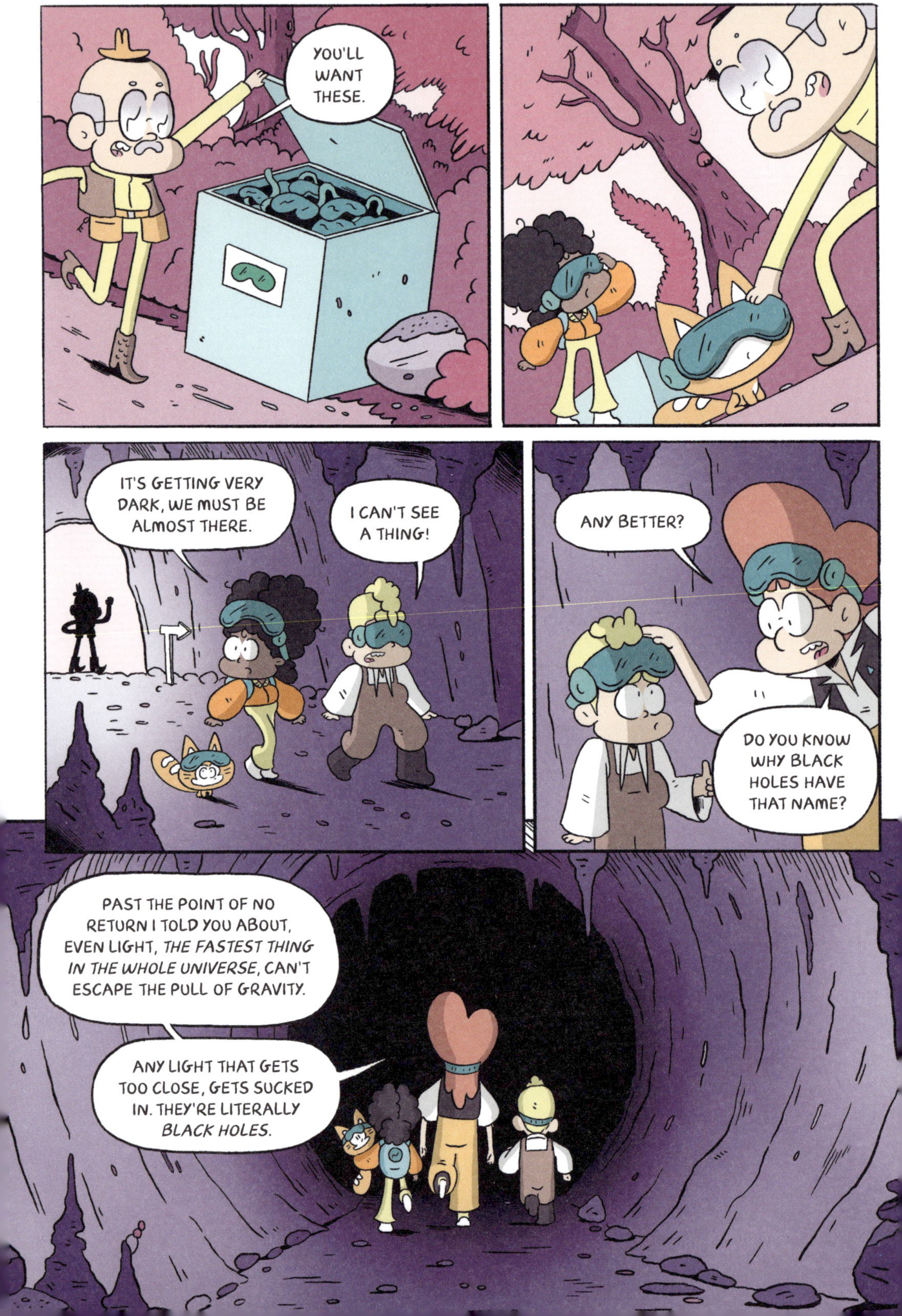
YOU'LL WANT THESE.
IT'S GETTING VERY DARK, WE MUST BE ALMOST THERE.
I CAN'T SEE A THING!
ANY BETTER?
DO YOU KNOW WHY BLACK HOLES HAVE THAT NAME?
PAST THE POINT OF NO RETURN I TOLD YOU ABOUT, EVEN LIGHT, *THE FASTEST THING IN THE WHOLE UNIVERSE*, CAN'T ESCAPE THE PULL OF GRAVITY.
ANY LIGHT THAT GETS TOO CLOSE, GETS SUCKED IN. THEY'RE LITERALLY *BLACK HOLES*.

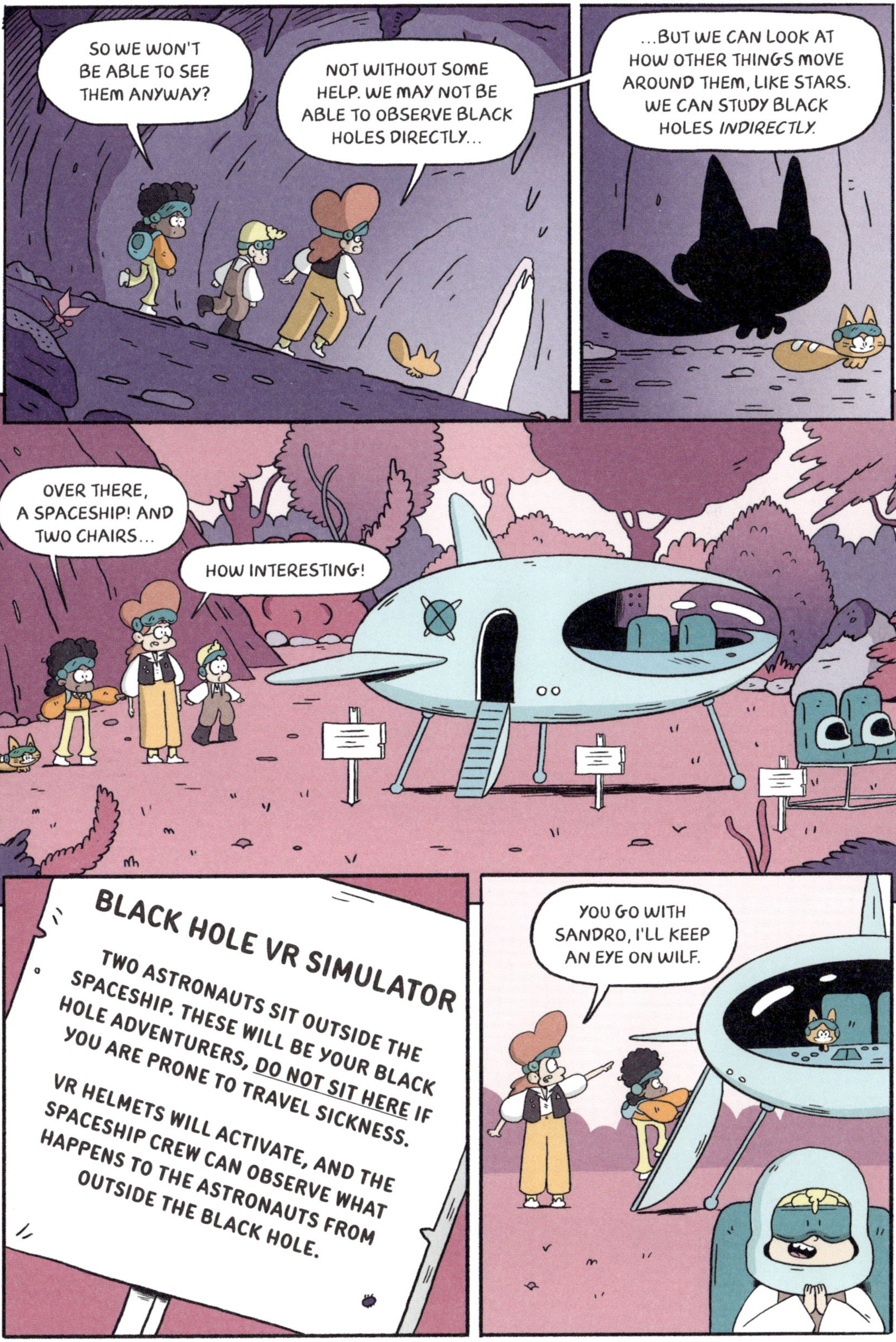

SO WE WON'T BE ABLE TO SEE THEM ANYWAY?
NOT WITHOUT SOME HELP. WE MAY NOT BE ABLE TO OBSERVE BLACK HOLES DIRECTLY...
...BUT WE CAN LOOK AT HOW OTHER THINGS MOVE AROUND THEM, LIKE STARS. WE CAN STUDY BLACK HOLES *INDIRECTLY.*
OVER THERE, A SPACESHIP! AND TWO CHAIRS...
HOW INTERESTING!
BLACK HOLE VR SIMULATOR
TWO ASTRONAUTS SIT OUTSIDE THE SPACESHIP. THESE WILL BE YOUR BLACK HOLE ADVENTURERS, DO NOT SIT HERE IF YOU ARE PRONE TO TRAVEL SICKNESS.
VR HELMETS WILL ACTIVATE, AND THE SPACESHIP CREW CAN OBSERVE WHAT HAPPENS TO THE ASTRONAUTS FROM OUTSIDE THE BLACK HOLE.
YOU GO WITH SANDRO, I'LL KEEP AN EYE ON WILF.

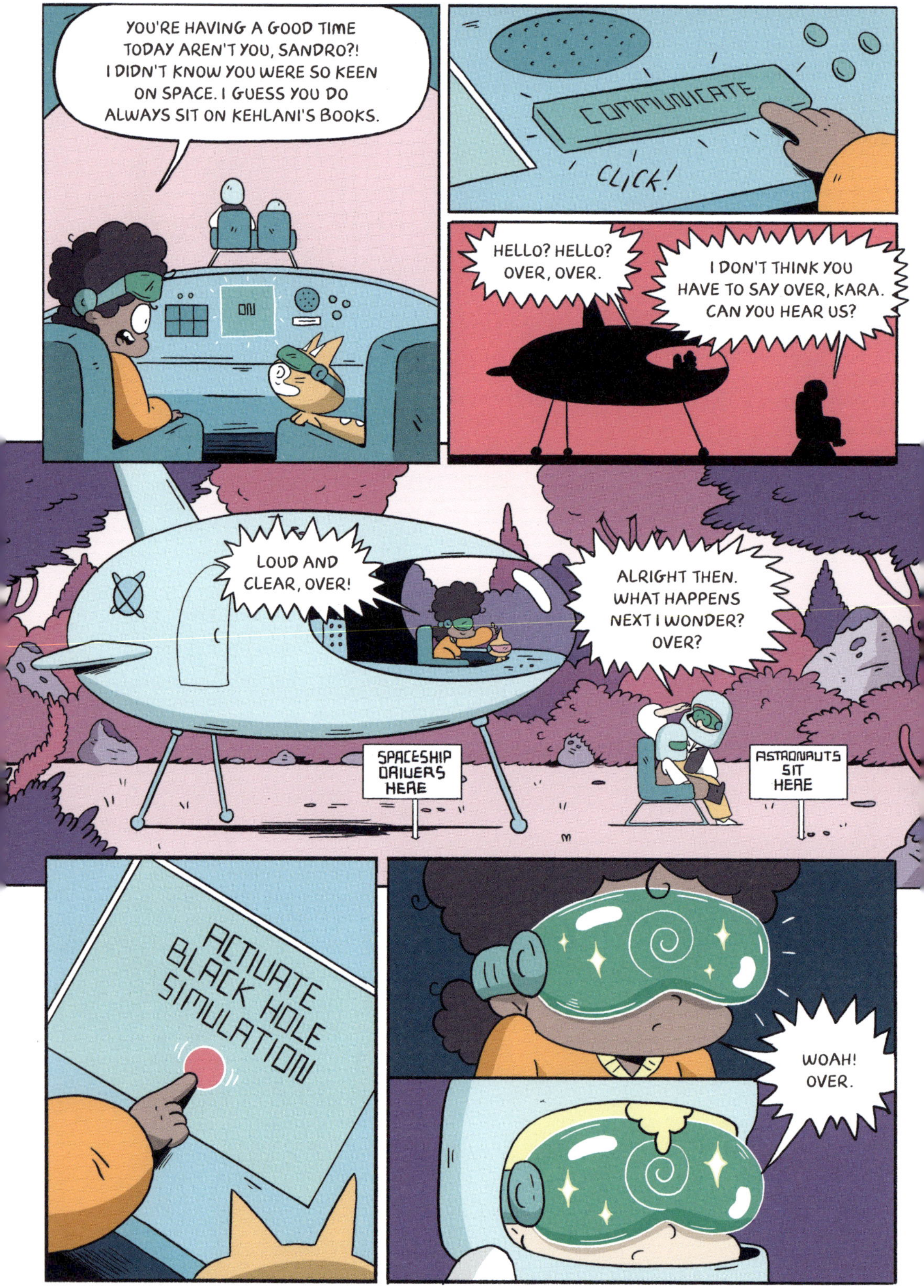

YOU'RE HAVING A GOOD TIME TODAY AREN'T YOU, SANDRO?! I DIDN'T KNOW YOU WERE SO KEEN ON SPACE. I GUESS YOU DO ALWAYS SIT ON KEHLANI'S BOOKS.
ON
COMMUNICATE
CLICK!
HELLO? HELLO? OVER, OVER.
I DON'T THINK YOU HAVE TO SAY OVER, KARA. CAN YOU HEAR US?
LOUD AND CLEAR, OVER!
ALRIGHT THEN. WHAT HAPPENS NEXT I WONDER? OVER?
SPACESHIP DRIVERS HERE
ASTRONAUTS SIT HERE
ACTIVATE BLACK HOLE SIMULATION
WOAH! OVER.

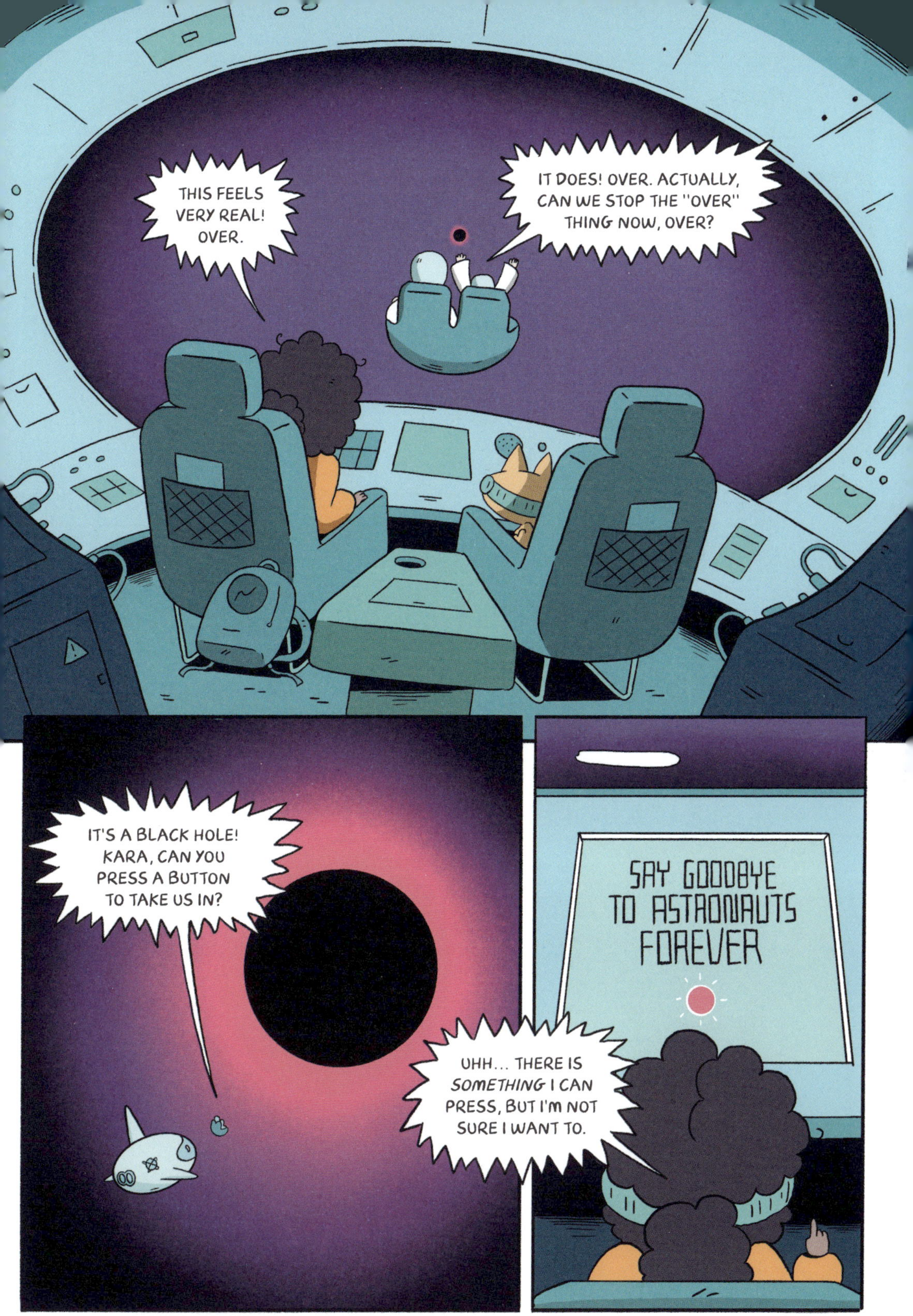
THIS FEELS VERY REAL! OVER.
IT DOES! OVER. ACTUALLY, CAN WE STOP THE "OVER" THING NOW, OVER?
IT'S A BLACK HOLE! KARA, CAN YOU PRESS A BUTTON TO TAKE US IN?
SAY GOODBYE TO ASTRONAUTS FOREVER
UHH... THERE IS *SOMETHING* I CAN PRESS, BUT I'M NOT SURE I WANT TO.

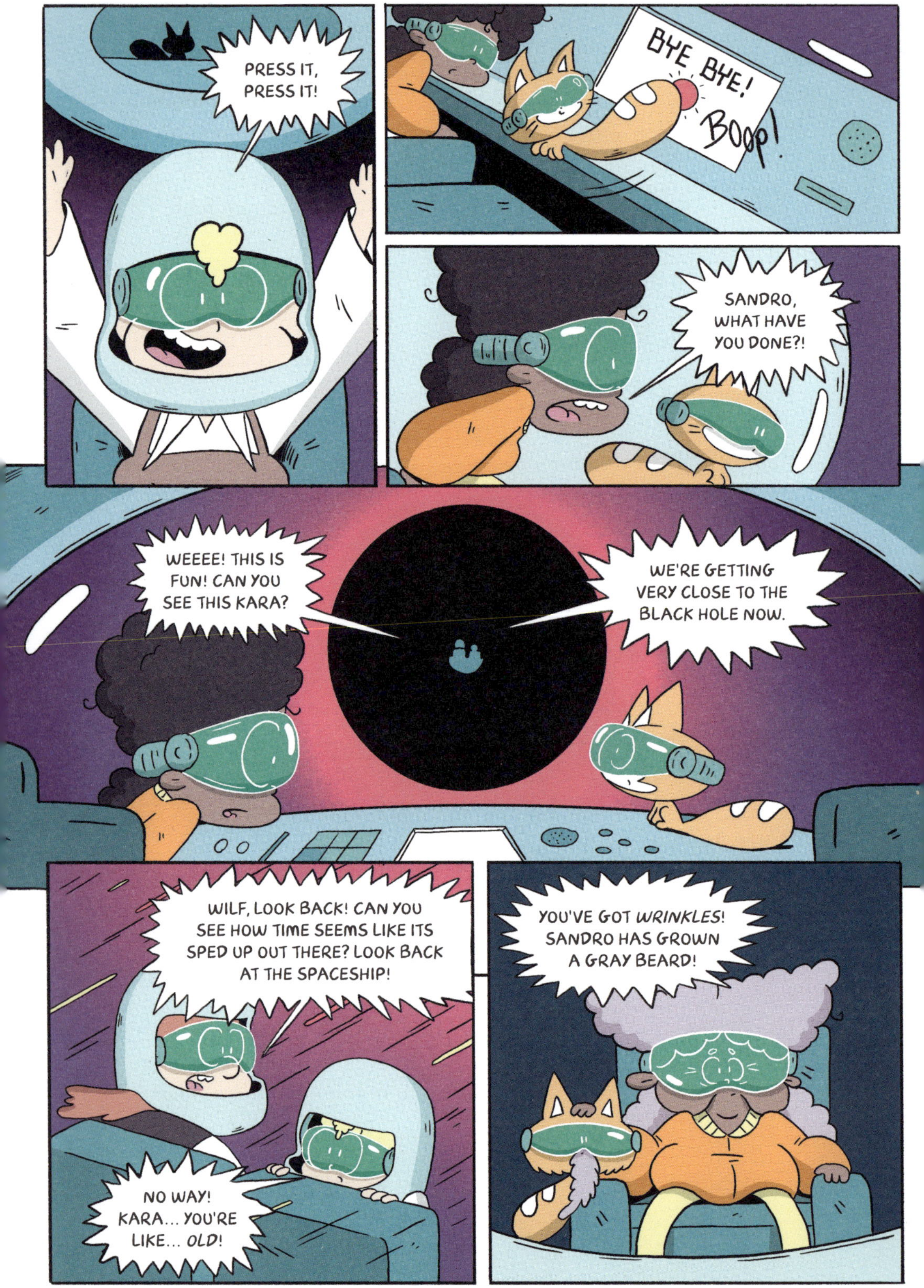
PRESS IT, PRESS IT!
BYE BYE!
BOOP!
SANDRO, WHAT HAVE YOU DONE?!
WEEEE! THIS IS FUN! CAN YOU SEE THIS KARA?
WE'RE GETTING VERY CLOSE TO THE BLACK HOLE NOW.
WILF, LOOK BACK! CAN YOU SEE HOW TIME SEEMS LIKE ITS SPED UP OUT THERE? LOOK BACK AT THE SPACESHIP!
NO WAY! KARA... YOU'RE LIKE... *OLD*!
YOU'VE GOT *WRINKLES*! SANDRO HAS GROWN A GRAY BEARD!

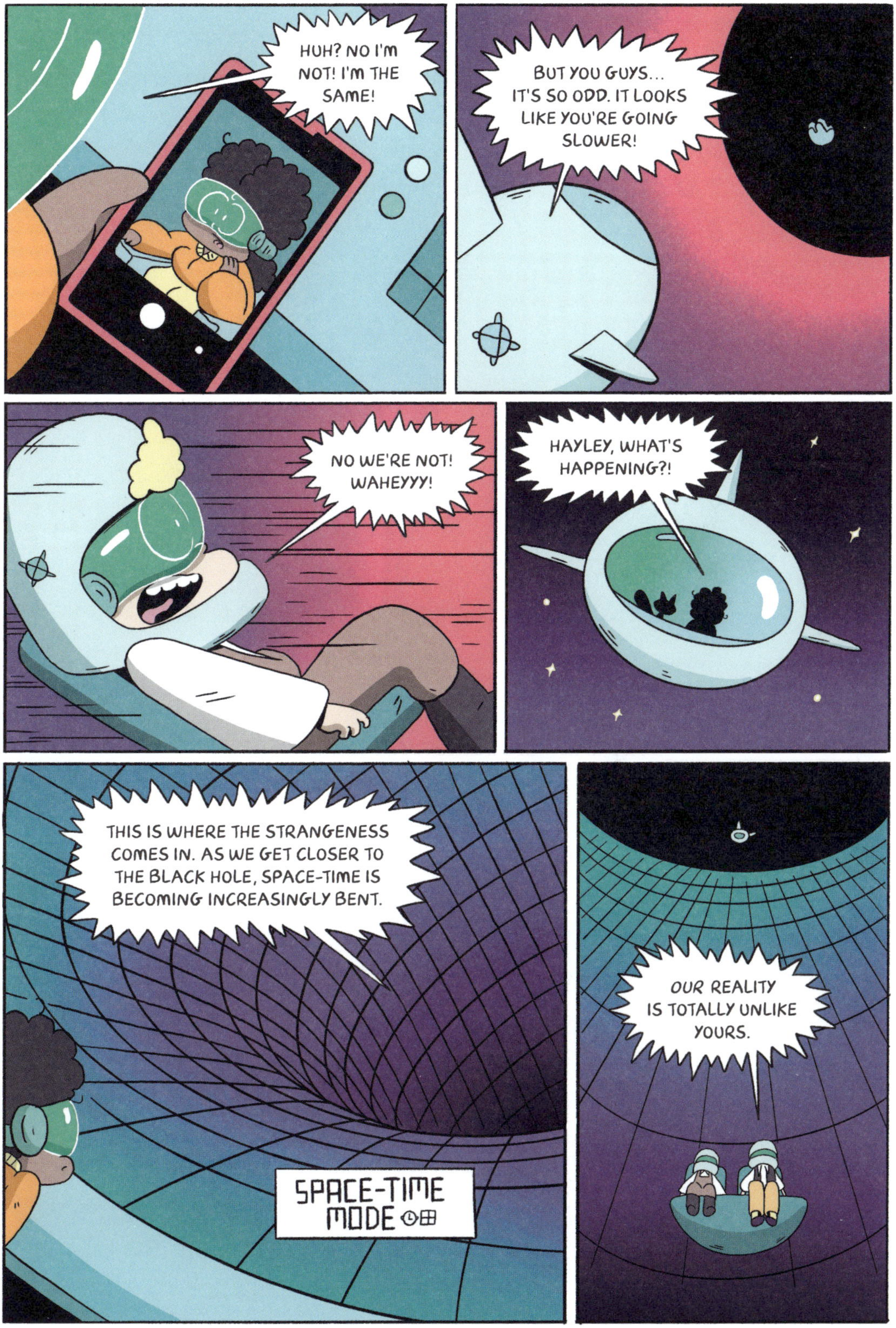
HUH? NO I'M NOT! I'M THE SAME!
BUT YOU GUYS... IT'S SO ODD. IT LOOKS LIKE YOU'RE GOING SLOWER!
NO WE'RE NOT! WAHEYYY!
HAYLEY, WHAT'S HAPPENING?!
THIS IS WHERE THE STRANGENESS COMES IN. AS WE GET CLOSER TO THE BLACK HOLE, SPACE-TIME IS BECOMING INCREASINGLY BENT.
SPACE-TIME MODE
OUR REALITY IS TOTALLY UNLIKE YOURS.

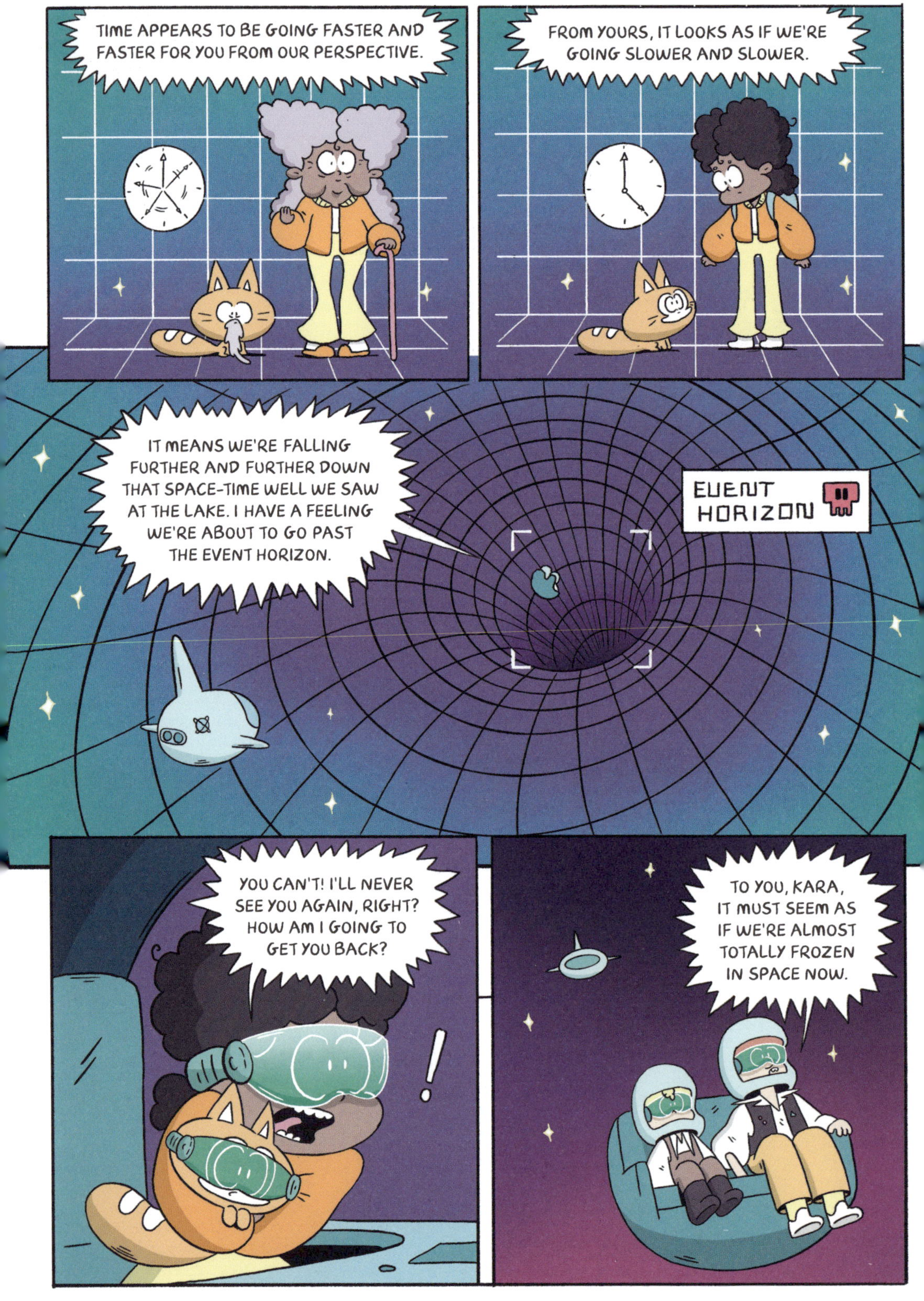
TIME APPEARS TO BE GOING FASTER AND FASTER FOR YOU FROM OUR PERSPECTIVE.
FROM YOURS, IT LOOKS AS IF WE'RE GOING SLOWER AND SLOWER.
IT MEANS WE'RE FALLING FURTHER AND FURTHER DOWN THAT SPACE-TIME WELL WE SAW AT THE LAKE. I HAVE A FEELING WE'RE ABOUT TO GO PAST THE EVENT HORIZON.
EVENT HORIZON
YOU CAN'T! I'LL NEVER SEE YOU AGAIN, RIGHT? HOW AM I GOING TO GET YOU BACK?
!
TO YOU, KARA, IT MUST SEEM AS IF WE'RE ALMOST TOTALLY FROZEN IN SPACE NOW.

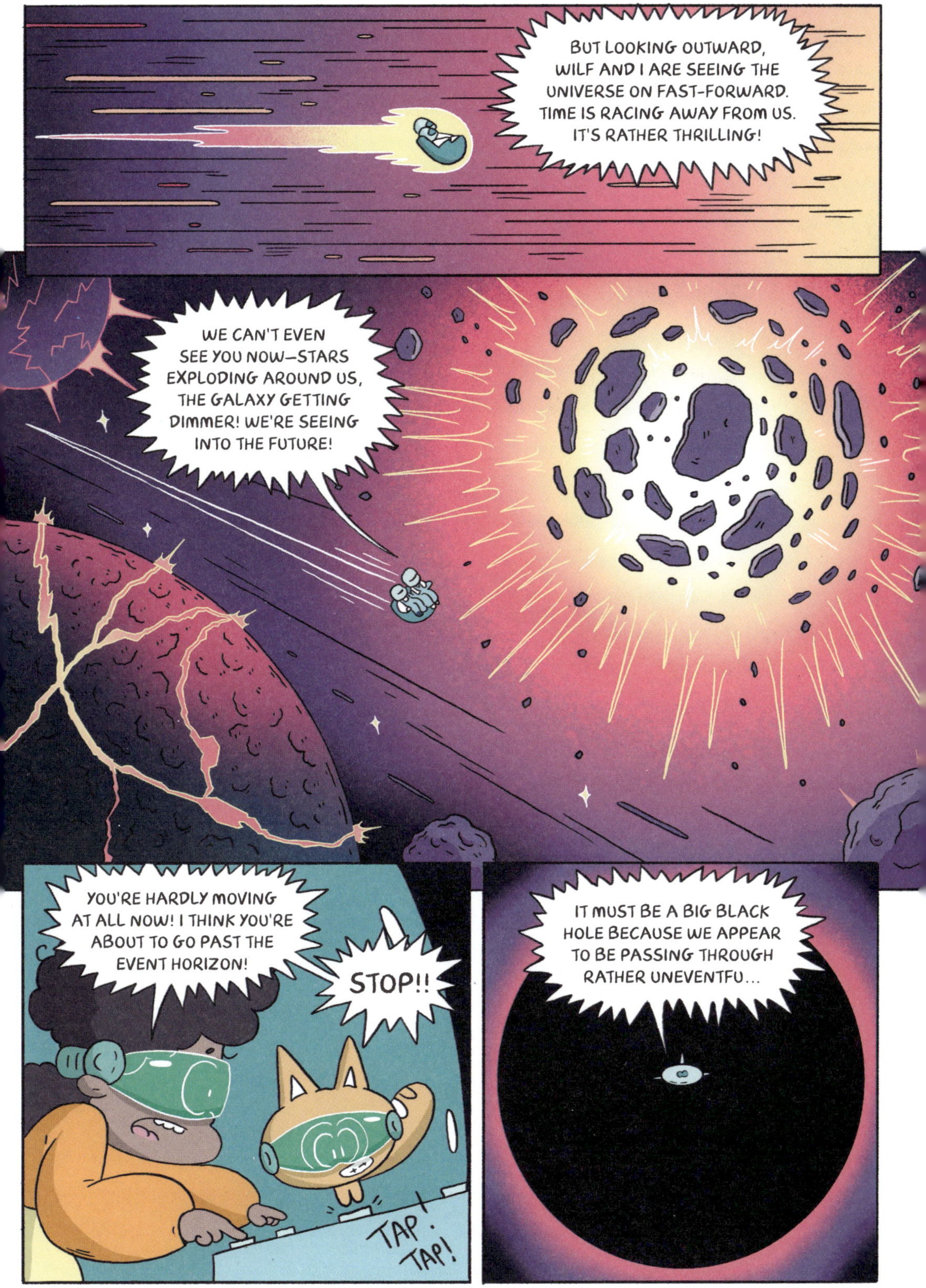
BUT LOOKING OUTWARD, WILF AND I ARE SEEING THE UNIVERSE ON FAST-FORWARD. TIME IS RACING AWAY FROM US. IT'S RATHER THRILLING!
WE CAN'T EVEN SEE YOU NOW—STARS EXPLODING AROUND US, THE GALAXY GETTING DIMMER! WE'RE SEEING INTO THE FUTURE!
YOU'RE HARDLY MOVING AT ALL NOW! I THINK YOU'RE ABOUT TO GO PAST THE EVENT HORIZON!
STOP!!
TAP! TAP!
IT MUST BE A BIG BLACK HOLE BECAUSE WE APPEAR TO BE PASSING THROUGH RATHER UNEVENTFU...

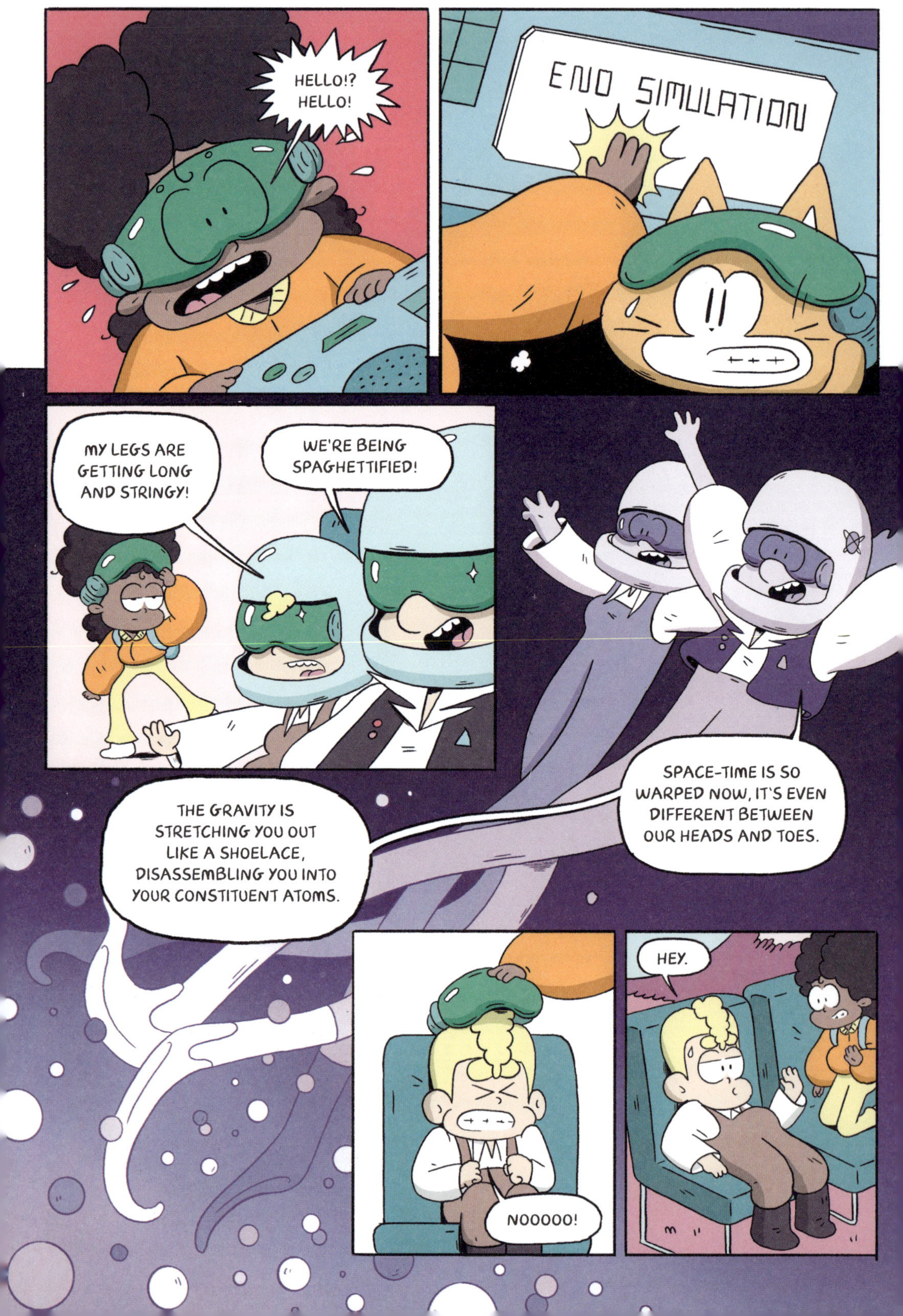
HELLO!? HELLO!
END SIMULATION
MY LEGS ARE GETTING LONG AND STRINGY!
WE'RE BEING SPAGHETTIFIED!
SPACE-TIME IS SO WARPED NOW, IT'S EVEN DIFFERENT BETWEEN OUR HEADS AND TOES.
THE GRAVITY IS STRETCHING YOU OUT LIKE A SHOELACE, DISASSEMBLING YOU INTO YOUR CONSTITUENT ATOMS.
NOOOOO!
HEY.

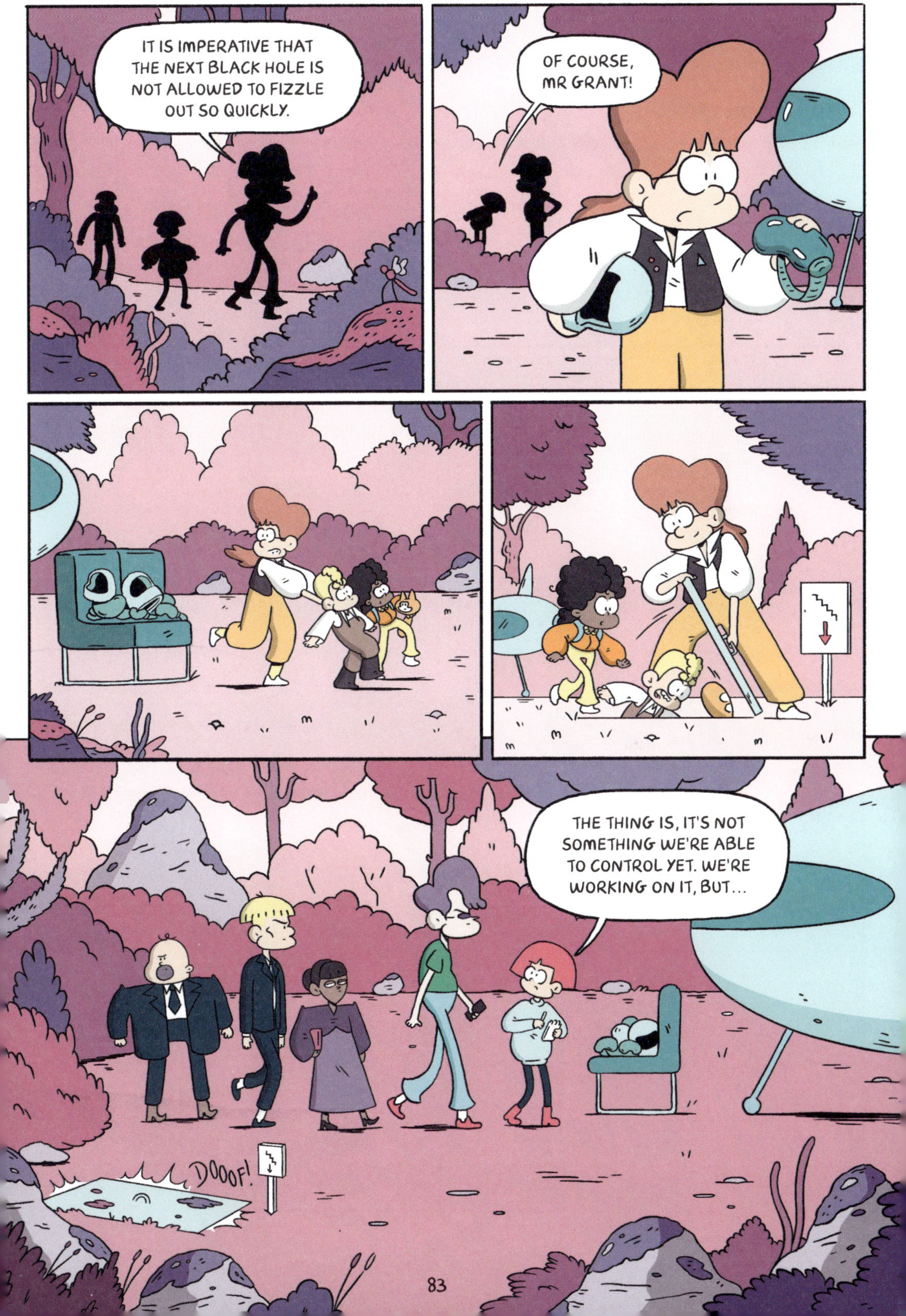
IT IS IMPERATIVE THAT THE NEXT BLACK HOLE IS NOT ALLOWED TO FIZZLE OUT SO QUICKLY.
OF COURSE, MR GRANT!
THE THING IS, IT'S NOT SOMETHING WE'RE ABLE TO CONTROL YET. WE'RE WORKING ON IT, BUT...
DOOOF!

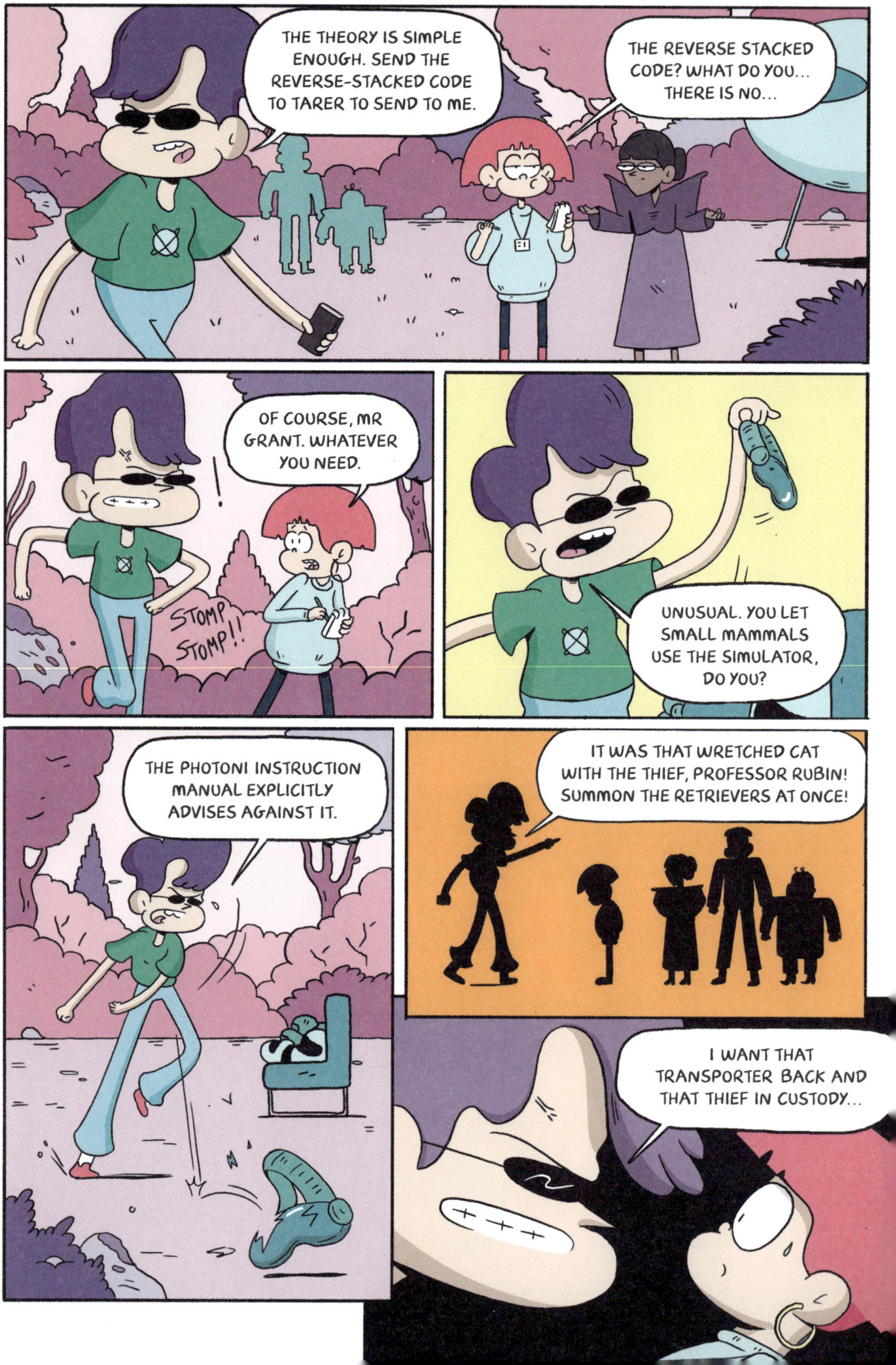
THE THEORY IS SIMPLE ENOUGH. SEND THE REVERSE-STACKED CODE TO TARER TO SEND TO ME.
THE REVERSE STACKED CODE? WHAT DO YOU... THERE IS NO...
OF COURSE, MR GRANT. WHATEVER YOU NEED.
STOMP STOMP!!
UNUSUAL. YOU LET SMALL MAMMALS USE THE SIMULATOR, DO YOU?
THE PHOTONI INSTRUCTION MANUAL EXPLICITLY ADVISES AGAINST IT.
IT WAS THAT WRETCHED CAT WITH THE THIEF, PROFESSOR RUBIN! SUMMON THE RETRIEVERS AT ONCE!
I WANT THAT TRANSPORTER BACK AND THAT THIEF IN CUSTODY...

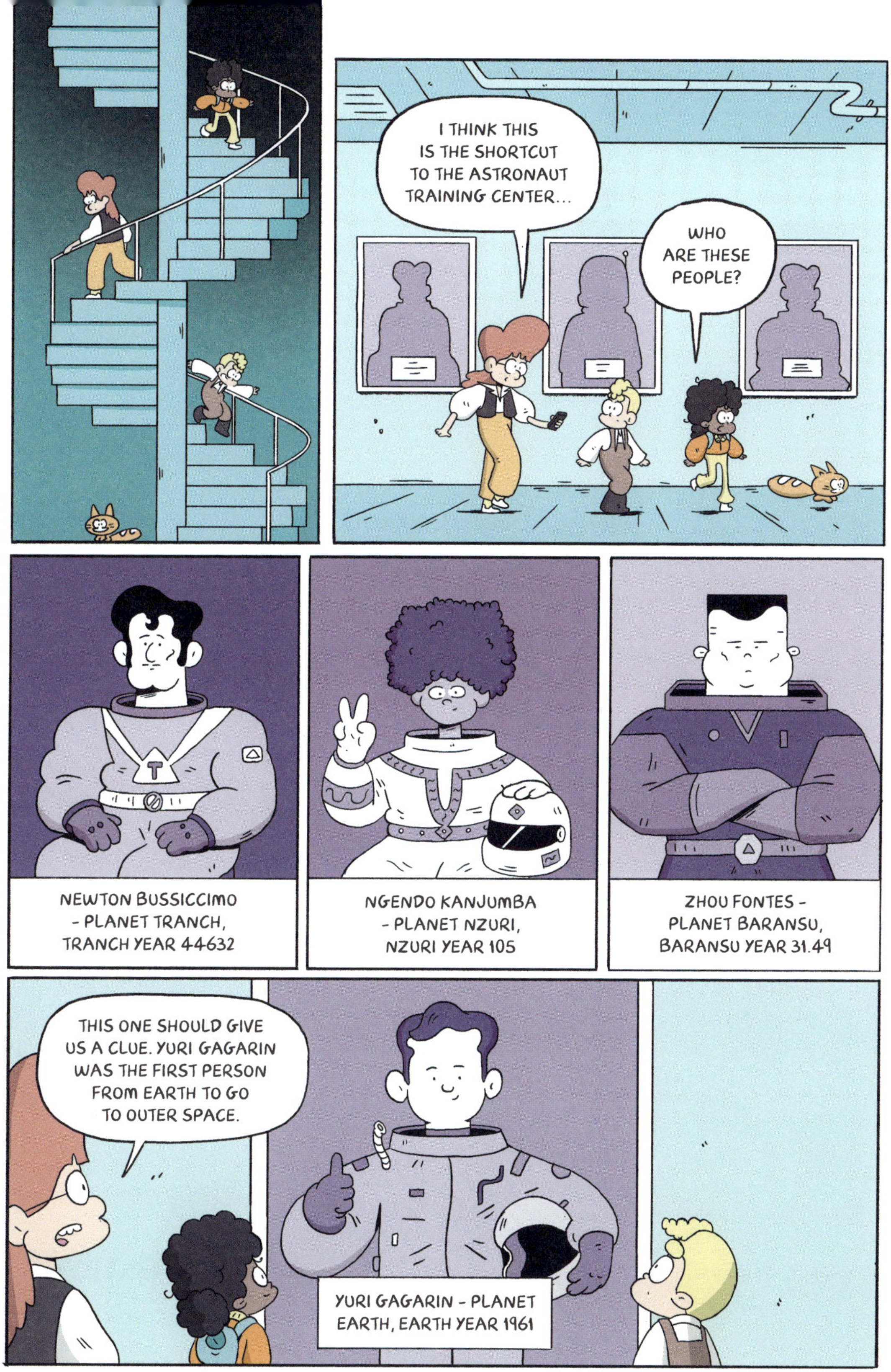
I THINK THIS IS THE SHORTCUT TO THE ASTRONAUT TRAINING CENTER...
WHO ARE THESE PEOPLE?
NEWTON BUSSICCIMO - PLANET TRANCH, TRANCH YEAR 44632
NGENDO KANJUMBA - PLANET NZURI, NZURI YEAR 105
ZHOU FONTES - PLANET BARANSU, BARANSU YEAR 31.49
THIS ONE SHOULD GIVE US A CLUE. YURI GAGARIN WAS THE FIRST PERSON FROM EARTH TO GO TO OUTER SPACE.
YURI GAGARIN - PLANET EARTH, EARTH YEAR 1961

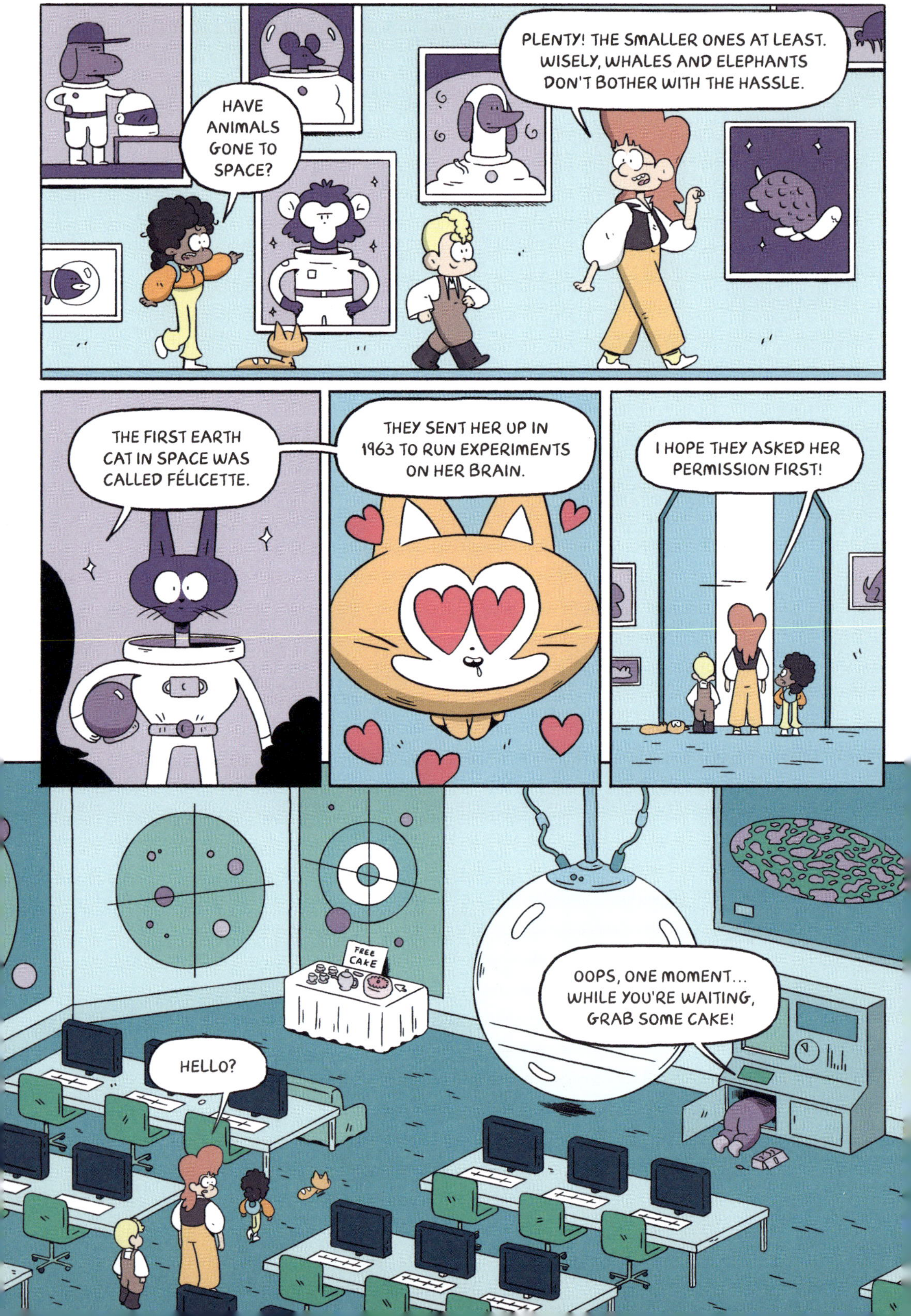
HAVE ANIMALS GONE TO SPACE?
PLENTY! THE SMALLER ONES AT LEAST. WISELY, WHALES AND ELEPHANTS DON'T BOTHER WITH THE HASSLE.
THE FIRST EARTH CAT IN SPACE WAS CALLED FÉLICETTE.
THEY SENT HER UP IN 1963 TO RUN EXPERIMENTS ON HER BRAIN.
I HOPE THEY ASKED HER PERMISSION FIRST!
FREE CAKE
HELLO?
OOPS, ONE MOMENT... WHILE YOU'RE WAITING, GRAB SOME CAKE!

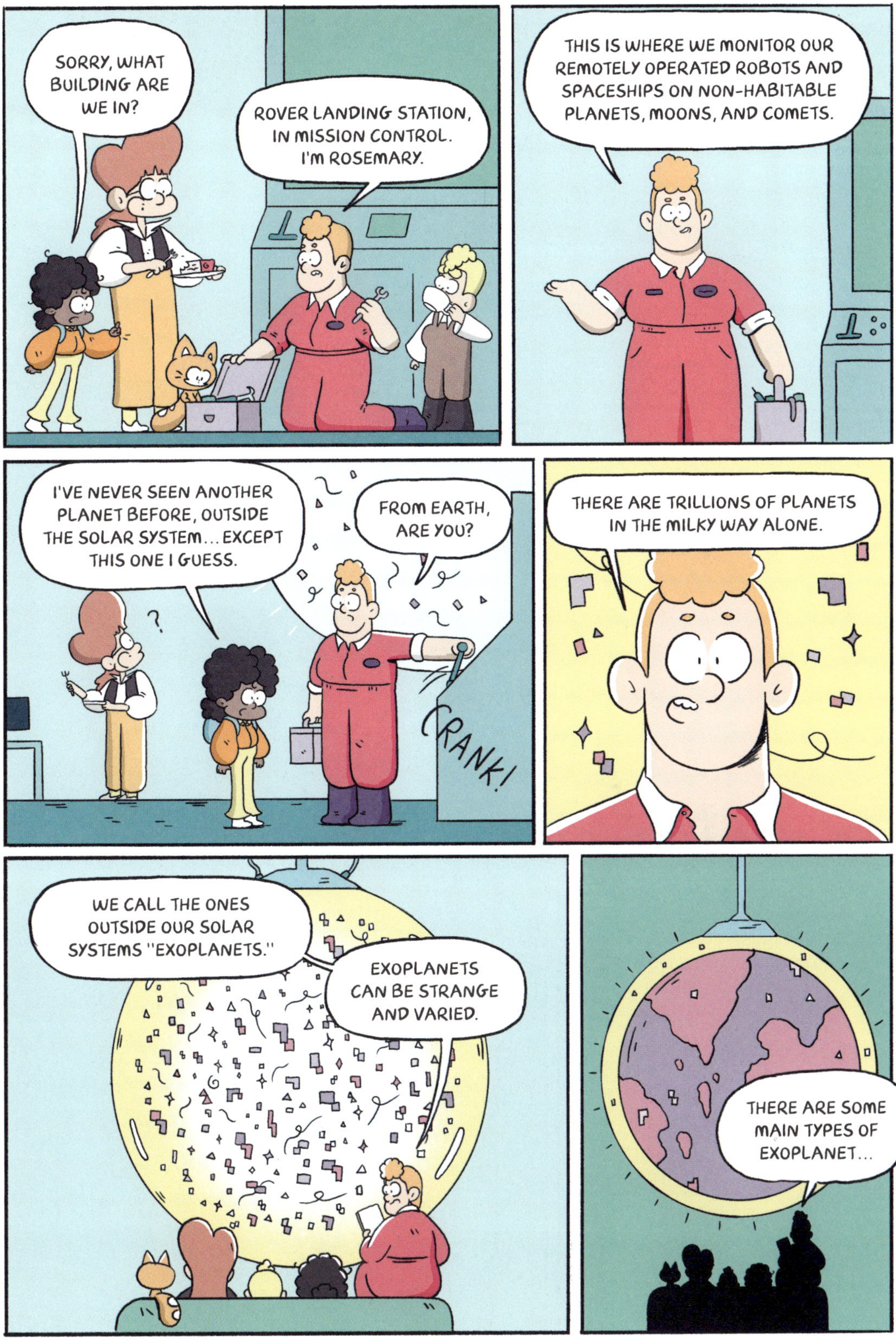
SORRY, WHAT BUILDING ARE WE IN?
ROVER LANDING STATION, IN MISSION CONTROL. I'M ROSEMARY.
THIS IS WHERE WE MONITOR OUR REMOTELY OPERATED ROBOTS AND SPACESHIPS ON NON-HABITABLE PLANETS, MOONS, AND COMETS.
I'VE NEVER SEEN ANOTHER PLANET BEFORE, OUTSIDE THE SOLAR SYSTEM... EXCEPT THIS ONE I GUESS.
?
FROM EARTH, ARE YOU?
CRANK!
THERE ARE TRILLIONS OF PLANETS IN THE MILKY WAY ALONE.
WE CALL THE ONES OUTSIDE OUR SOLAR SYSTEMS "EXOPLANETS."
EXOPLANETS CAN BE STRANGE AND VARIED.
THERE ARE SOME MAIN TYPES OF EXOPLANET...

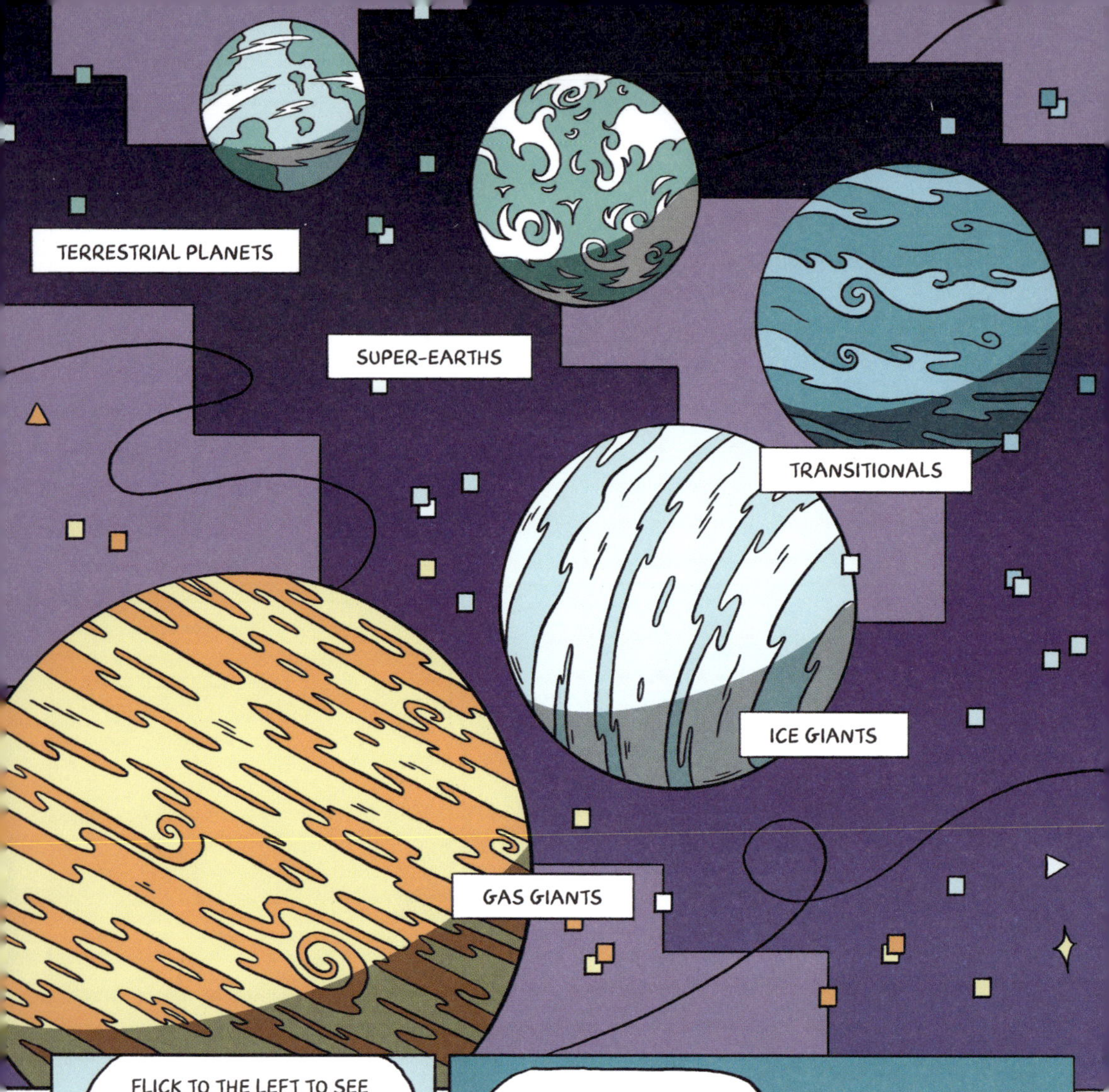
TERRESTRIAL PLANETS
SUPER-EARTHS
TRANSITIONALS
ICE GIANTS
GAS GIANTS

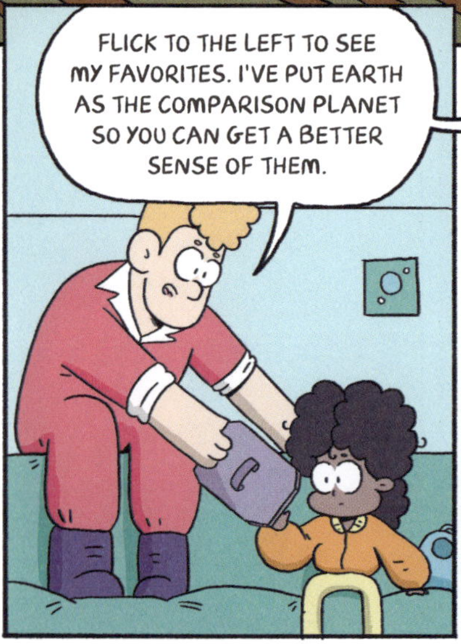
FLICK TO THE LEFT TO SEE MY FAVORITES. I'VE PUT EARTH AS THE COMPARISON PLANET SO YOU CAN GET A BETTER SENSE OF THEM.

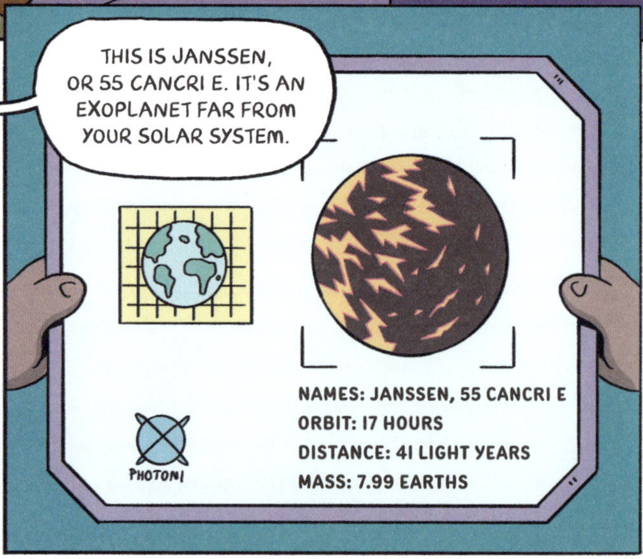
THIS IS JANSSEN, OR 55 CANCRI E. IT'S AN EXOPLANET FAR FROM YOUR SOLAR SYSTEM.
PHOTONI
NAMES: JANSSEN, 55 CANCRI E
ORBIT: 17 HOURS
DISTANCE: 41 LIGHT YEARS
MASS: 7.99 EARTHS

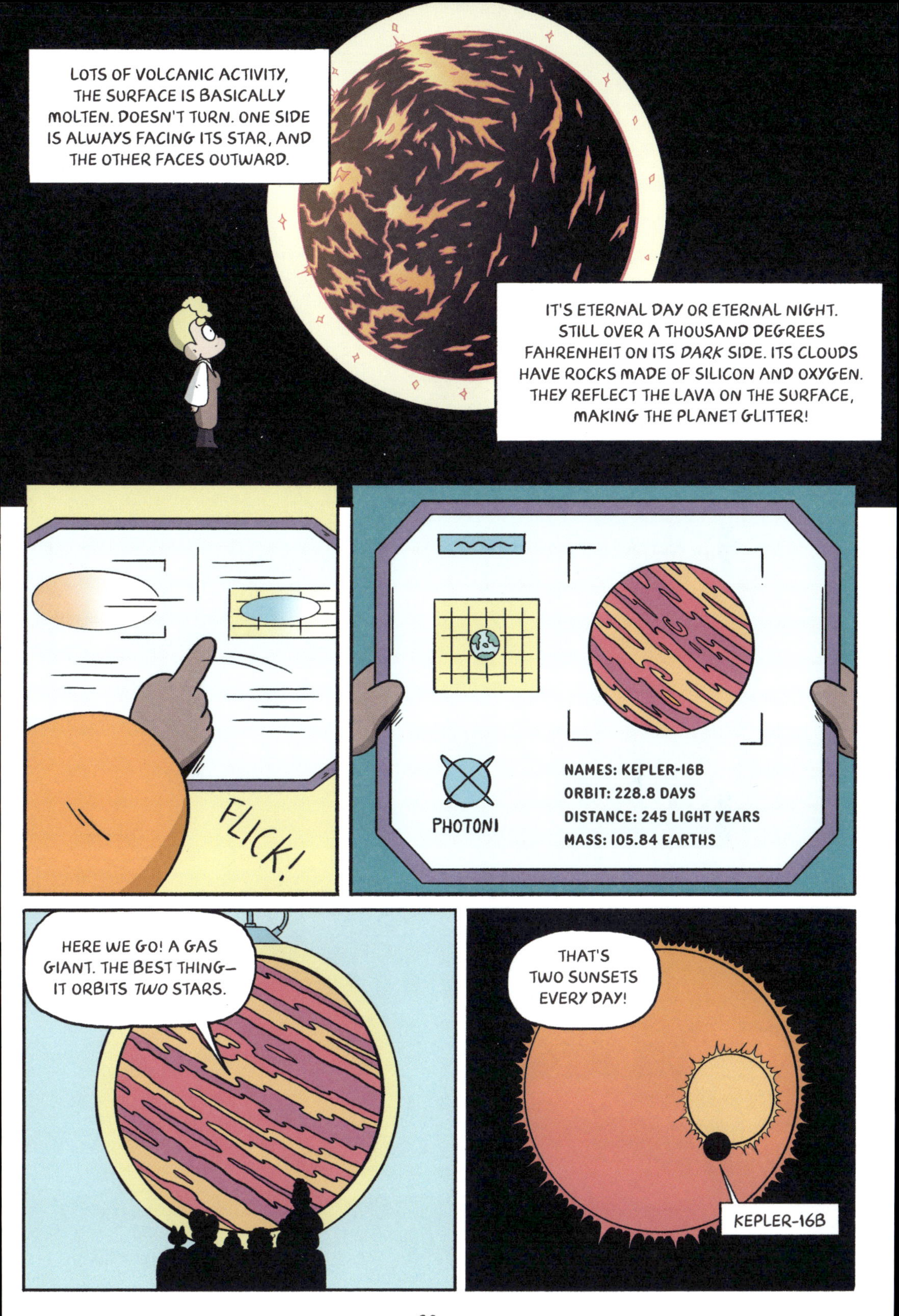
LOTS OF VOLCANIC ACTIVITY, THE SURFACE IS BASICALLY MOLTEN. DOESN'T TURN. ONE SIDE IS ALWAYS FACING ITS STAR, AND THE OTHER FACES OUTWARD.
IT'S ETERNAL DAY OR ETERNAL NIGHT. STILL OVER A THOUSAND DEGREES FAHRENHEIT ON ITS *DARK* SIDE. ITS CLOUDS HAVE ROCKS MADE OF SILICON AND OXYGEN. THEY REFLECT THE LAVA ON THE SURFACE, MAKING THE PLANET GLITTER!
FLICK!
PHOTONI
NAMES: KEPLER-16B
ORBIT: 228.8 DAYS
DISTANCE: 245 LIGHT YEARS
MASS: 105.84 EARTHS
HERE WE GO! A GAS GIANT. THE BEST THING— IT ORBITS *TWO* STARS.
THAT'S TWO SUNSETS EVERY DAY!
KEPLER-16B

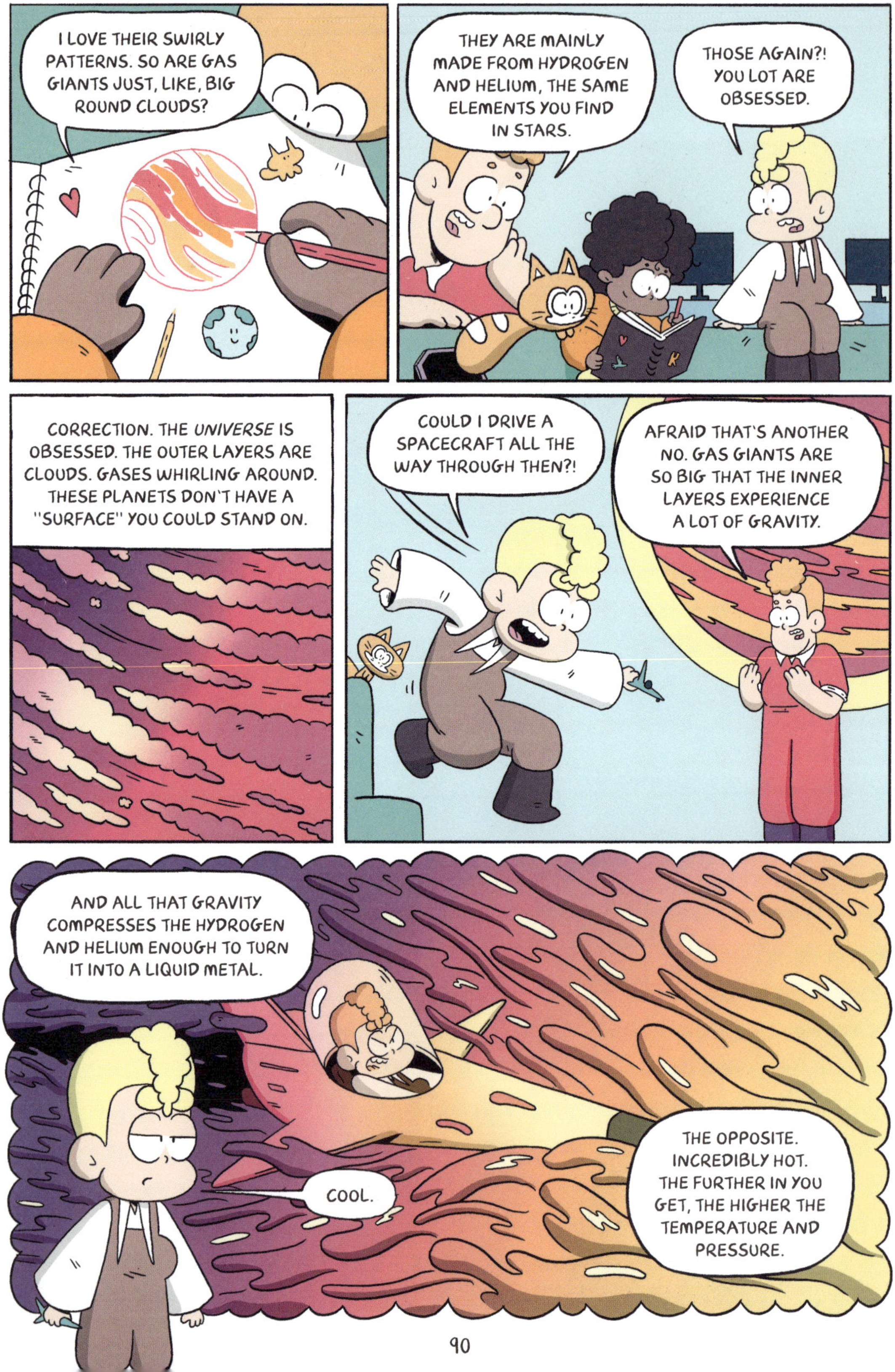
I LOVE THEIR SWIRLY PATTERNS. SO ARE GAS GIANTS JUST, LIKE, BIG ROUND CLOUDS?
THEY ARE MAINLY MADE FROM HYDROGEN AND HELIUM, THE SAME ELEMENTS YOU FIND IN STARS.
THOSE AGAIN?! YOU LOT ARE OBSESSED.
CORRECTION. THE *UNIVERSE* IS OBSESSED. THE OUTER LAYERS ARE CLOUDS. GASES WHIRLING AROUND. THESE PLANETS DON'T HAVE A "SURFACE" YOU COULD STAND ON.
COULD I DRIVE A SPACECRAFT ALL THE WAY THROUGH THEN?!
AFRAID THAT'S ANOTHER NO. GAS GIANTS ARE SO BIG THAT THE INNER LAYERS EXPERIENCE A LOT OF GRAVITY.
AND ALL THAT GRAVITY COMPRESSES THE HYDROGEN AND HELIUM ENOUGH TO TURN IT INTO A LIQUID METAL.
COOL.
THE OPPOSITE. INCREDIBLY HOT. THE FURTHER IN YOU GET, THE HIGHER THE TEMPERATURE AND PRESSURE.

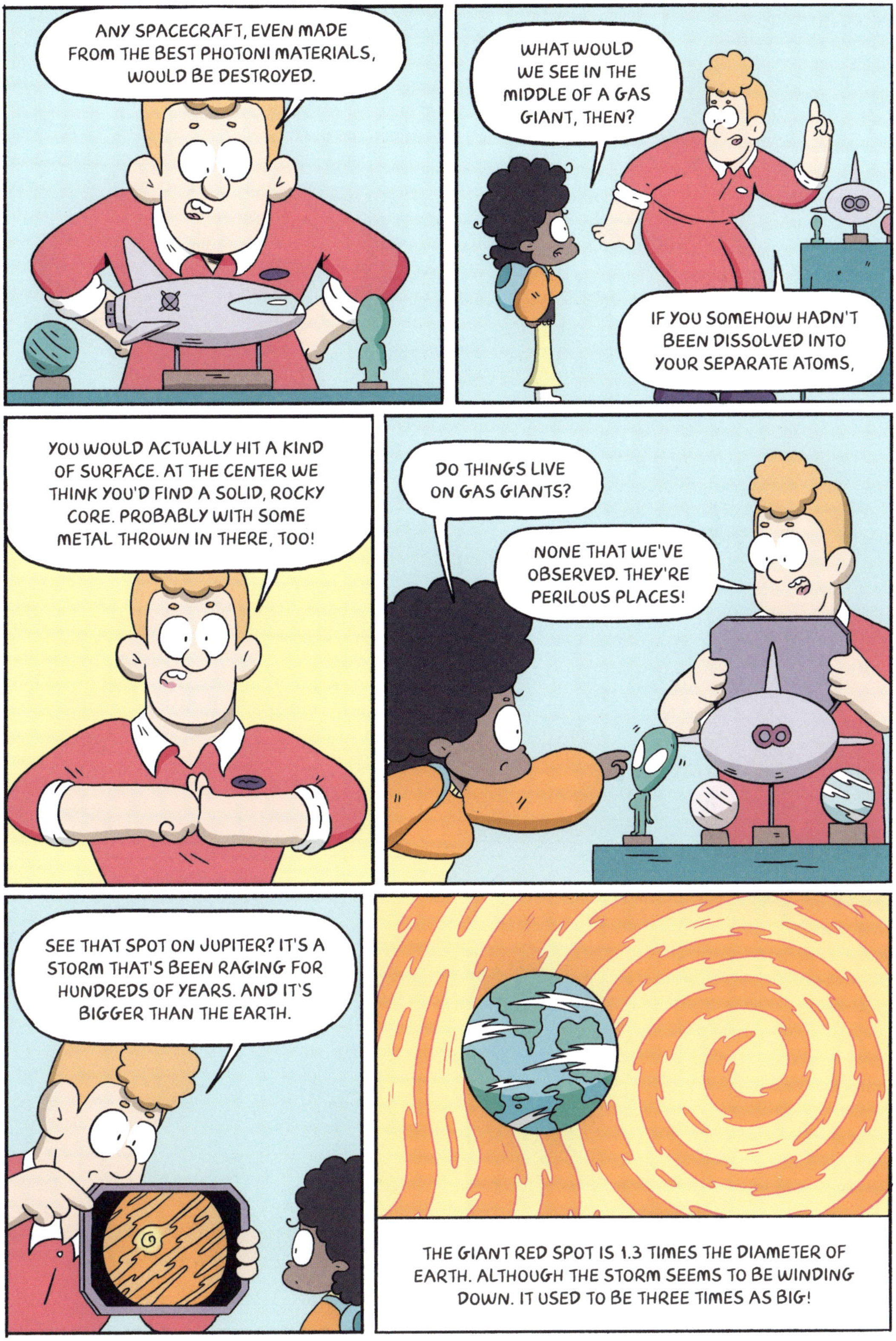
ANY SPACECRAFT, EVEN MADE FROM THE BEST PHOTONI MATERIALS, WOULD BE DESTROYED.
WHAT WOULD WE SEE IN THE MIDDLE OF A GAS GIANT, THEN?
IF YOU SOMEHOW HADN'T BEEN DISSOLVED INTO YOUR SEPARATE ATOMS,
YOU WOULD ACTUALLY HIT A KIND OF SURFACE. AT THE CENTER WE THINK YOU'D FIND A SOLID, ROCKY CORE. PROBABLY WITH SOME METAL THROWN IN THERE, TOO!
DO THINGS LIVE ON GAS GIANTS?
NONE THAT WE'VE OBSERVED. THEY'RE PERILOUS PLACES!
SEE THAT SPOT ON JUPITER? IT'S A STORM THAT'S BEEN RAGING FOR HUNDREDS OF YEARS. AND IT'S BIGGER THAN THE EARTH.
THE GIANT RED SPOT IS 1.3 TIMES THE DIAMETER OF EARTH. ALTHOUGH THE STORM SEEMS TO BE WINDING DOWN. IT USED TO BE THREE TIMES AS BIG!

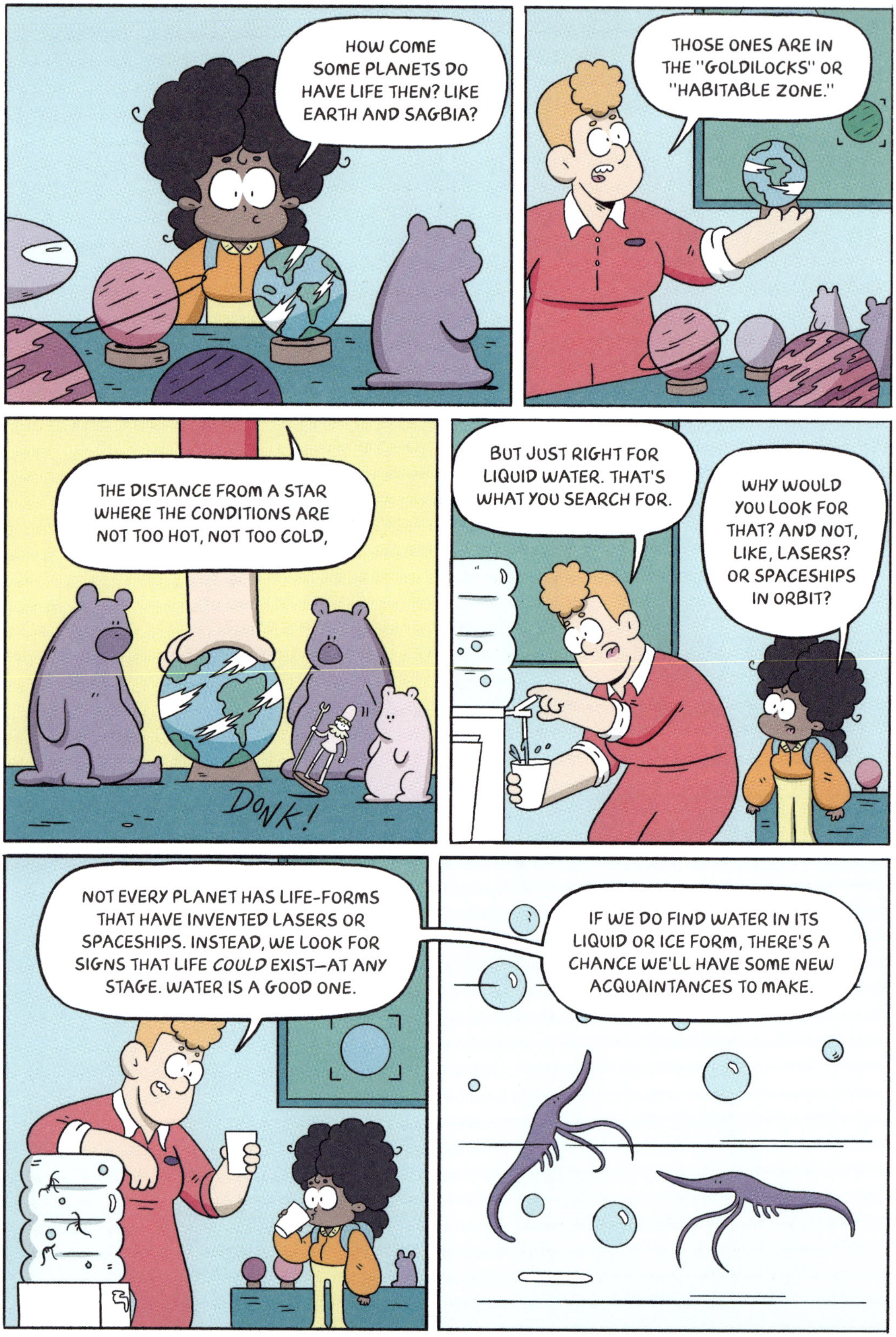
HOW COME SOME PLANETS DO HAVE LIFE THEN? LIKE EARTH AND SAGBIA?
THOSE ONES ARE IN THE "GOLDILOCKS" OR "HABITABLE ZONE."
THE DISTANCE FROM A STAR WHERE THE CONDITIONS ARE NOT TOO HOT, NOT TOO COLD,
DONK!
BUT JUST RIGHT FOR LIQUID WATER. THAT'S WHAT YOU SEARCH FOR.
WHY WOULD YOU LOOK FOR THAT? AND NOT, LIKE, LASERS? OR SPACESHIPS IN ORBIT?
NOT EVERY PLANET HAS LIFE-FORMS THAT HAVE INVENTED LASERS OR SPACESHIPS. INSTEAD, WE LOOK FOR SIGNS THAT LIFE *COULD* EXIST—AT ANY STAGE. WATER IS A GOOD ONE.
IF WE DO FIND WATER IN ITS LIQUID OR ICE FORM, THERE'S A CHANCE WE'LL HAVE SOME NEW ACQUAINTANCES TO MAKE.

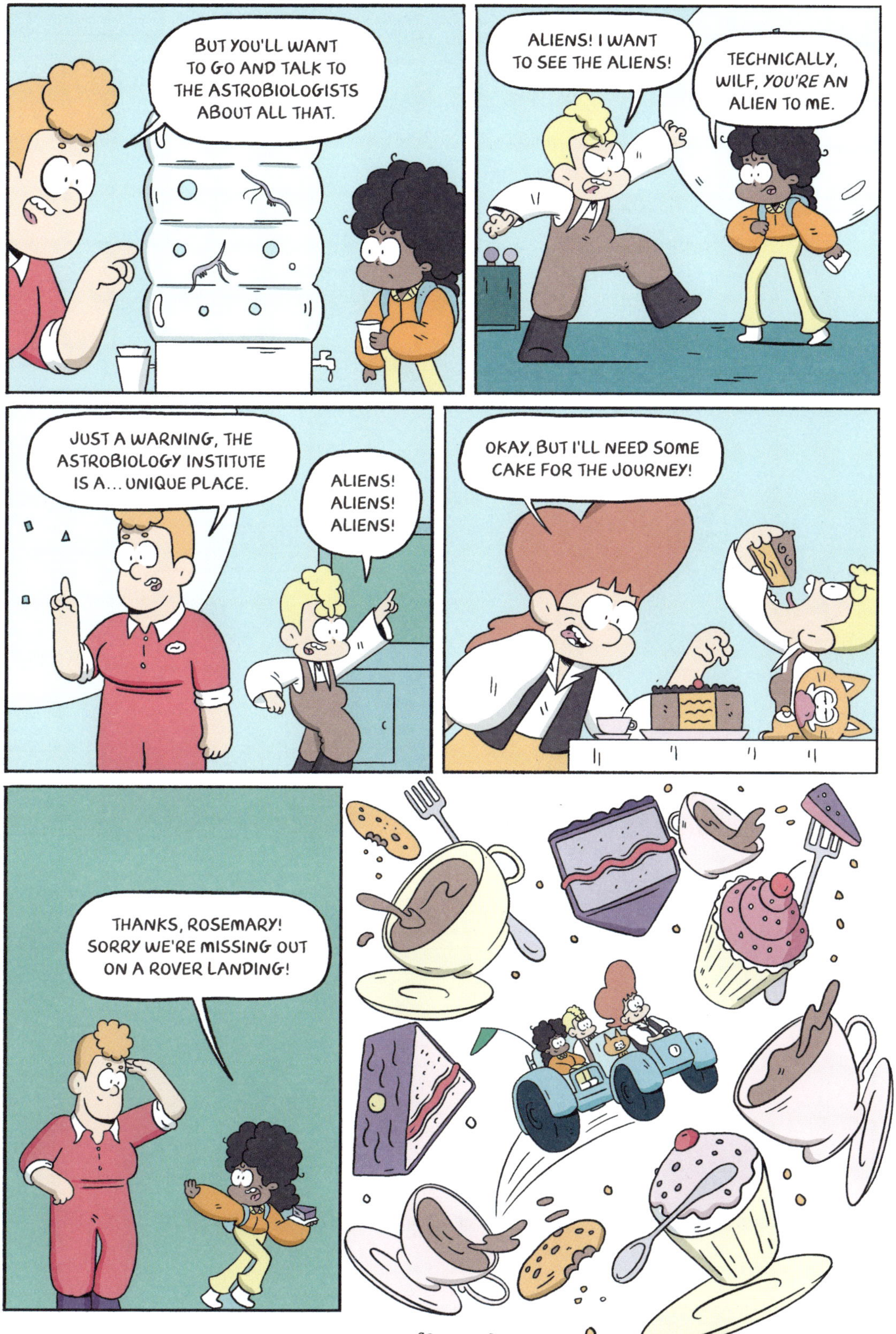
BUT YOU'LL WANT TO GO AND TALK TO THE ASTROBIOLOGISTS ABOUT ALL THAT.
ALIENS! I WANT TO SEE THE ALIENS!
TECHNICALLY, WILF, *YOU'RE* AN ALIEN TO ME.
JUST A WARNING, THE ASTROBIOLOGY INSTITUTE IS A... UNIQUE PLACE.
ALIENS! ALIENS! ALIENS!
OKAY, BUT I'LL NEED SOME CAKE FOR THE JOURNEY!
THANKS, ROSEMARY! SORRY WE'RE MISSING OUT ON A ROVER LANDING!

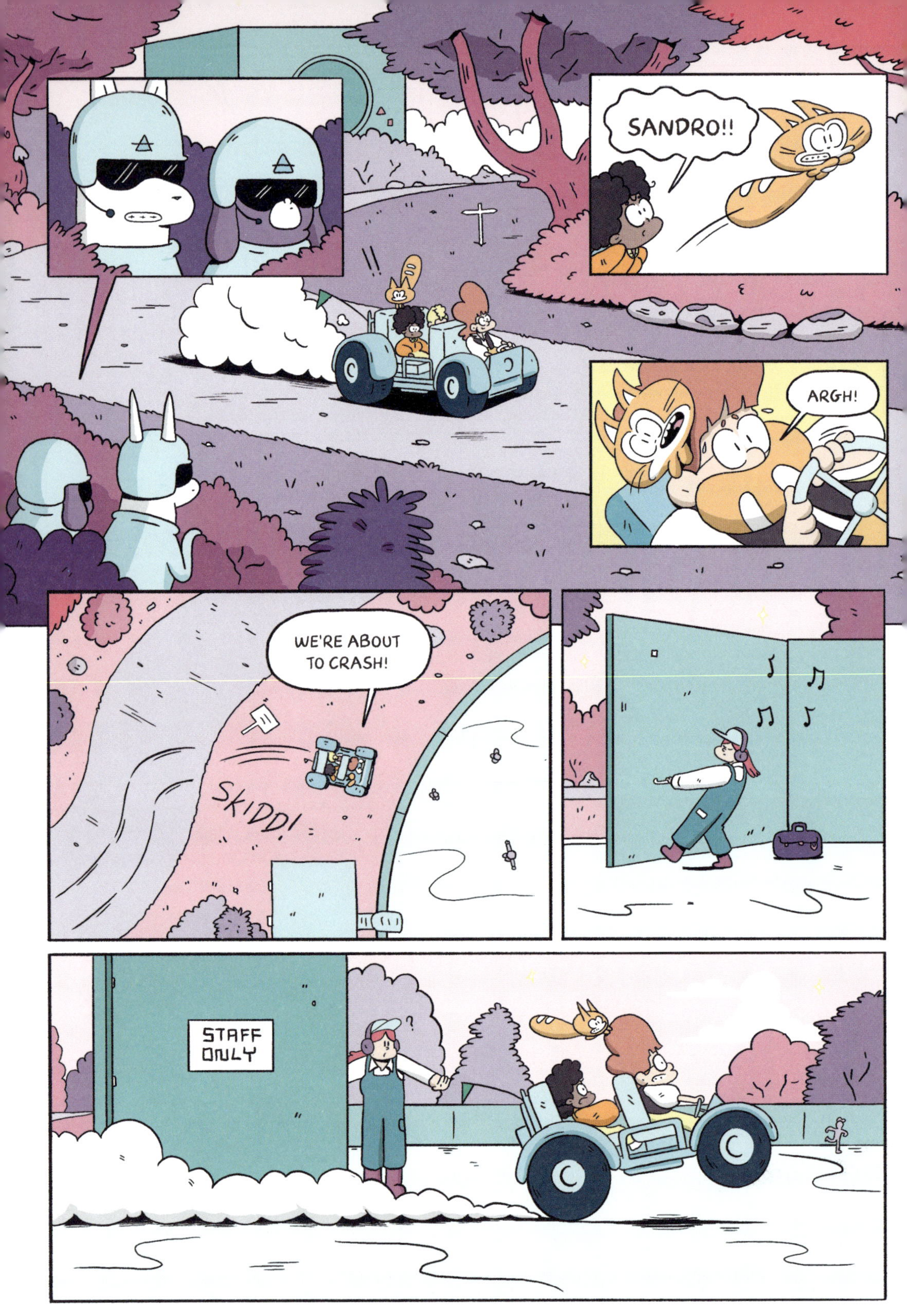
SANDRO!!
ARGH!
WE'RE ABOUT TO CRASH!
SKIDD!
STAFF ONLY

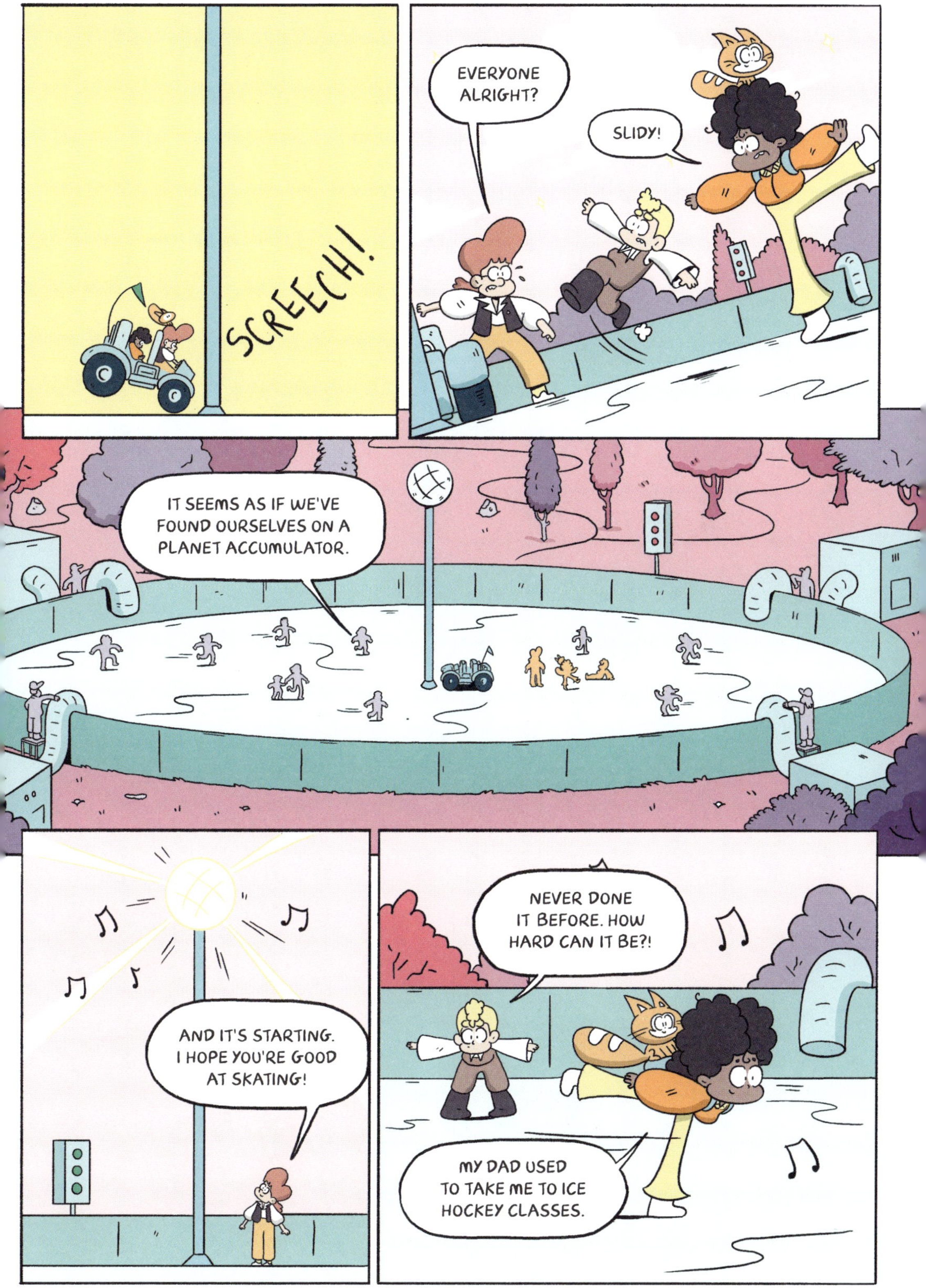
SCREECH!
EVERYONE ALRIGHT?
SLIDY!
IT SEEMS AS IF WE'VE FOUND OURSELVES ON A PLANET ACCUMULATOR.
AND IT'S STARTING. I HOPE YOU'RE GOOD AT SKATING!
NEVER DONE IT BEFORE. HOW HARD CAN IT BE?!
MY DAD USED TO TAKE ME TO ICE HOCKEY CLASSES.

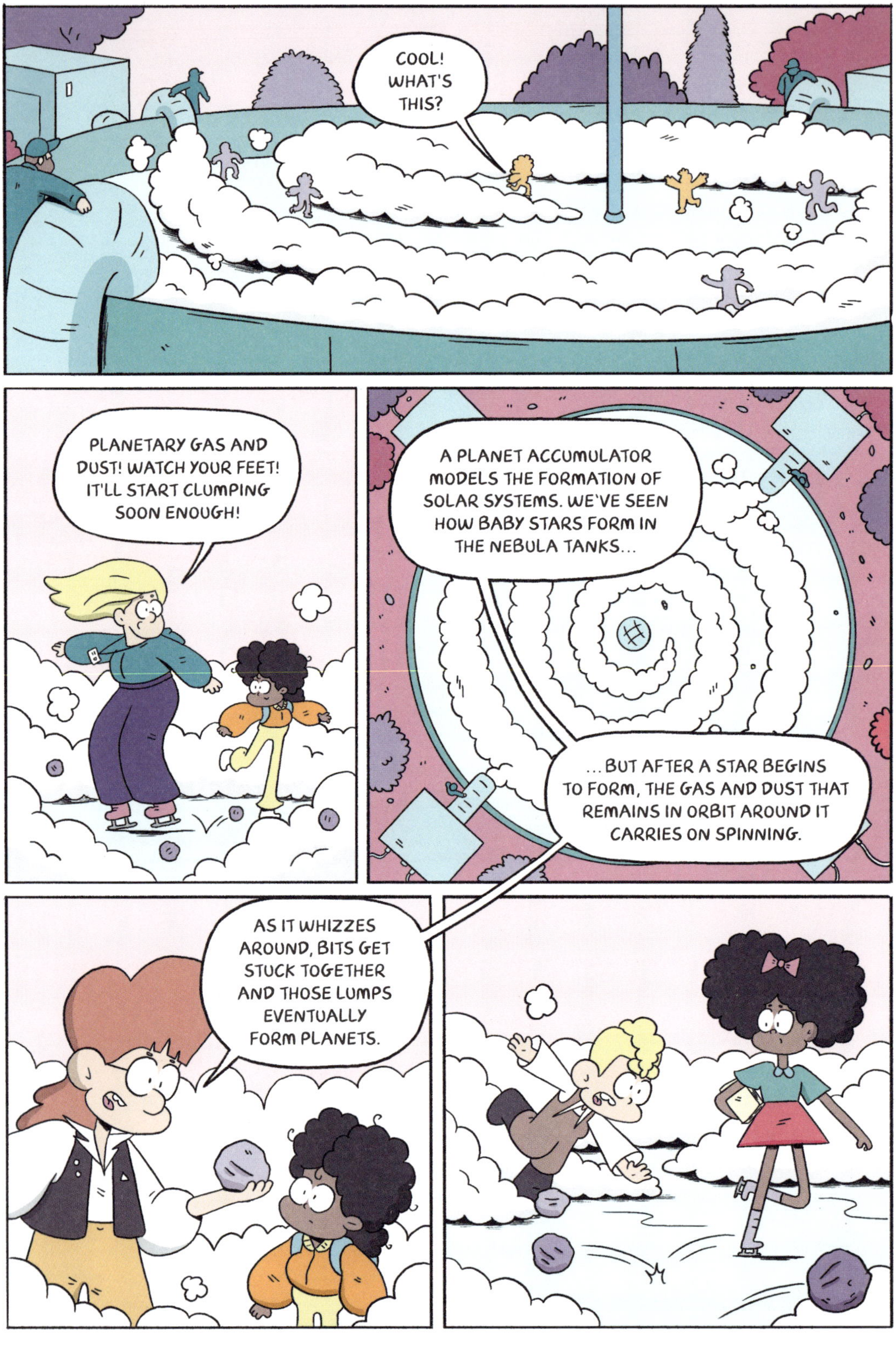
COOL! WHAT'S THIS?
PLANETARY GAS AND DUST! WATCH YOUR FEET! IT'LL START CLUMPING SOON ENOUGH!
A PLANET ACCUMULATOR MODELS THE FORMATION OF SOLAR SYSTEMS. WE'VE SEEN HOW BABY STARS FORM IN THE NEBULA TANKS...
...BUT AFTER A STAR BEGINS TO FORM, THE GAS AND DUST THAT REMAINS IN ORBIT AROUND IT CARRIES ON SPINNING.
AS IT WHIZZES AROUND, BITS GET STUCK TOGETHER AND THOSE LUMPS EVENTUALLY FORM PLANETS.

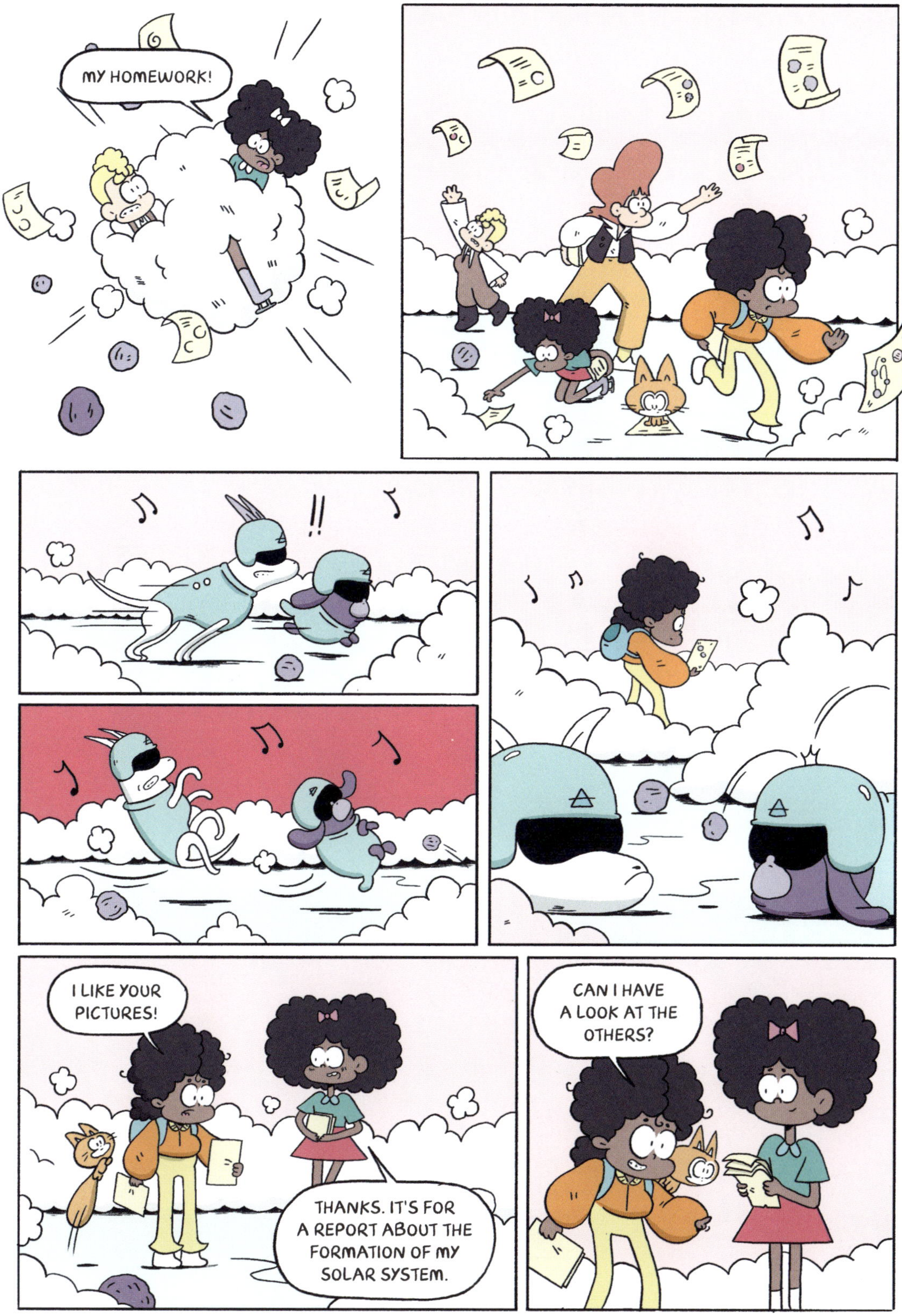
MY HOMEWORK!
!!
I LIKE YOUR PICTURES!
THANKS. IT'S FOR A REPORT ABOUT THE FORMATION OF MY SOLAR SYSTEM.
CAN I HAVE A LOOK AT THE OTHERS?

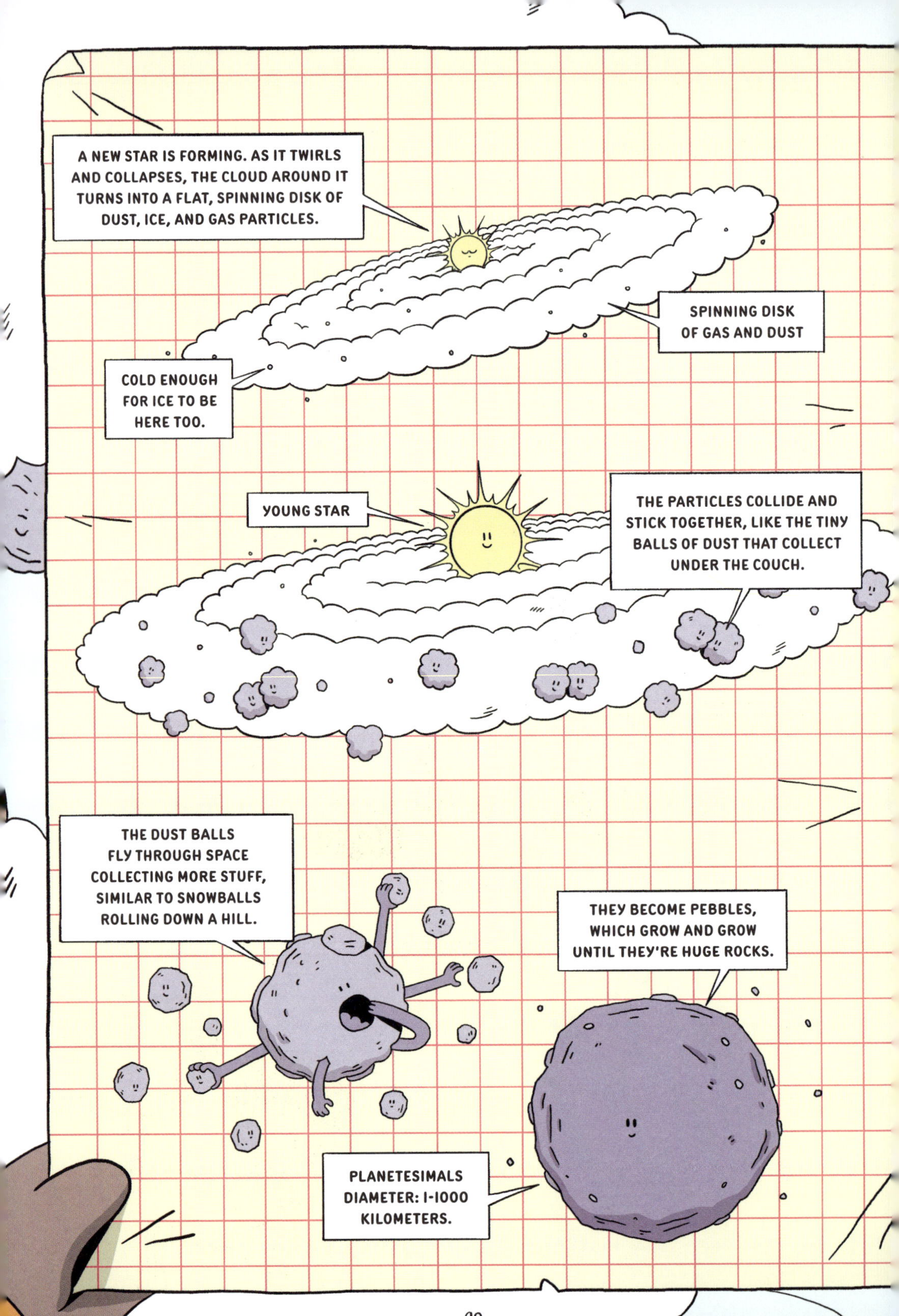
A NEW STAR IS FORMING. AS IT TWIRLS AND COLLAPSES, THE CLOUD AROUND IT TURNS INTO A FLAT, SPINNING DISK OF DUST, ICE, AND GAS PARTICLES.
SPINNING DISK OF GAS AND DUST
COLD ENOUGH FOR ICE TO BE HERE TOO.
YOUNG STAR
THE PARTICLES COLLIDE AND STICK TOGETHER, LIKE THE TINY BALLS OF DUST THAT COLLECT UNDER THE COUCH.
THE DUST BALLS FLY THROUGH SPACE COLLECTING MORE STUFF, SIMILAR TO SNOWBALLS ROLLING DOWN A HILL.
THEY BECOME PEBBLES, WHICH GROW AND GROW UNTIL THEY'RE HUGE ROCKS.
PLANETESIMALS DIAMETER: 1-1000 KILOMETERS.

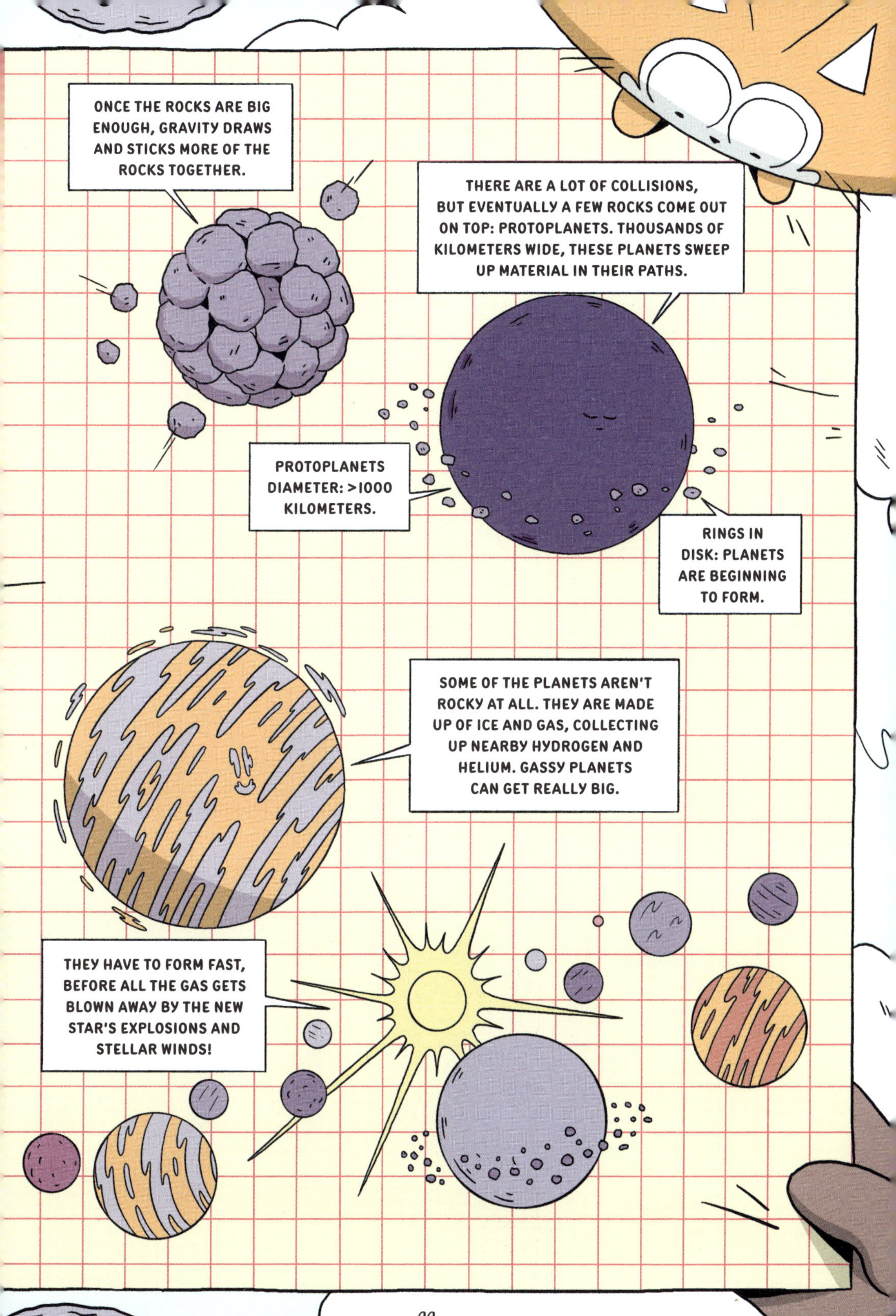
ONCE THE ROCKS ARE BIG ENOUGH, GRAVITY DRAWS AND STICKS MORE OF THE ROCKS TOGETHER.
THERE ARE A LOT OF COLLISIONS, BUT EVENTUALLY A FEW ROCKS COME OUT ON TOP: PROTOPLANETS. THOUSANDS OF KILOMETERS WIDE, THESE PLANETS SWEEP UP MATERIAL IN THEIR PATHS.
PROTOPLANETS DIAMETER: >1000 KILOMETERS.
RINGS IN DISK: PLANETS ARE BEGINNING TO FORM.
SOME OF THE PLANETS AREN'T ROCKY AT ALL. THEY ARE MADE UP OF ICE AND GAS, COLLECTING UP NEARBY HYDROGEN AND HELIUM. GASSY PLANETS CAN GET REALLY BIG.
THEY HAVE TO FORM FAST, BEFORE ALL THE GAS GETS BLOWN AWAY BY THE NEW STAR'S EXPLOSIONS AND STELLAR WINDS!

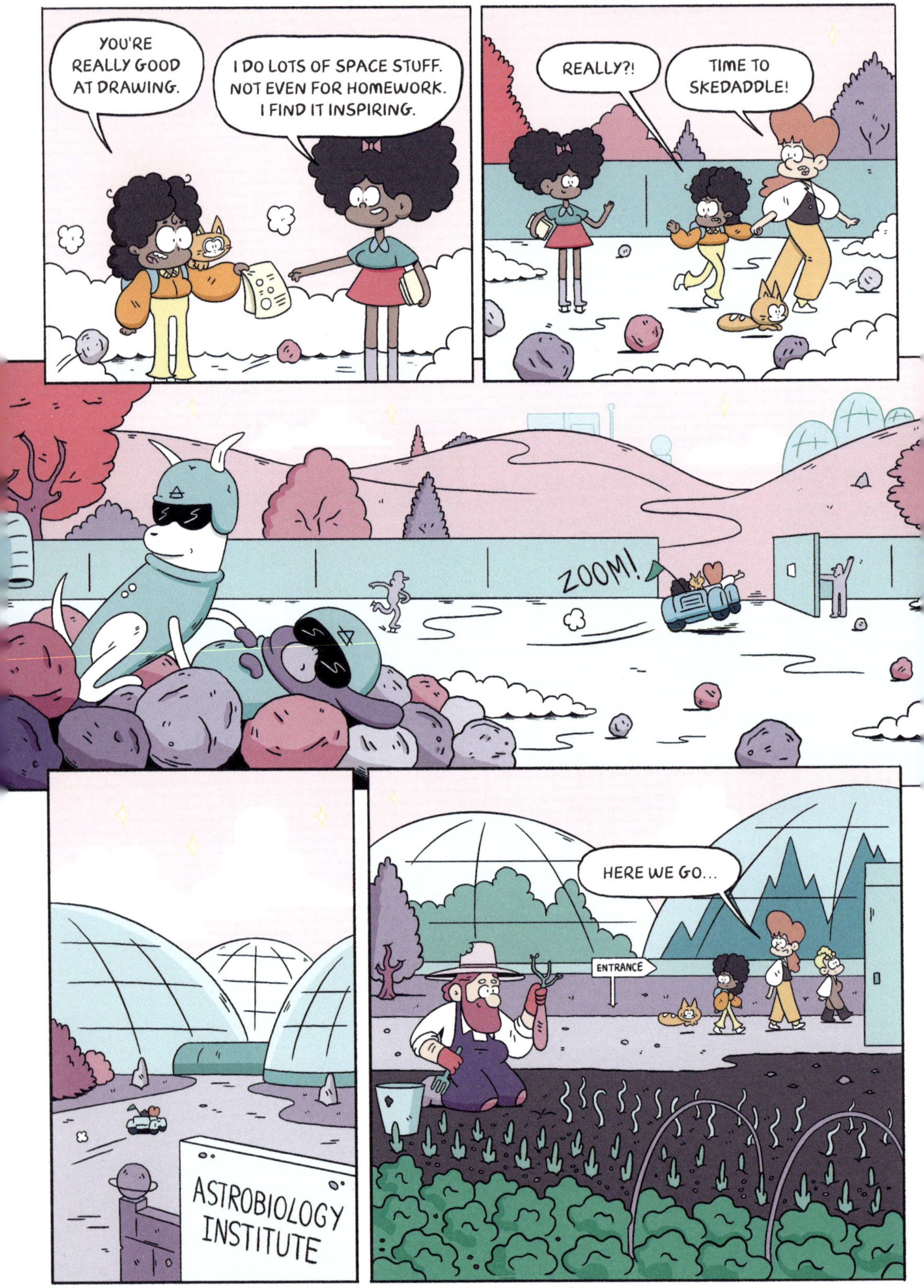
YOU'RE REALLY GOOD AT DRAWING.
I DO LOTS OF SPACE STUFF. NOT EVEN FOR HOMEWORK. I FIND IT INSPIRING.
REALLY?!
TIME TO SKEDADDLE!
ZOOM!
ASTROBIOLOGY INSTITUTE
HERE WE GO...
ENTRANCE

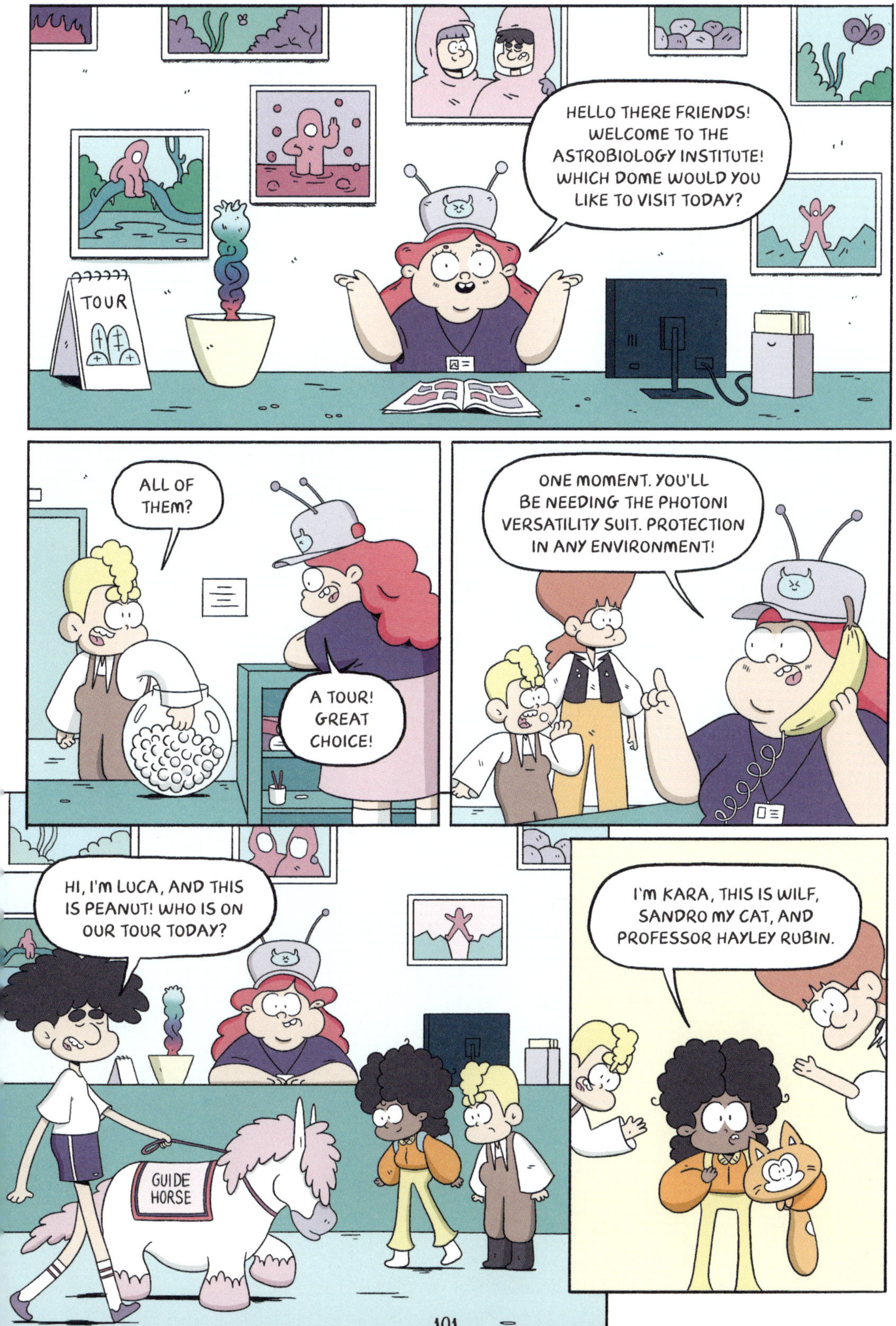
HELLO THERE FRIENDS! WELCOME TO THE ASTROBIOLOGY INSTITUTE! WHICH DOME WOULD YOU LIKE TO VISIT TODAY?
TOUR
ALL OF THEM?
A TOUR! GREAT CHOICE!
ONE MOMENT. YOU'LL BE NEEDING THE PHOTONI VERSATILITY SUIT. PROTECTION IN ANY ENVIRONMENT!
HI, I'M LUCA, AND THIS IS PEANUT! WHO IS ON OUR TOUR TODAY?
GUIDE HORSE
I'M KARA, THIS IS WILF, SANDRO MY CAT, AND PROFESSOR HAYLEY RUBIN.

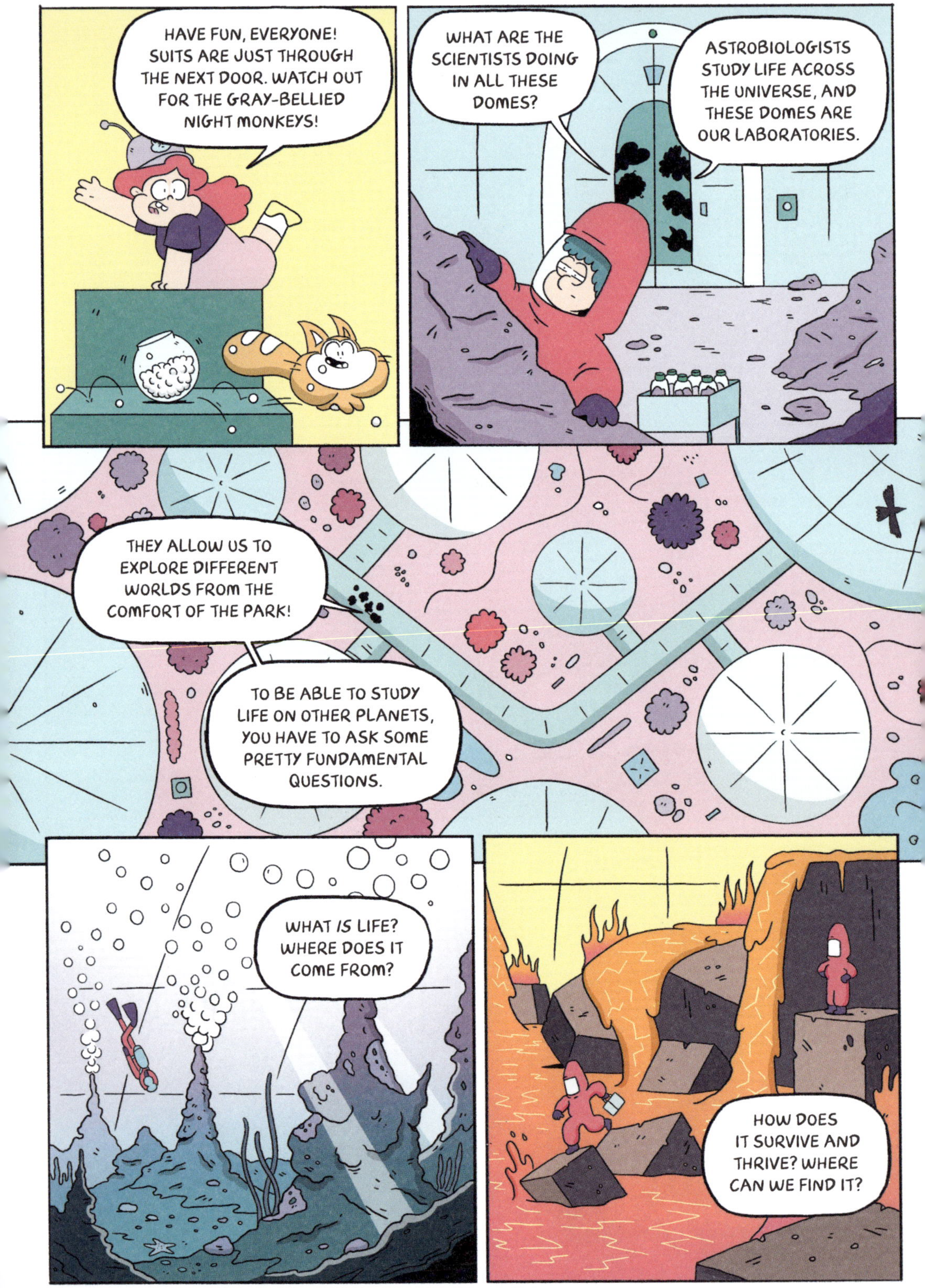
HAVE FUN, EVERYONE! SUITS ARE JUST THROUGH THE NEXT DOOR. WATCH OUT FOR THE GRAY-BELLIED NIGHT MONKEYS!
WHAT ARE THE SCIENTISTS DOING IN ALL THESE DOMES?
ASTROBIOLOGISTS STUDY LIFE ACROSS THE UNIVERSE, AND THESE DOMES ARE OUR LABORATORIES.
THEY ALLOW US TO EXPLORE DIFFERENT WORLDS FROM THE COMFORT OF THE PARK!
TO BE ABLE TO STUDY LIFE ON OTHER PLANETS, YOU HAVE TO ASK SOME PRETTY FUNDAMENTAL QUESTIONS.
WHAT *IS* LIFE? WHERE DOES IT COME FROM?
HOW DOES IT SURVIVE AND THRIVE? WHERE CAN WE FIND IT?

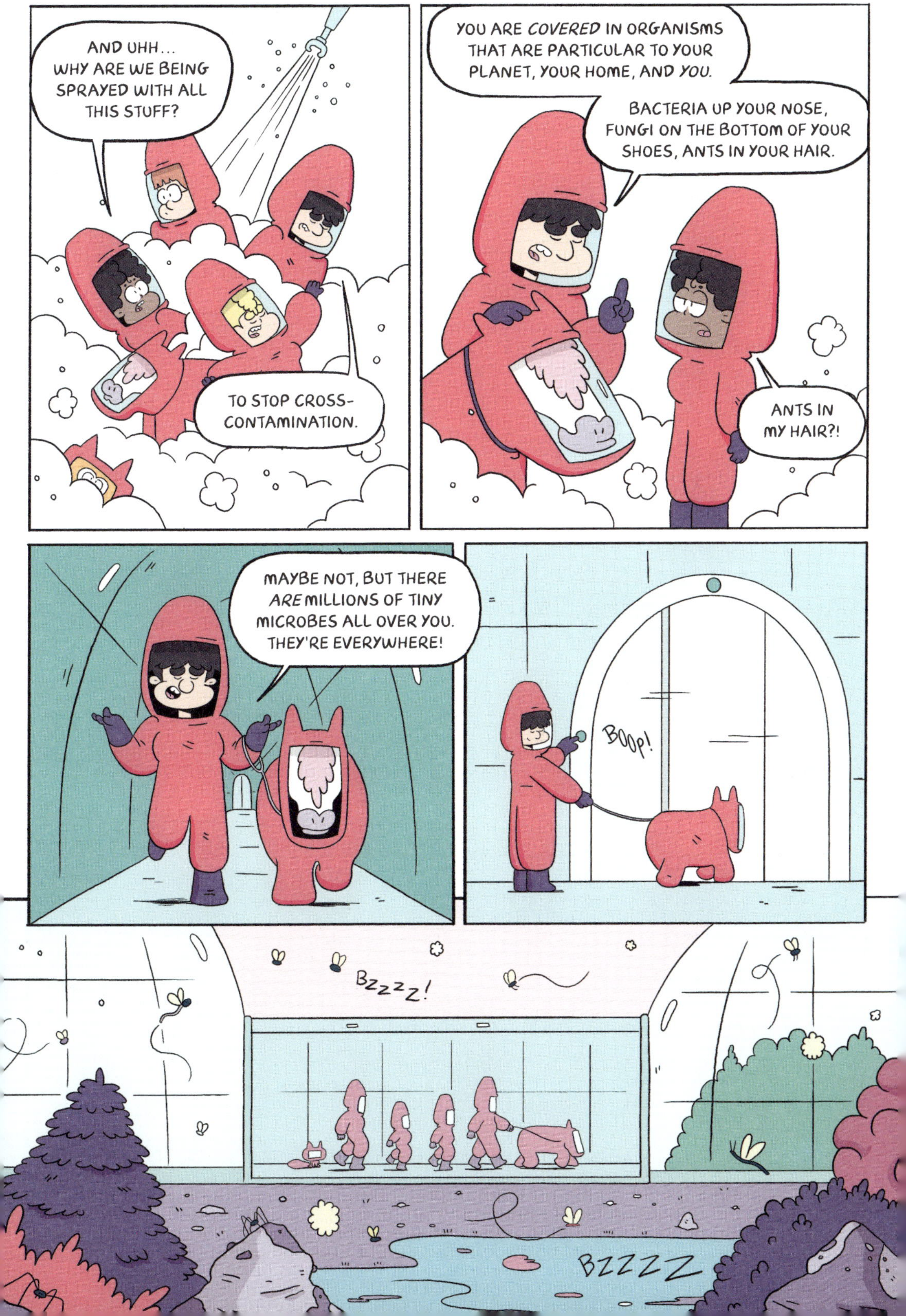
AND UHH... WHY ARE WE BEING SPRAYED WITH ALL THIS STUFF?
TO STOP CROSS-CONTAMINATION.
YOU ARE COVERED IN ORGANISMS THAT ARE PARTICULAR TO YOUR PLANET, YOUR HOME, AND YOU.
BACTERIA UP YOUR NOSE, FUNGI ON THE BOTTOM OF YOUR SHOES, ANTS IN YOUR HAIR.
ANTS IN MY HAIR?!
MAYBE NOT, BUT THERE ARE MILLIONS OF TINY MICROBES ALL OVER YOU. THEY'RE EVERYWHERE!
BOOP!
BZZZZ!
BZZZZ

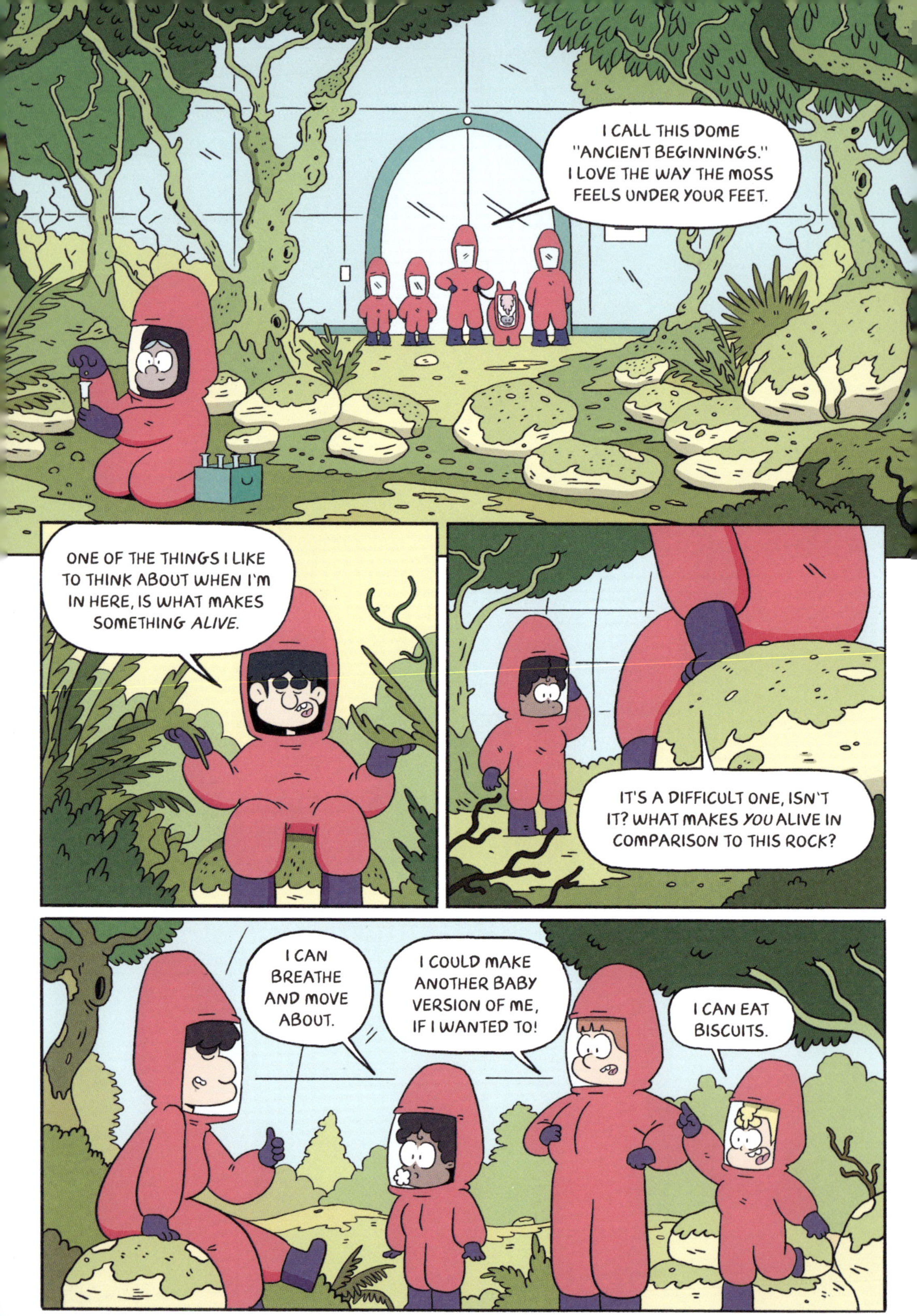
I CALL THIS DOME "ANCIENT BEGINNINGS." I LOVE THE WAY THE MOSS FEELS UNDER YOUR FEET.
ONE OF THE THINGS I LIKE TO THINK ABOUT WHEN I'M IN HERE, IS WHAT MAKES SOMETHING *ALIVE*.
IT'S A DIFFICULT ONE, ISN'T IT? WHAT MAKES *YOU* ALIVE IN COMPARISON TO THIS ROCK?
I CAN BREATHE AND MOVE ABOUT.
I COULD MAKE ANOTHER BABY VERSION OF ME, IF I WANTED TO!
I CAN EAT BISCUITS.

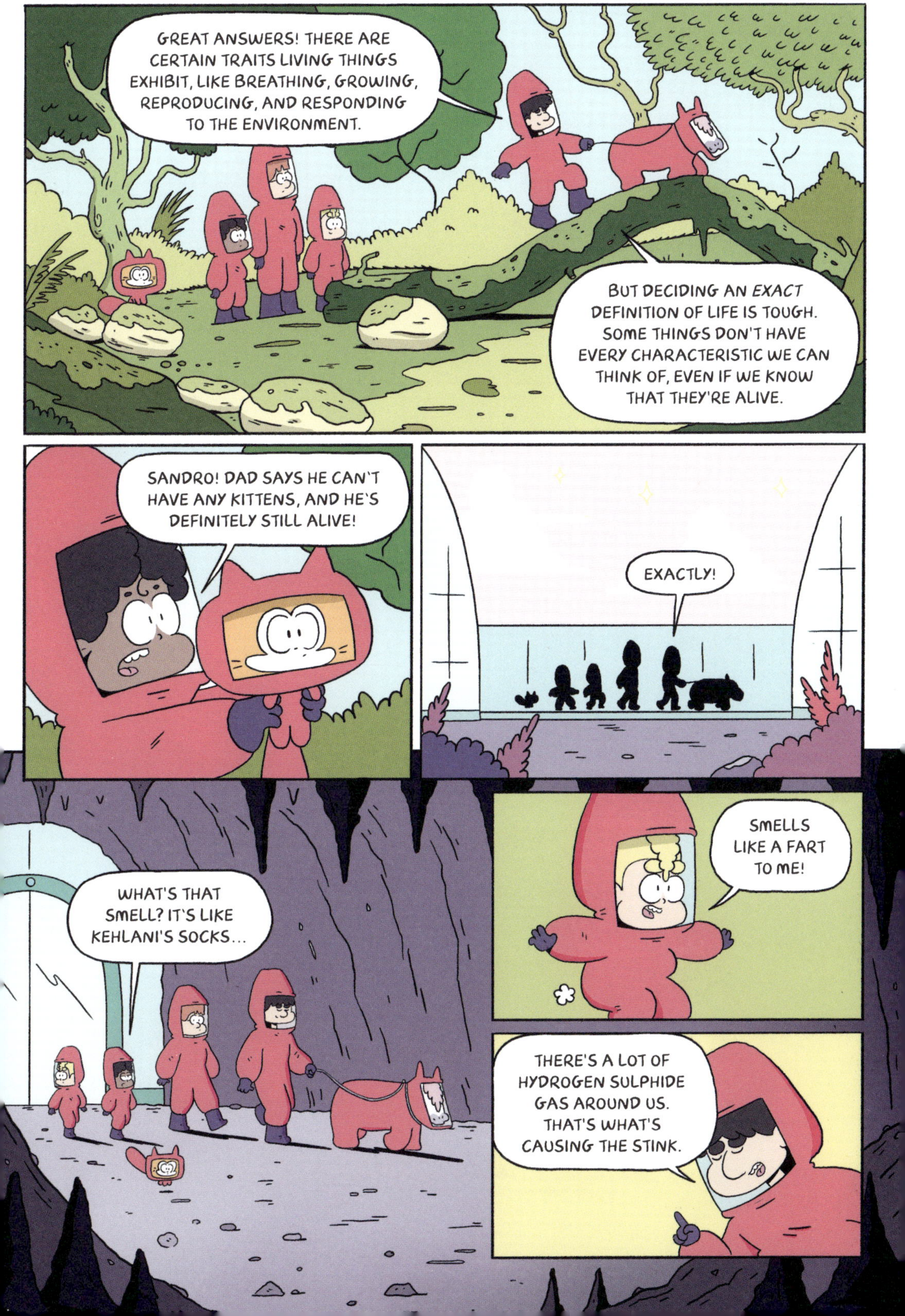
GREAT ANSWERS! THERE ARE CERTAIN TRAITS LIVING THINGS EXHIBIT, LIKE BREATHING, GROWING, REPRODUCING, AND RESPONDING TO THE ENVIRONMENT.
BUT DECIDING AN *EXACT* DEFINITION OF LIFE IS TOUGH. SOME THINGS DON'T HAVE EVERY CHARACTERISTIC WE CAN THINK OF, EVEN IF WE KNOW THAT THEY'RE ALIVE.
SANDRO! DAD SAYS HE CAN'T HAVE ANY KITTENS, AND HE'S DEFINITELY STILL ALIVE!
EXACTLY!
WHAT'S THAT SMELL? IT'S LIKE KEHLANI'S SOCKS...
SMELLS LIKE A FART TO ME!
THERE'S A LOT OF HYDROGEN SULPHIDE GAS AROUND US. THAT'S WHAT'S CAUSING THE STINK.

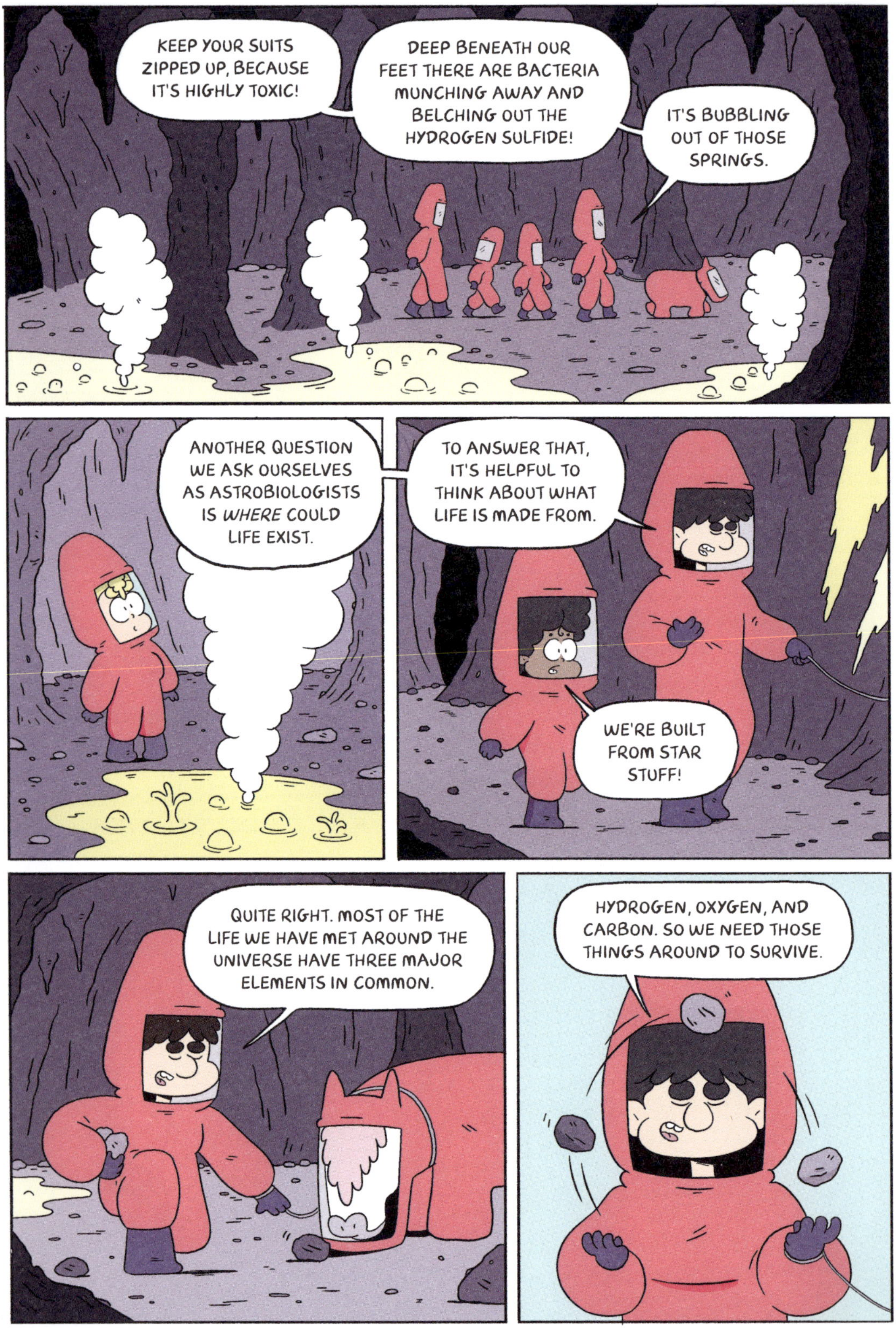
KEEP YOUR SUITS ZIPPED UP, BECAUSE IT'S HIGHLY TOXIC!
DEEP BENEATH OUR FEET THERE ARE BACTERIA MUNCHING AWAY AND BELCHING OUT THE HYDROGEN SULFIDE!
IT'S BUBBLING OUT OF THOSE SPRINGS.
ANOTHER QUESTION WE ASK OURSELVES AS ASTROBIOLOGISTS IS *WHERE* COULD LIFE EXIST.
TO ANSWER THAT, IT'S HELPFUL TO THINK ABOUT WHAT LIFE IS MADE FROM.
WE'RE BUILT FROM STAR STUFF!
QUITE RIGHT. MOST OF THE LIFE WE HAVE MET AROUND THE UNIVERSE HAVE THREE MAJOR ELEMENTS IN COMMON.
HYDROGEN, OXYGEN, AND CARBON. SO WE NEED THOSE THINGS AROUND TO SURVIVE.

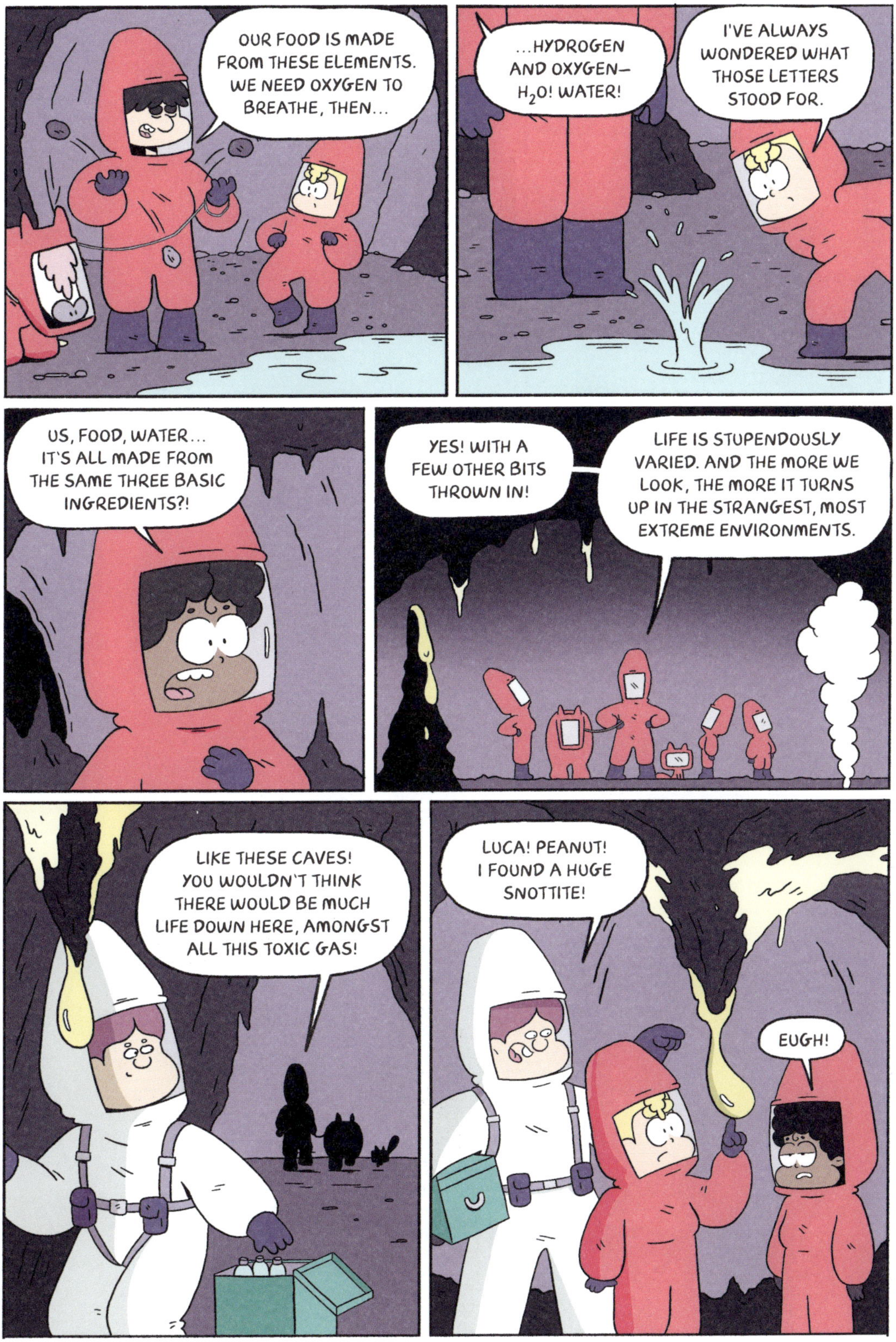
OUR FOOD IS MADE FROM THESE ELEMENTS. WE NEED OXYGEN TO BREATHE, THEN...
...HYDROGEN AND OXYGEN— H_2O! WATER!
I'VE ALWAYS WONDERED WHAT THOSE LETTERS STOOD FOR.
US, FOOD, WATER... IT'S ALL MADE FROM THE SAME THREE BASIC INGREDIENTS?!
YES! WITH A FEW OTHER BITS THROWN IN!
LIFE IS STUPENDOUSLY VARIED. AND THE MORE WE LOOK, THE MORE IT TURNS UP IN THE STRANGEST, MOST EXTREME ENVIRONMENTS.
LIKE THESE CAVES! YOU WOULDN'T THINK THERE WOULD BE MUCH LIFE DOWN HERE, AMONGST ALL THIS TOXIC GAS!
LUCA! PEANUT! I FOUND A HUGE SNOTTITE!
EUGH!

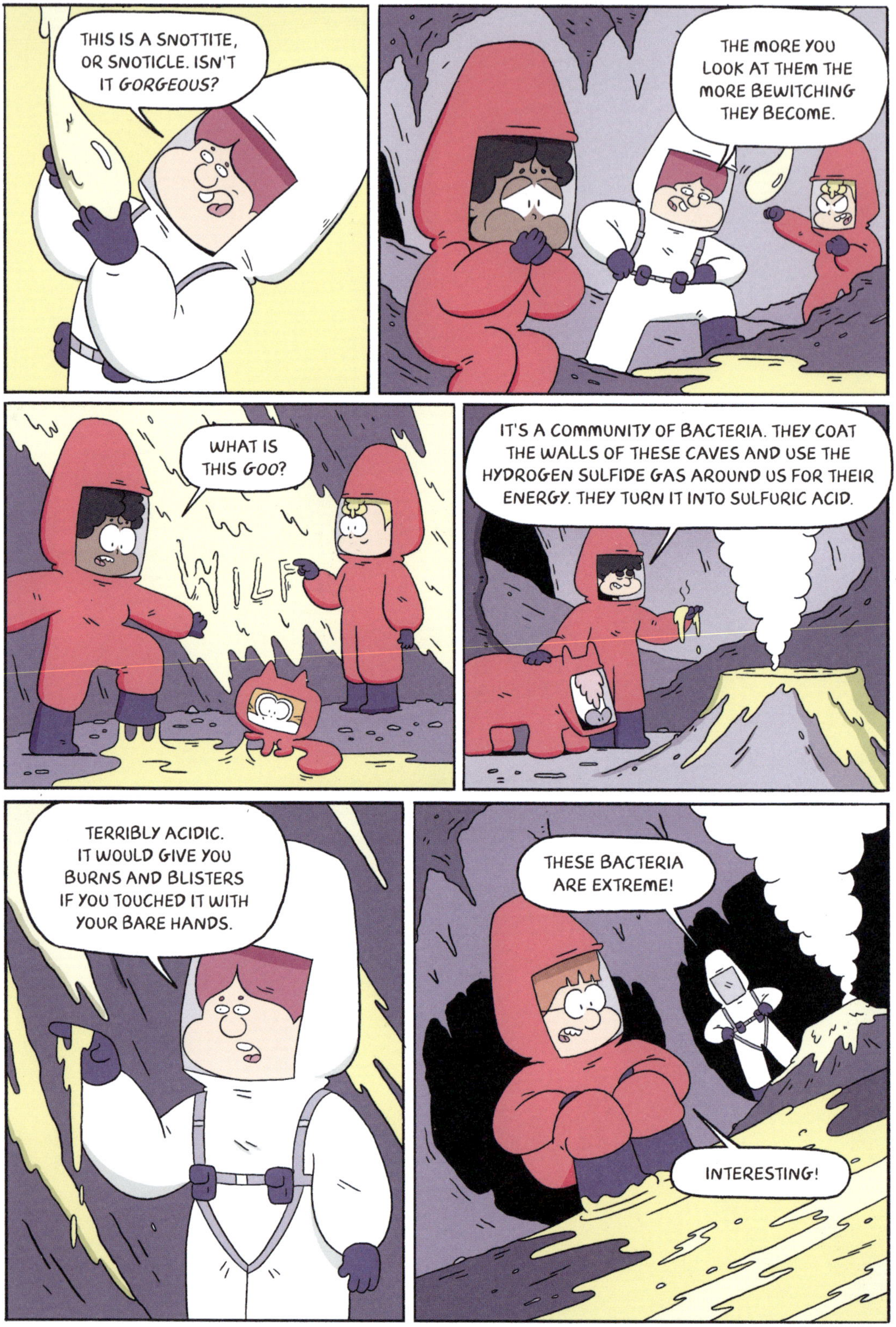

THIS IS A SNOTTITE, OR SNOTICLE. ISN'T IT *GORGEOUS?*
THE MORE YOU LOOK AT THEM THE MORE BEWITCHING THEY BECOME.
WHAT IS THIS *GOO*?
WILF
IT'S A COMMUNITY OF BACTERIA. THEY COAT THE WALLS OF THESE CAVES AND USE THE HYDROGEN SULFIDE GAS AROUND US FOR THEIR ENERGY. THEY TURN IT INTO SULFURIC ACID.
TERRIBLY ACIDIC. IT WOULD GIVE YOU BURNS AND BLISTERS IF YOU TOUCHED IT WITH YOUR BARE HANDS.
THESE BACTERIA ARE EXTREME!
INTERESTING!

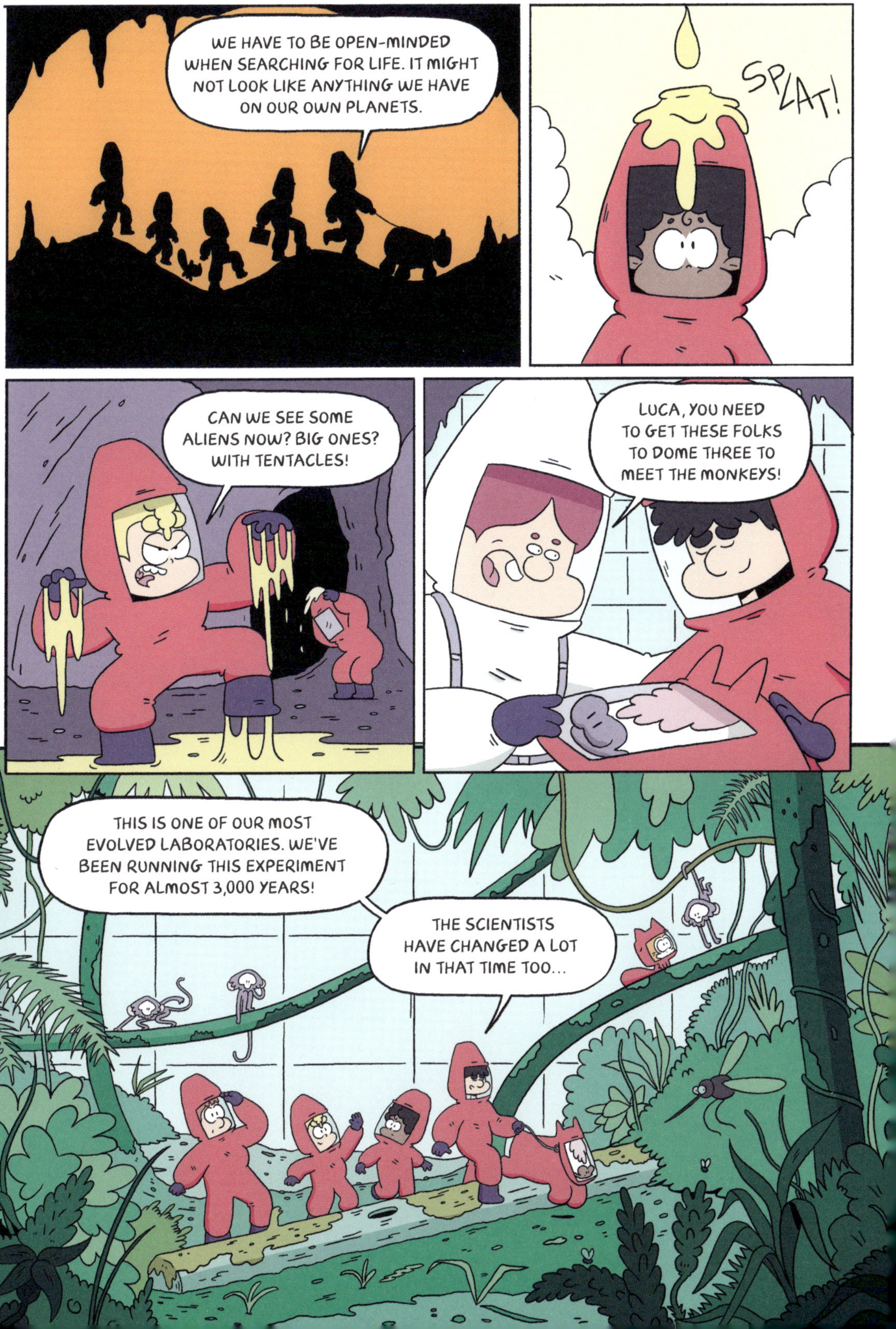
WE HAVE TO BE OPEN-MINDED WHEN SEARCHING FOR LIFE. IT MIGHT NOT LOOK LIKE ANYTHING WE HAVE ON OUR OWN PLANETS.
SPLAT!
CAN WE SEE SOME ALIENS NOW? BIG ONES? WITH TENTACLES!
LUCA, YOU NEED TO GET THESE FOLKS TO DOME THREE TO MEET THE MONKEYS!
THIS IS ONE OF OUR MOST EVOLVED LABORATORIES. WE'VE BEEN RUNNING THIS EXPERIMENT FOR ALMOST 3,000 YEARS!
THE SCIENTISTS HAVE CHANGED A LOT IN THAT TIME TOO...

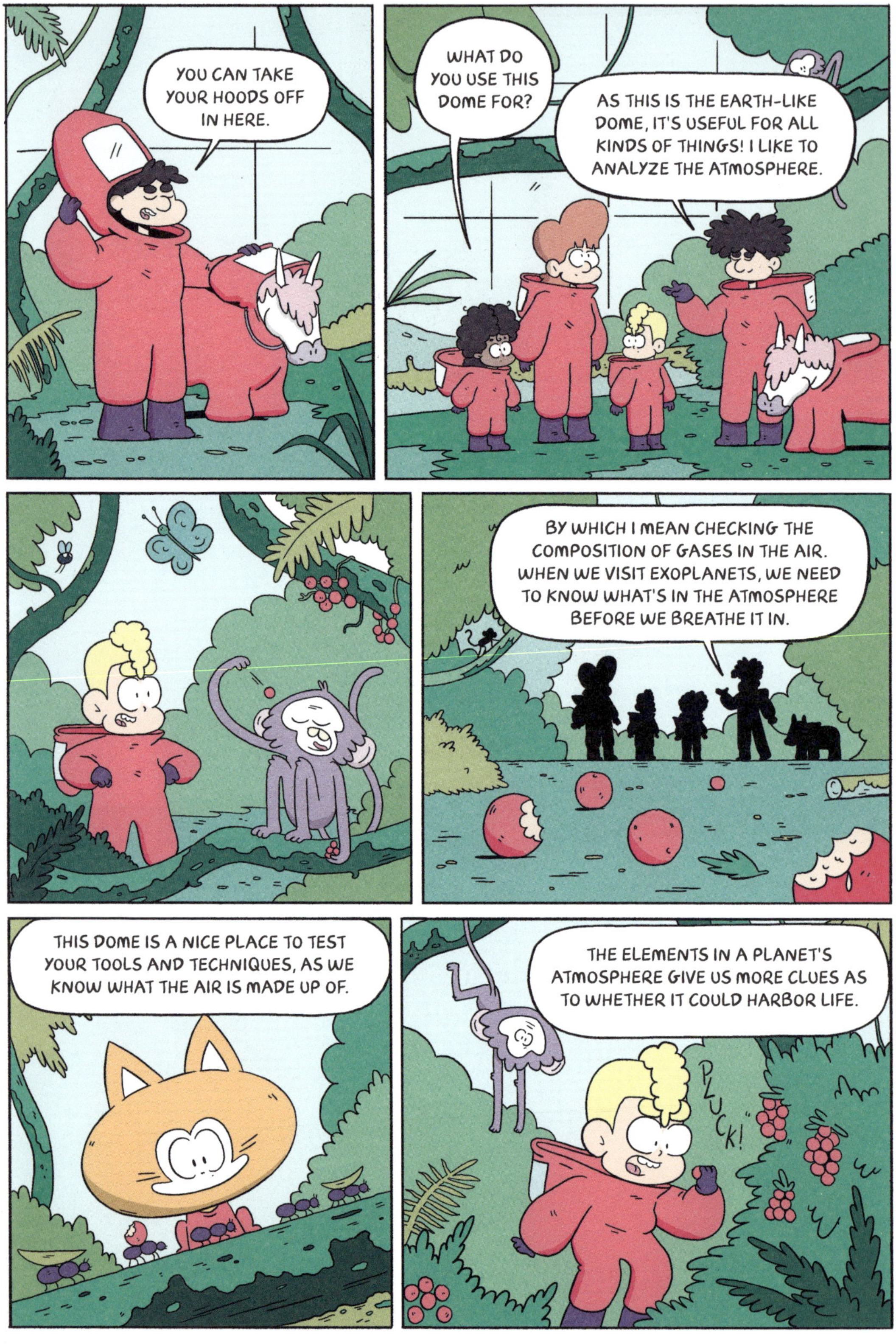
YOU CAN TAKE YOUR HOODS OFF IN HERE.
WHAT DO YOU USE THIS DOME FOR?
AS THIS IS THE EARTH-LIKE DOME, IT'S USEFUL FOR ALL KINDS OF THINGS! I LIKE TO ANALYZE THE ATMOSPHERE.
BY WHICH I MEAN CHECKING THE COMPOSITION OF GASES IN THE AIR. WHEN WE VISIT EXOPLANETS, WE NEED TO KNOW WHAT'S IN THE ATMOSPHERE BEFORE WE BREATHE IT IN.
THIS DOME IS A NICE PLACE TO TEST YOUR TOOLS AND TECHNIQUES, AS WE KNOW WHAT THE AIR IS MADE UP OF.
THE ELEMENTS IN A PLANET'S ATMOSPHERE GIVE US MORE CLUES AS TO WHETHER IT COULD HARBOR LIFE.
PLUCK!

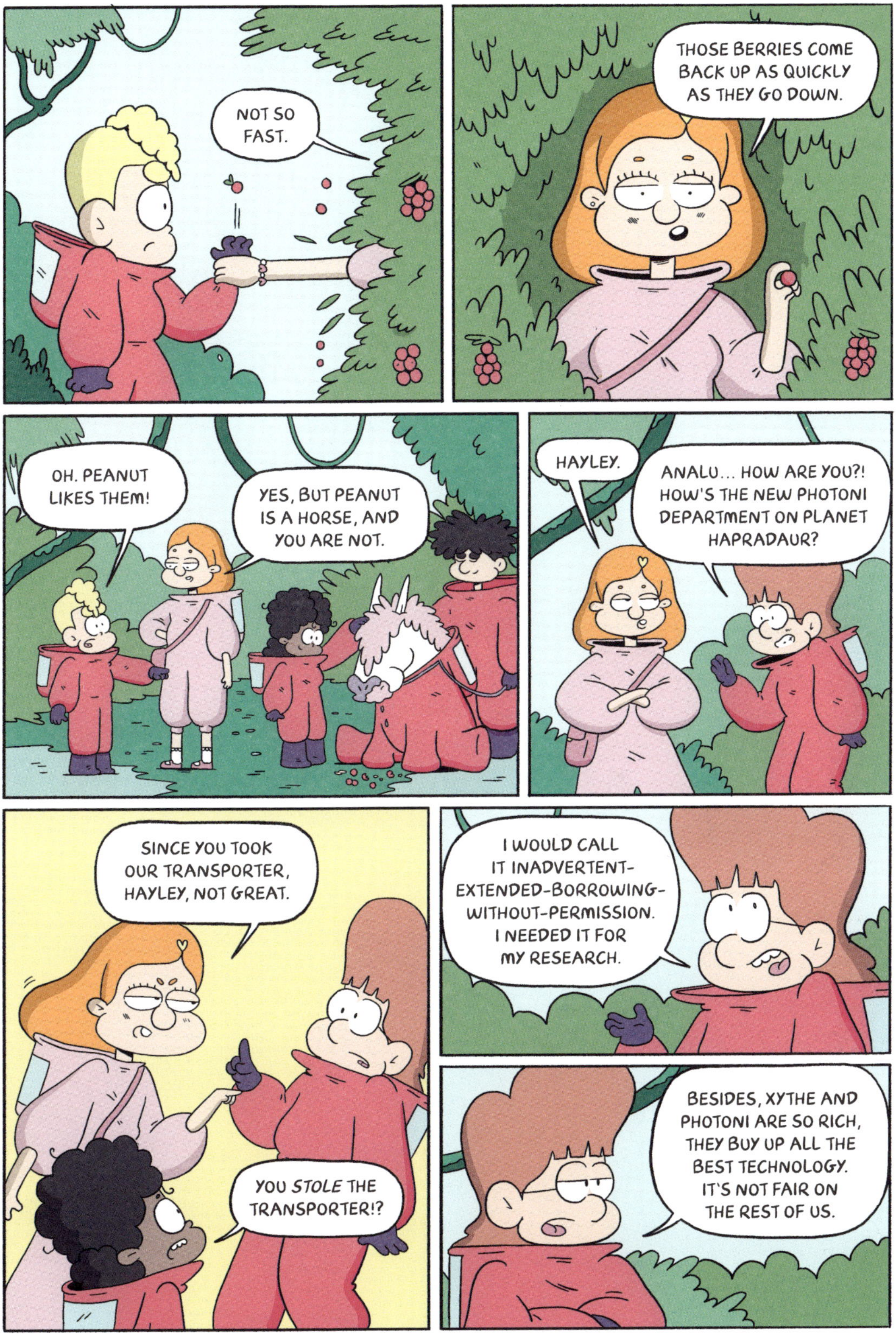
NOT SO FAST.
THOSE BERRIES COME BACK UP AS QUICKLY AS THEY GO DOWN.
OH. PEANUT LIKES THEM!
YES, BUT PEANUT IS A HORSE, AND YOU ARE NOT.
HAYLEY.
ANALU... HOW ARE YOU?! HOW'S THE NEW PHOTONI DEPARTMENT ON PLANET HAPRADAUR?
SINCE YOU TOOK OUR TRANSPORTER, HAYLEY, NOT GREAT.
YOU *STOLE* THE TRANSPORTER!?
I WOULD CALL IT INADVERTENT-EXTENDED-BORROWING-WITHOUT-PERMISSION. I NEEDED IT FOR MY RESEARCH.
BESIDES, XYTHE AND PHOTONI ARE SO RICH, THEY BUY UP ALL THE BEST TECHNOLOGY. IT'S NOT FAIR ON THE REST OF US.

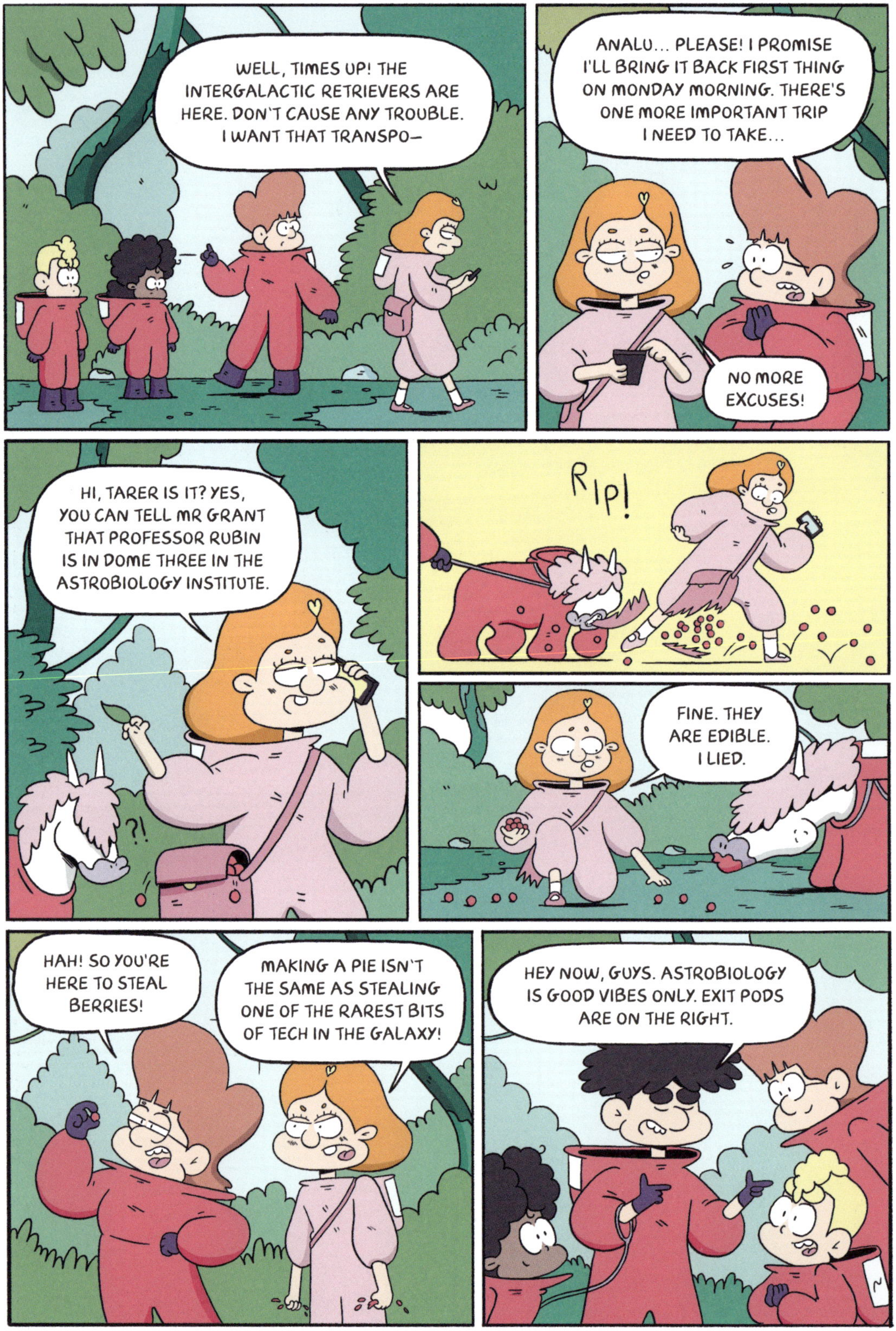
WELL, TIMES UP! THE INTERGALACTIC RETRIEVERS ARE HERE. DON'T CAUSE ANY TROUBLE. I WANT THAT TRANSPO—
ANALU... PLEASE! I PROMISE I'LL BRING IT BACK FIRST THING ON MONDAY MORNING. THERE'S ONE MORE IMPORTANT TRIP I NEED TO TAKE...
NO MORE EXCUSES!
HI, TARER IS IT? YES, YOU CAN TELL MR GRANT THAT PROFESSOR RUBIN IS IN DOME THREE IN THE ASTROBIOLOGY INSTITUTE.
?!
RIP!
FINE. THEY ARE EDIBLE. I LIED.
HAH! SO YOU'RE HERE TO STEAL BERRIES!
MAKING A PIE ISN'T THE SAME AS STEALING ONE OF THE RAREST BITS OF TECH IN THE GALAXY!
HEY NOW, GUYS. ASTROBIOLOGY IS GOOD VIBES ONLY. EXIT PODS ARE ON THE RIGHT.

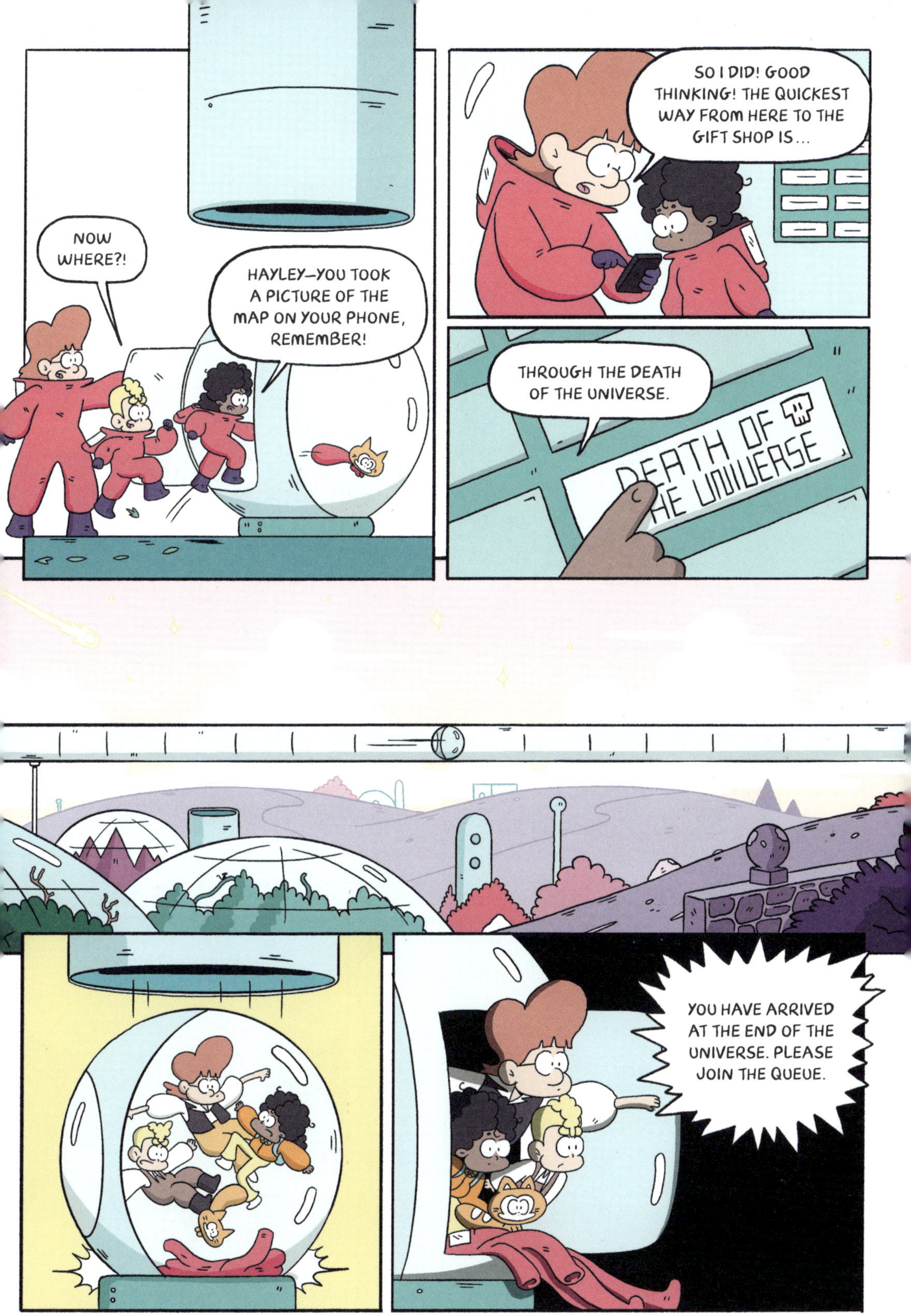
NOW WHERE?!
HAYLEY—YOU TOOK A PICTURE OF THE MAP ON YOUR PHONE, REMEMBER!
SO I DID! GOOD THINKING! THE QUICKEST WAY FROM HERE TO THE GIFT SHOP IS...
THROUGH THE DEATH OF THE UNIVERSE.
DEATH OF THE UNIVERSE
YOU HAVE ARRIVED AT THE END OF THE UNIVERSE. PLEASE JOIN THE QUEUE.

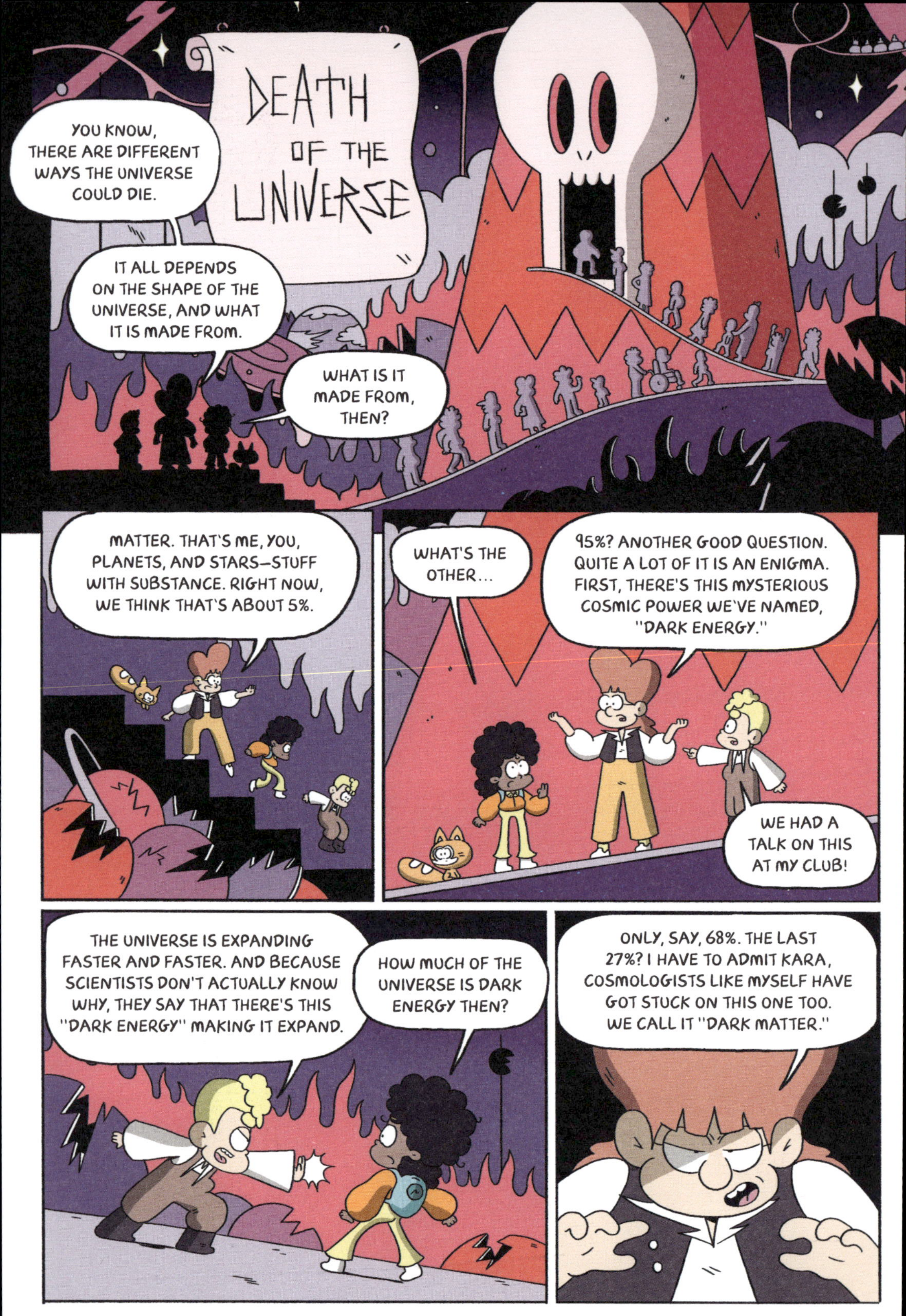
DEATH OF THE UNIVERSE
YOU KNOW, THERE ARE DIFFERENT WAYS THE UNIVERSE COULD DIE.
IT ALL DEPENDS ON THE SHAPE OF THE UNIVERSE, AND WHAT IT IS MADE FROM.
WHAT IS IT MADE FROM, THEN?
MATTER. THAT'S ME, YOU, PLANETS, AND STARS—STUFF WITH SUBSTANCE. RIGHT NOW, WE THINK THAT'S ABOUT 5%.
WHAT'S THE OTHER...
95%? ANOTHER GOOD QUESTION. QUITE A LOT OF IT IS AN ENIGMA. FIRST, THERE'S THIS MYSTERIOUS COSMIC POWER WE'VE NAMED, "DARK ENERGY."
WE HAD A TALK ON THIS AT MY CLUB!
THE UNIVERSE IS EXPANDING FASTER AND FASTER. AND BECAUSE SCIENTISTS DON'T ACTUALLY KNOW WHY, THEY SAY THAT THERE'S THIS "DARK ENERGY" MAKING IT EXPAND.
HOW MUCH OF THE UNIVERSE IS DARK ENERGY THEN?
ONLY, SAY, 68%. THE LAST 27%? I HAVE TO ADMIT KARA, COSMOLOGISTS LIKE MYSELF HAVE GOT STUCK ON THIS ONE TOO. WE CALL IT "DARK MATTER."

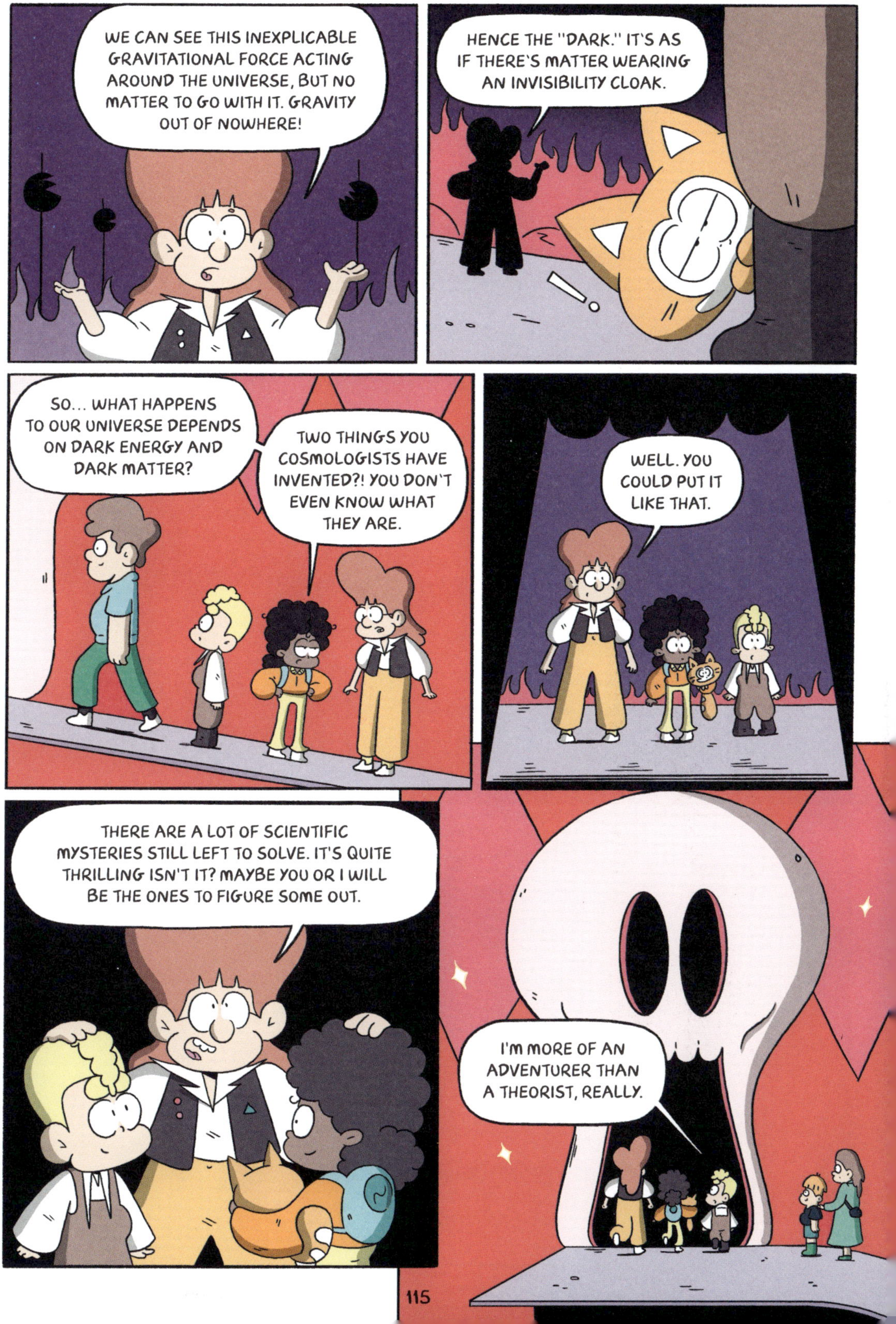
WE CAN SEE THIS INEXPLICABLE GRAVITATIONAL FORCE ACTING AROUND THE UNIVERSE, BUT NO MATTER TO GO WITH IT. GRAVITY OUT OF NOWHERE!
HENCE THE "DARK." IT'S AS IF THERE'S MATTER WEARING AN INVISIBILITY CLOAK.
!
SO... WHAT HAPPENS TO OUR UNIVERSE DEPENDS ON DARK ENERGY AND DARK MATTER?
TWO THINGS YOU COSMOLOGISTS HAVE INVENTED?! YOU DON'T EVEN KNOW WHAT THEY ARE.
WELL. YOU COULD PUT IT LIKE THAT.
THERE ARE A LOT OF SCIENTIFIC MYSTERIES STILL LEFT TO SOLVE. IT'S QUITE THRILLING ISN'T IT? MAYBE YOU OR I WILL BE THE ONES TO FIGURE SOME OUT.
I'M MORE OF AN ADVENTURER THAN A THEORIST, REALLY.

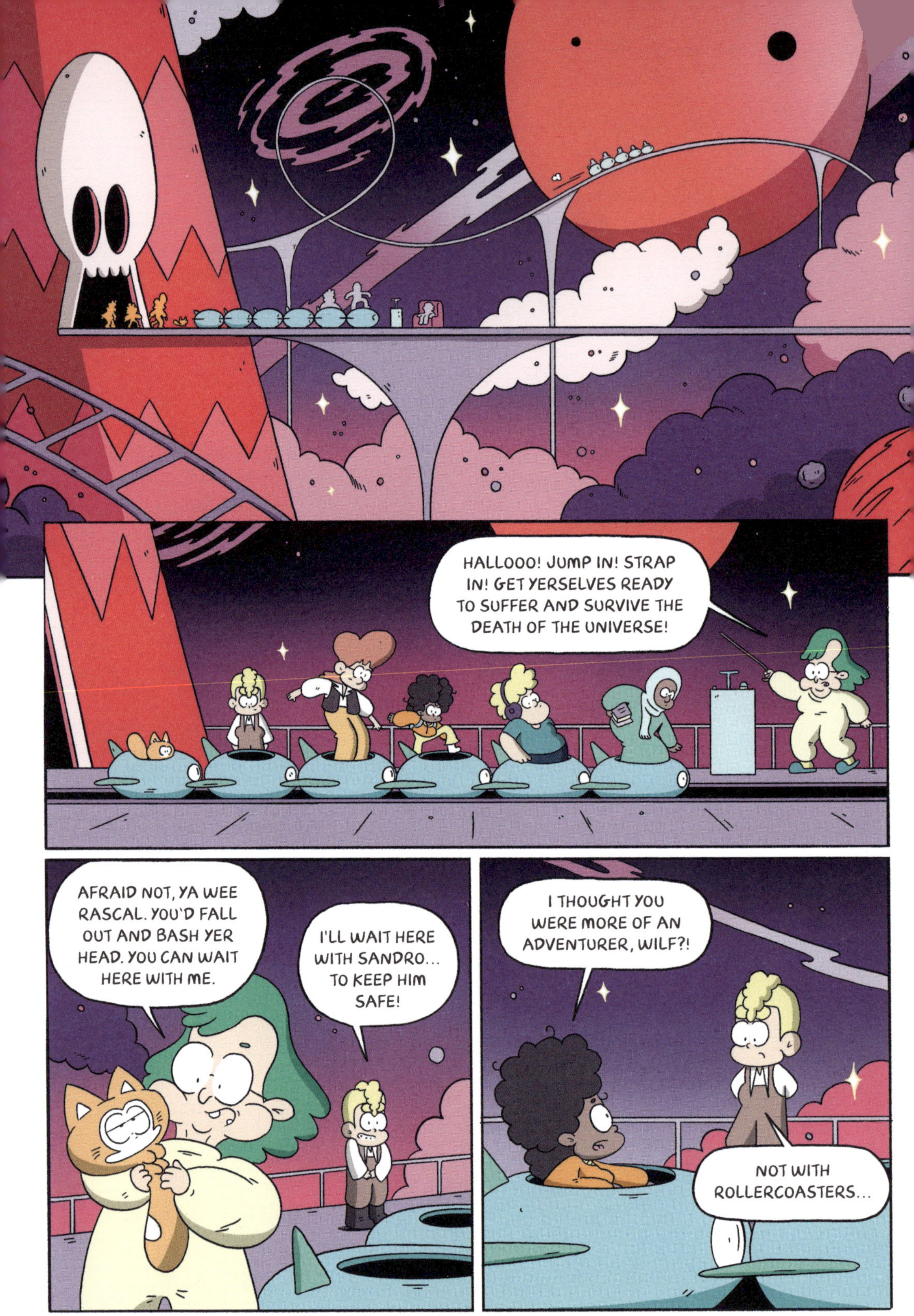
HALLOOO! JUMP IN! STRAP IN! GET YERSELVES READY TO SUFFER AND SURVIVE THE DEATH OF THE UNIVERSE!
AFRAID NOT, YA WEE RASCAL. YOU'D FALL OUT AND BASH YER HEAD. YOU CAN WAIT HERE WITH ME.
I'LL WAIT HERE WITH SANDRO... TO KEEP HIM SAFE!
I THOUGHT YOU WERE MORE OF AN ADVENTURER, WILF?!
NOT WITH ROLLERCOASTERS...

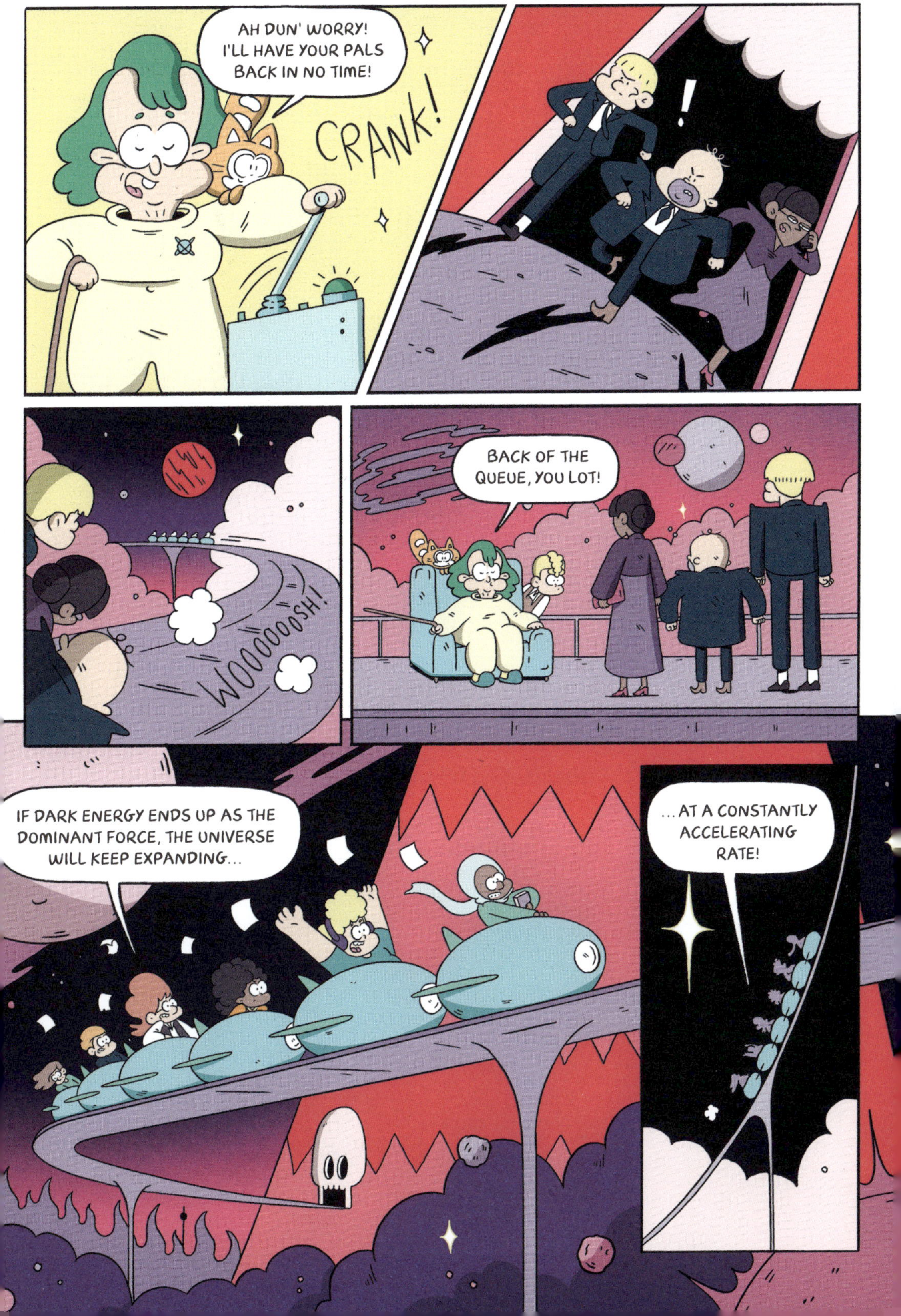

AH DUN' WORRY! I'LL HAVE YOUR PALS BACK IN NO TIME!
CRANK!
!
WOOOOOOSH!
BACK OF THE QUEUE, YOU LOT!
IF DARK ENERGY ENDS UP AS THE DOMINANT FORCE, THE UNIVERSE WILL KEEP EXPANDING...
...AT A CONSTANTLY ACCELERATING RATE!

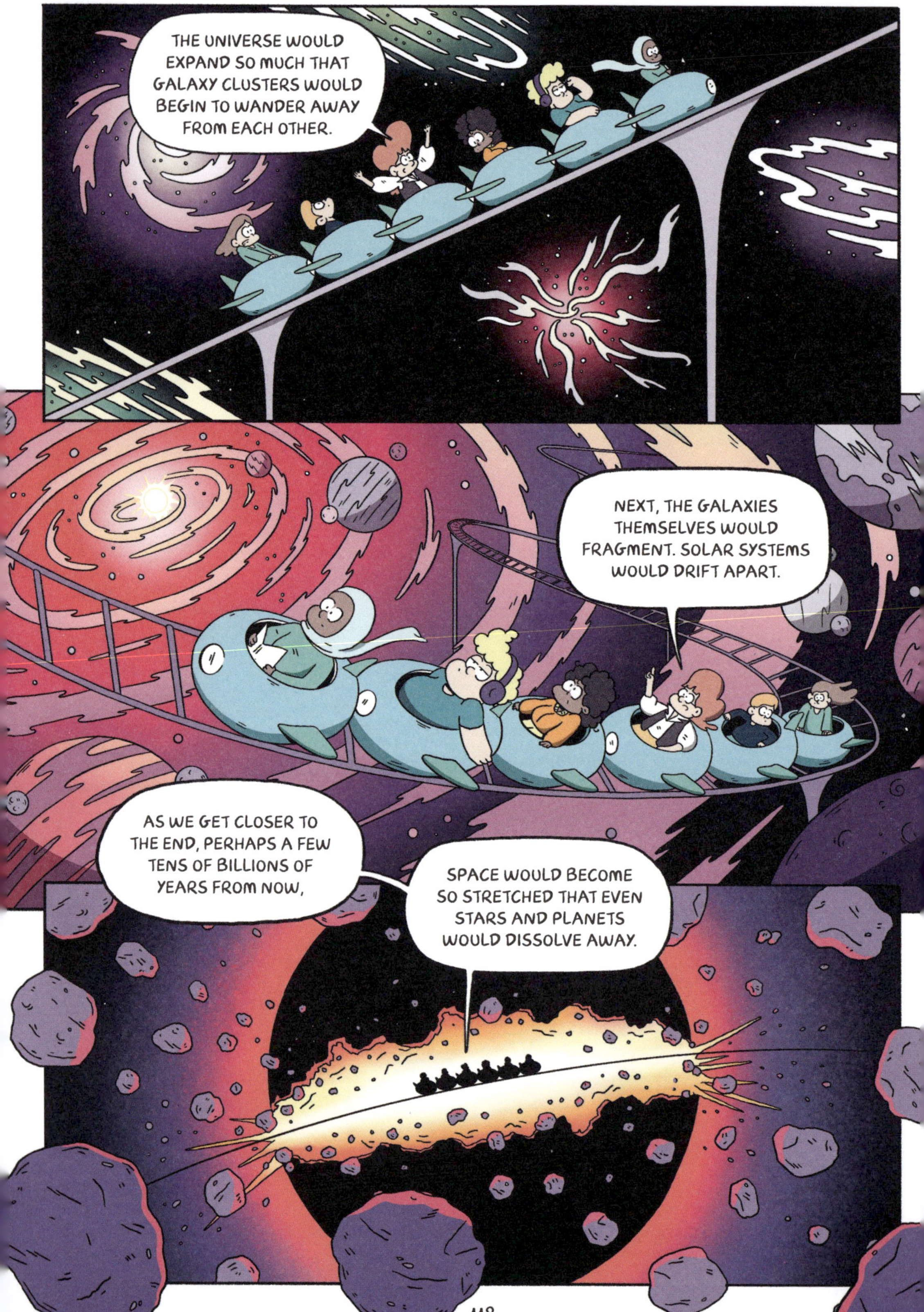
THE UNIVERSE WOULD EXPAND SO MUCH THAT GALAXY CLUSTERS WOULD BEGIN TO WANDER AWAY FROM EACH OTHER.
NEXT, THE GALAXIES THEMSELVES WOULD FRAGMENT. SOLAR SYSTEMS WOULD DRIFT APART.
AS WE GET CLOSER TO THE END, PERHAPS A FEW TENS OF BILLIONS OF YEARS FROM NOW,
SPACE WOULD BECOME SO STRETCHED THAT EVEN STARS AND PLANETS WOULD DISSOLVE AWAY.

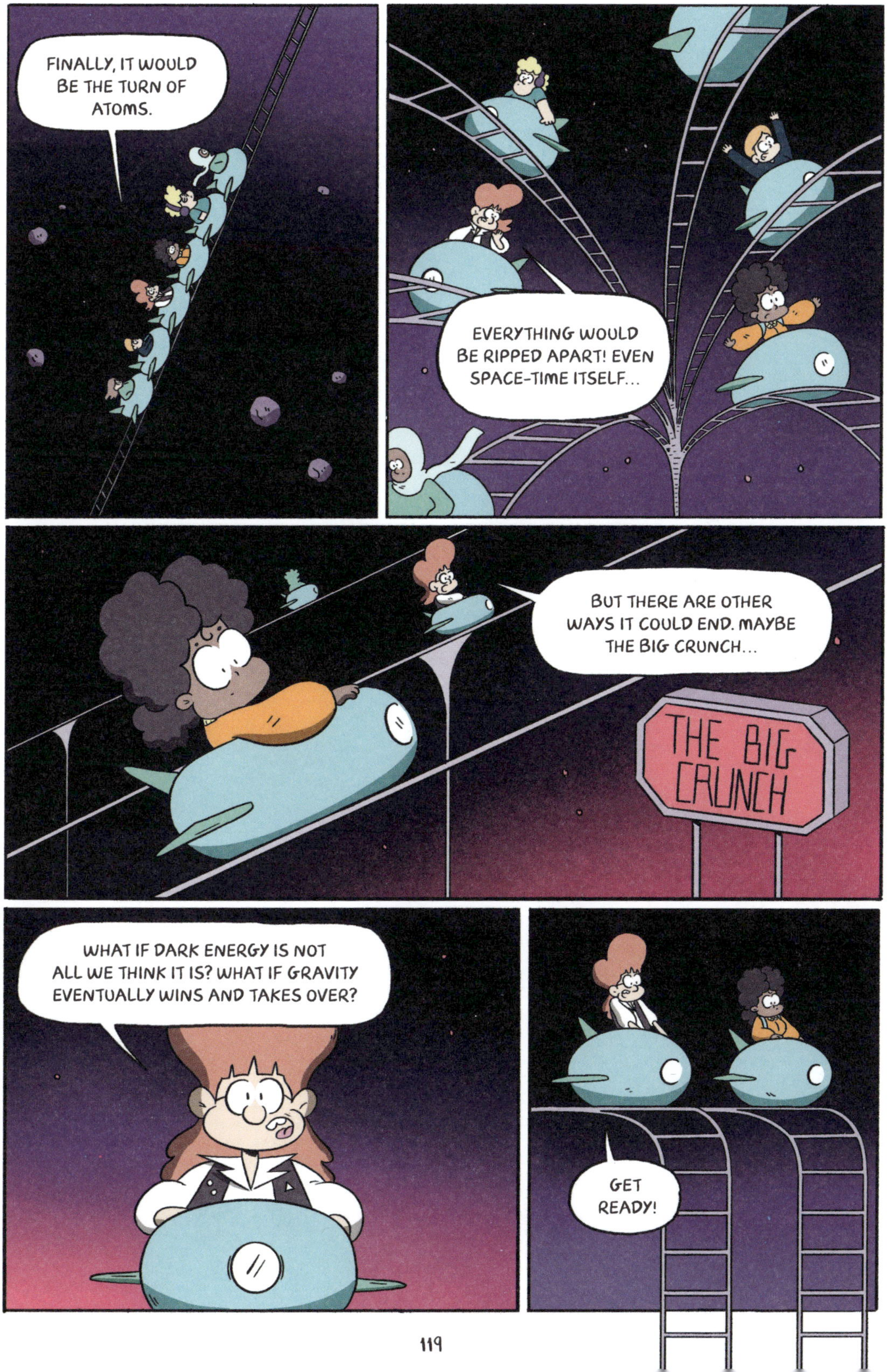
FINALLY, IT WOULD BE THE TURN OF ATOMS.
EVERYTHING WOULD BE RIPPED APART! EVEN SPACE-TIME ITSELF...
BUT THERE ARE OTHER WAYS IT COULD END. MAYBE THE BIG CRUNCH...
THE BIG CRUNCH
WHAT IF DARK ENERGY IS NOT ALL WE THINK IT IS? WHAT IF GRAVITY EVENTUALLY WINS AND TAKES OVER?
GET READY!

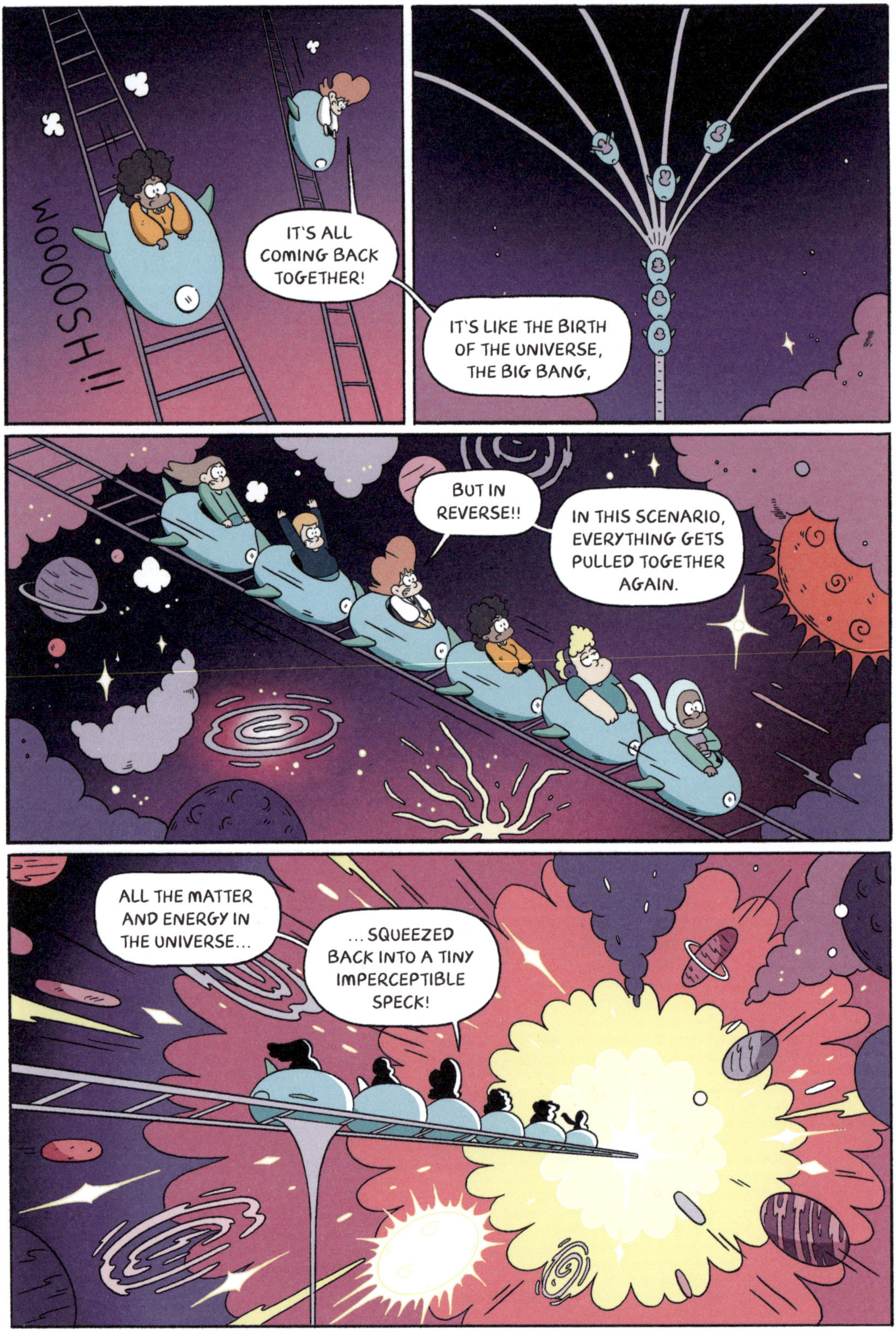
WOOOOSH!!
IT'S ALL COMING BACK TOGETHER!
IT'S LIKE THE BIRTH OF THE UNIVERSE, THE BIG BANG,
BUT IN REVERSE!!
IN THIS SCENARIO, EVERYTHING GETS PULLED TOGETHER AGAIN.
ALL THE MATTER AND ENERGY IN THE UNIVERSE...
...SQUEEZED BACK INTO A TINY IMPERCEPTIBLE SPECK!

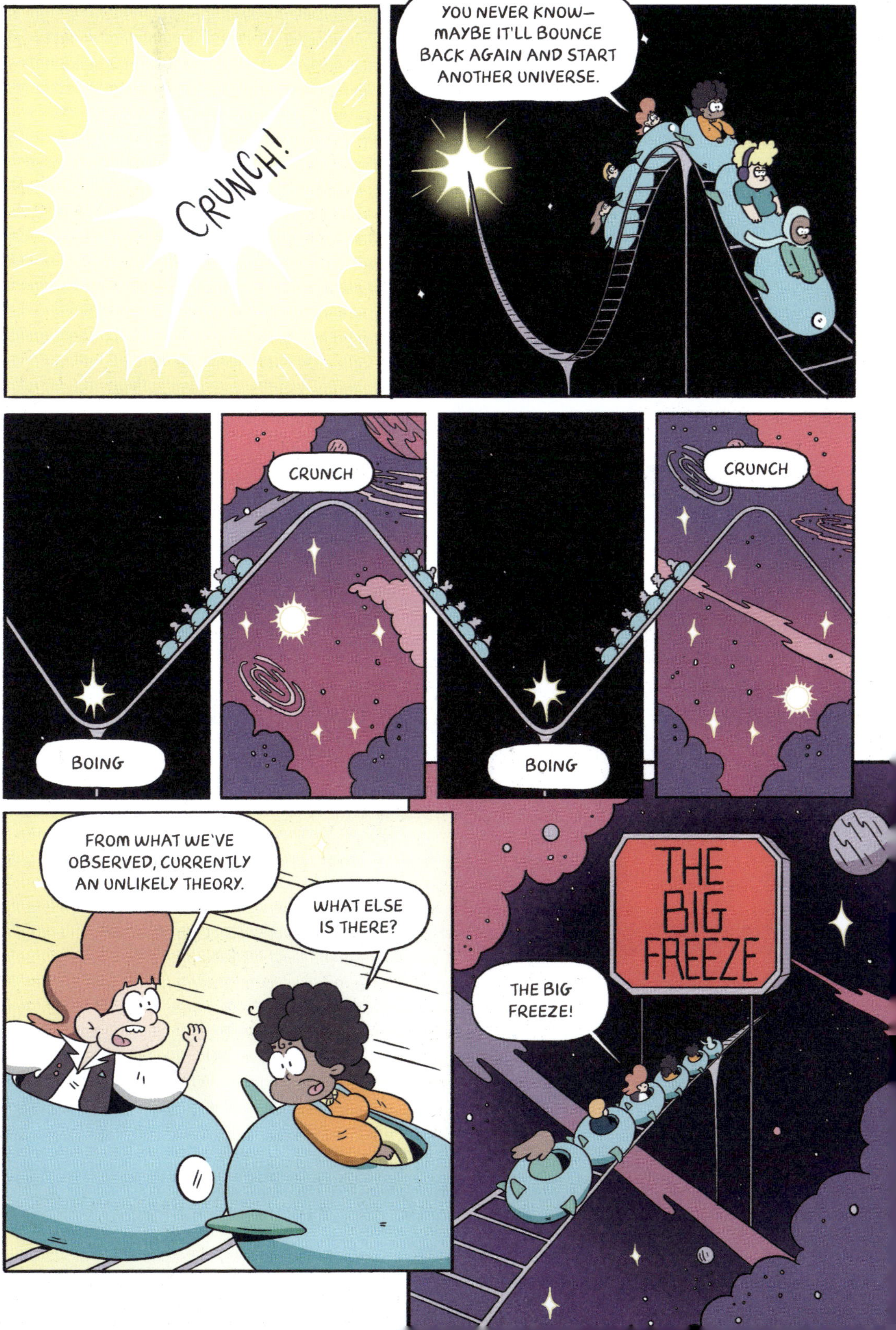
CRUNCH!
YOU NEVER KNOW— MAYBE IT'LL BOUNCE BACK AGAIN AND START ANOTHER UNIVERSE.
BOING
CRUNCH
BOING
CRUNCH
FROM WHAT WE'VE OBSERVED, CURRENTLY AN UNLIKELY THEORY.
WHAT ELSE IS THERE?
THE BIG FREEZE
THE BIG FREEZE!

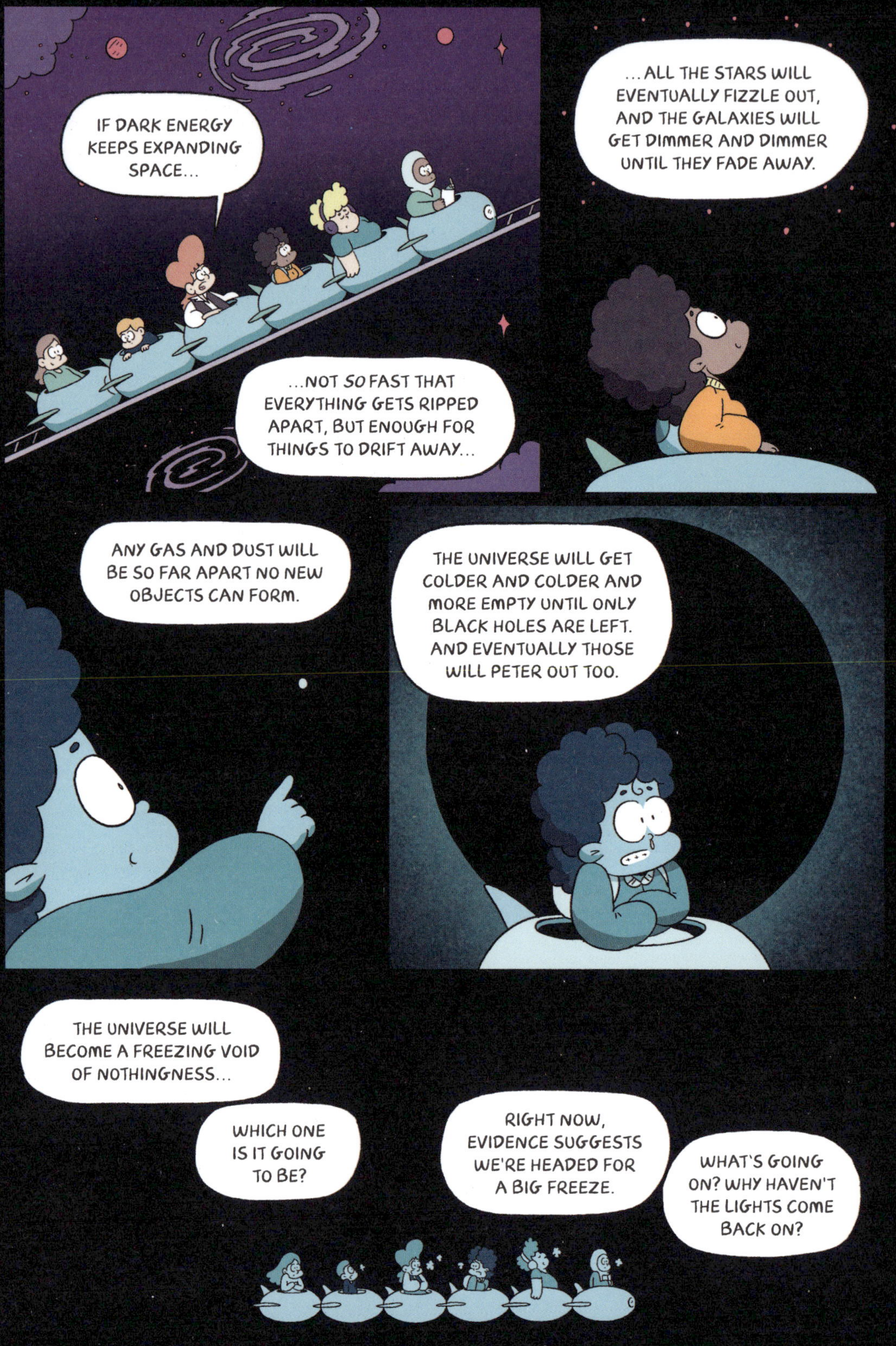
IF DARK ENERGY KEEPS EXPANDING SPACE...
...NOT SO FAST THAT EVERYTHING GETS RIPPED APART, BUT ENOUGH FOR THINGS TO DRIFT AWAY...
...ALL THE STARS WILL EVENTUALLY FIZZLE OUT, AND THE GALAXIES WILL GET DIMMER AND DIMMER UNTIL THEY FADE AWAY.
ANY GAS AND DUST WILL BE SO FAR APART NO NEW OBJECTS CAN FORM.
THE UNIVERSE WILL GET COLDER AND COLDER AND MORE EMPTY UNTIL ONLY BLACK HOLES ARE LEFT. AND EVENTUALLY THOSE WILL PETER OUT TOO.
THE UNIVERSE WILL BECOME A FREEZING VOID OF NOTHINGNESS...
WHICH ONE IS IT GOING TO BE?
RIGHT NOW, EVIDENCE SUGGESTS WE'RE HEADED FOR A BIG FREEZE.
WHAT'S GOING ON? WHY HAVEN'T THE LIGHTS COME BACK ON?

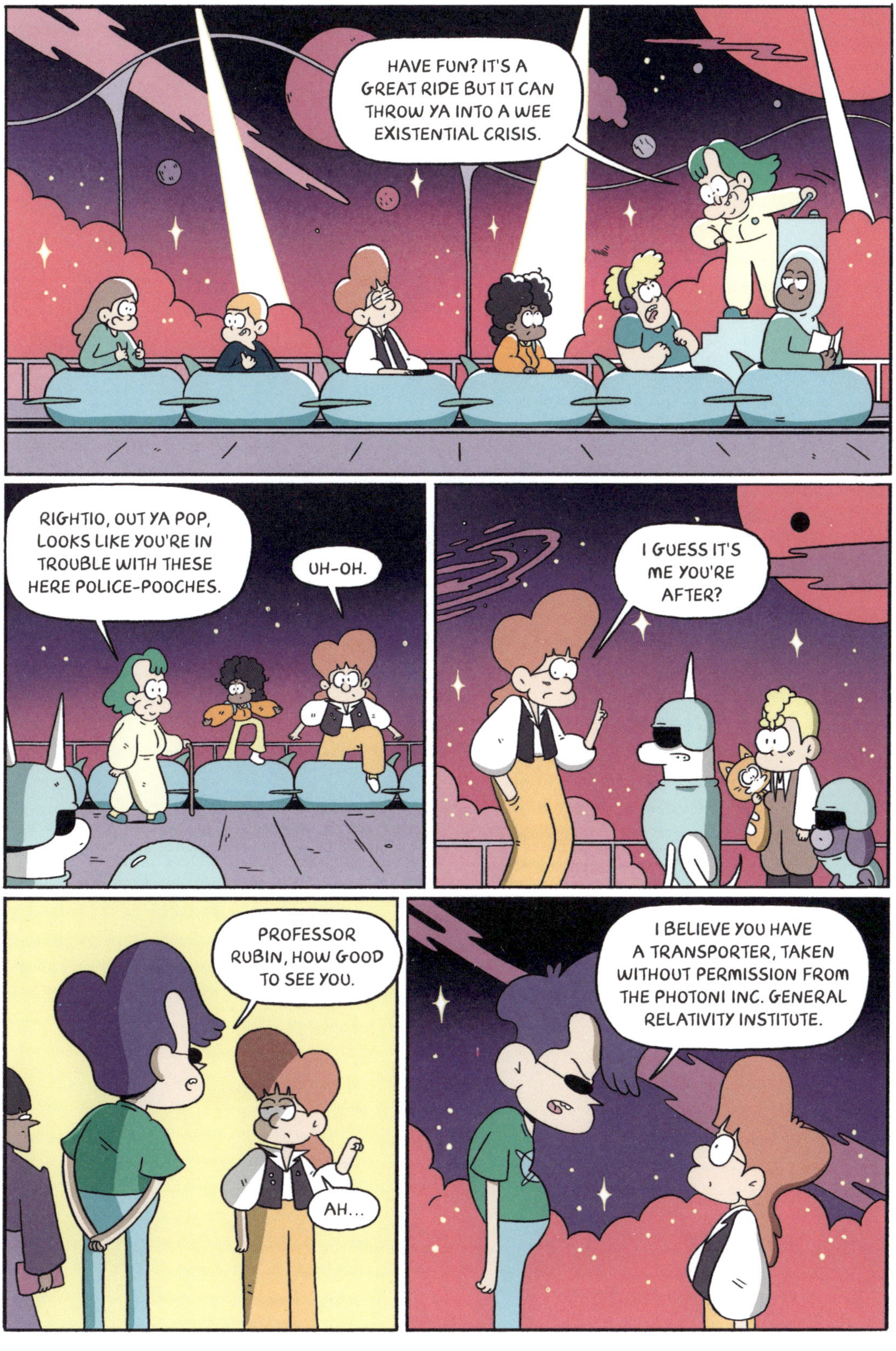
HAVE FUN? IT'S A GREAT RIDE BUT IT CAN THROW YA INTO A WEE EXISTENTIAL CRISIS.
RIGHTIO, OUT YA POP, LOOKS LIKE YOU'RE IN TROUBLE WITH THESE HERE POLICE-POOCHES.
UH-OH.
I GUESS IT'S ME YOU'RE AFTER?
PROFESSOR RUBIN, HOW GOOD TO SEE YOU.
AH...
I BELIEVE YOU HAVE A TRANSPORTER, TAKEN WITHOUT PERMISSION FROM THE PHOTONI INC. GENERAL RELATIVITY INSTITUTE.

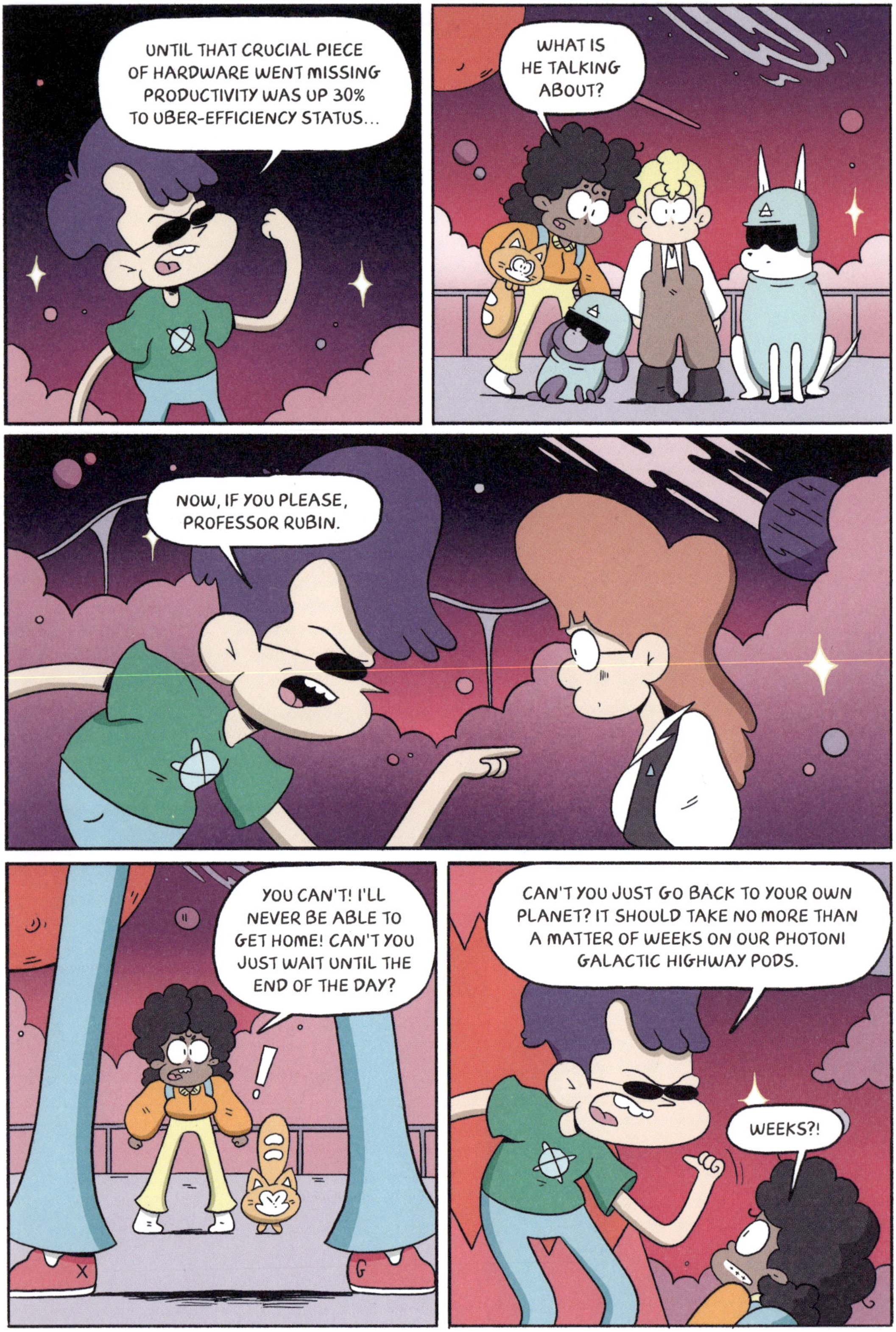
UNTIL THAT CRUCIAL PIECE OF HARDWARE WENT MISSING PRODUCTIVITY WAS UP 30% TO UBER-EFFICIENCY STATUS...
WHAT IS HE TALKING ABOUT?
NOW, IF YOU PLEASE, PROFESSOR RUBIN.
YOU CAN'T! I'LL NEVER BE ABLE TO GET HOME! CAN'T YOU JUST WAIT UNTIL THE END OF THE DAY?
!
CAN'T YOU JUST GO BACK TO YOUR OWN PLANET? IT SHOULD TAKE NO MORE THAN A MATTER OF WEEKS ON OUR PHOTONI GALACTIC HIGHWAY PODS.
WEEKS?!

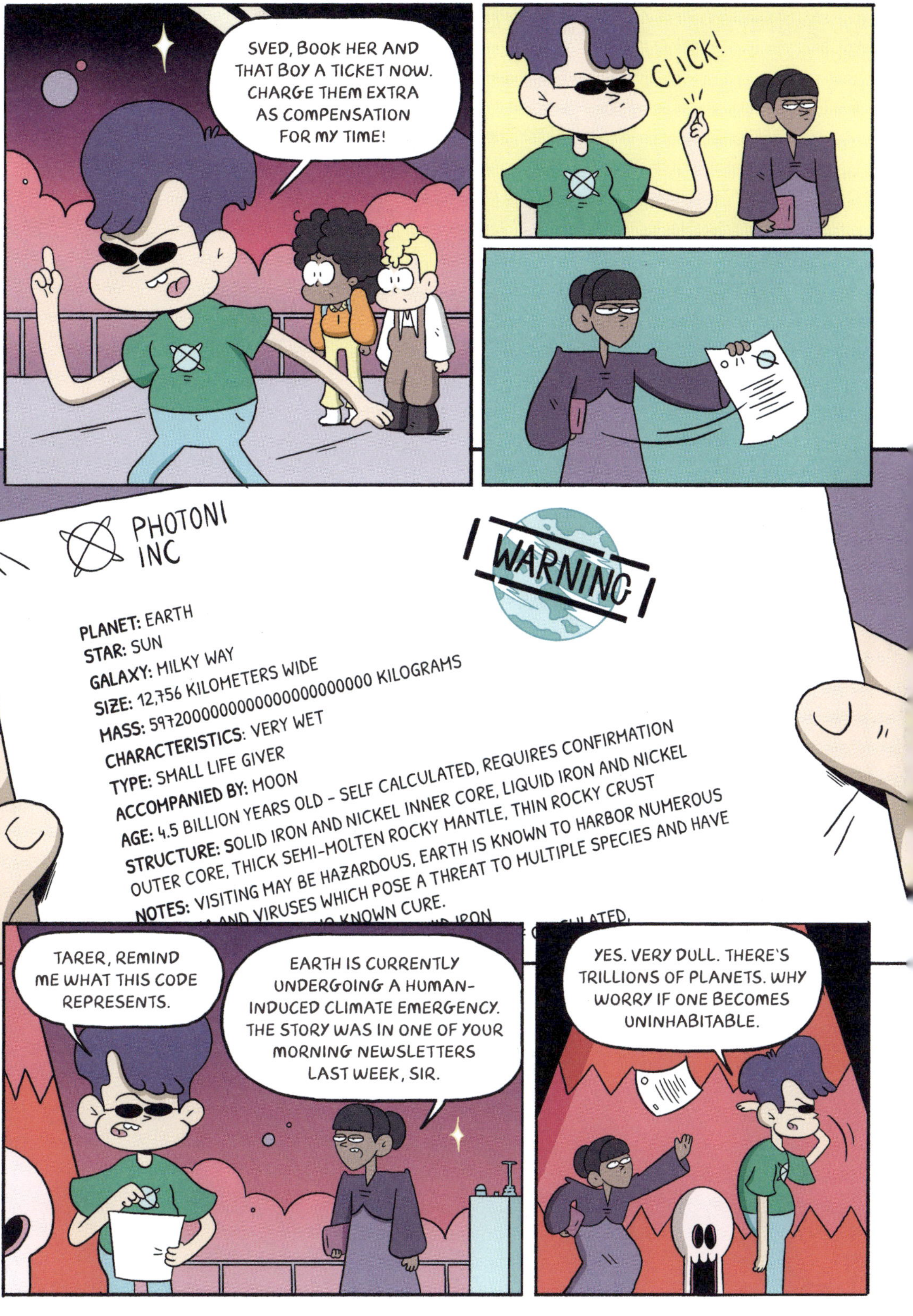

SVED, BOOK HER AND THAT BOY A TICKET NOW. CHARGE THEM EXTRA AS COMPENSATION FOR MY TIME!
CLICK!
PHOTONI INC
WARNING
PLANET: EARTH
STAR: SUN
GALAXY: MILKY WAY
SIZE: 12,756 KILOMETERS WIDE
MASS: 5972000000000000000000000 KILOGRAMS
CHARACTERISTICS: VERY WET
TYPE: SMALL LIFE GIVER
ACCOMPANIED BY: MOON
AGE: 4.5 BILLION YEARS OLD - SELF CALCULATED, REQUIRES CONFIRMATION
STRUCTURE: SOLID IRON AND NICKEL INNER CORE, LIQUID IRON AND NICKEL OUTER CORE, THICK SEMI-MOLTEN ROCKY MANTLE, THIN ROCKY CRUST
NOTES: VISITING MAY BE HAZARDOUS. EARTH IS KNOWN TO HARBOR NUMEROUS
AND VIRUSES WHICH POSE A THREAT TO MULTIPLE SPECIES AND HAVE
KNOWN CURE.
TARER, REMIND ME WHAT THIS CODE REPRESENTS.
EARTH IS CURRENTLY UNDERGOING A HUMAN-INDUCED CLIMATE EMERGENCY. THE STORY WAS IN ONE OF YOUR MORNING NEWSLETTERS LAST WEEK, SIR.
YES. VERY DULL. THERE'S TRILLIONS OF PLANETS. WHY WORRY IF ONE BECOMES UNINHABITABLE.

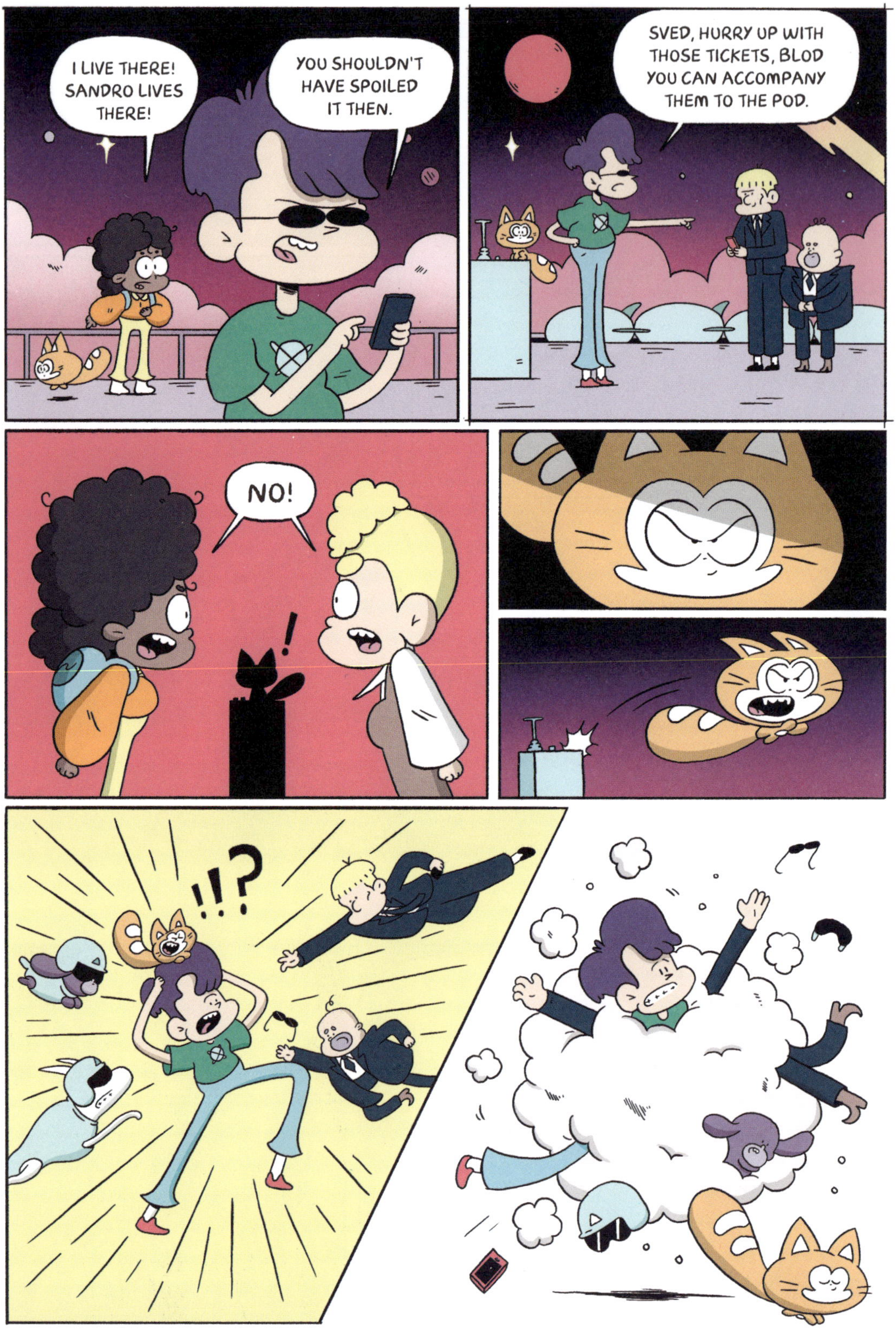
I LIVE THERE! SANDRO LIVES THERE!
YOU SHOULDN'T HAVE SPOILED IT THEN.
SVED, HURRY UP WITH THOSE TICKETS, BLOD YOU CAN ACCOMPANY THEM TO THE POD.
NO!
!
!!?

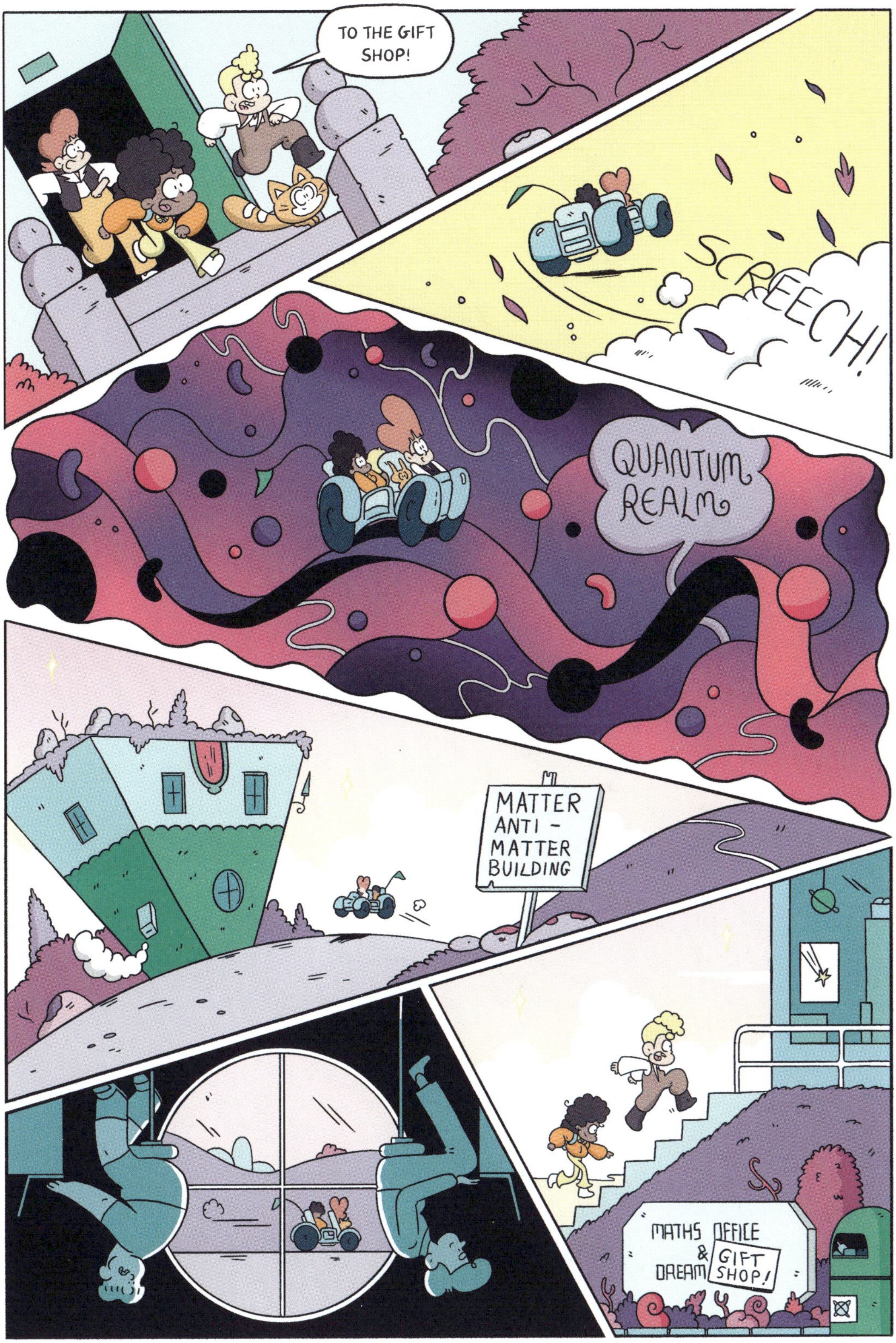
TO THE GIFT SHOP!
SCREECH!
QUANTUM REALM
MATTER ANTI-MATTER BUILDING
MATHS OFFICE & DREAM GIFT SHOP!

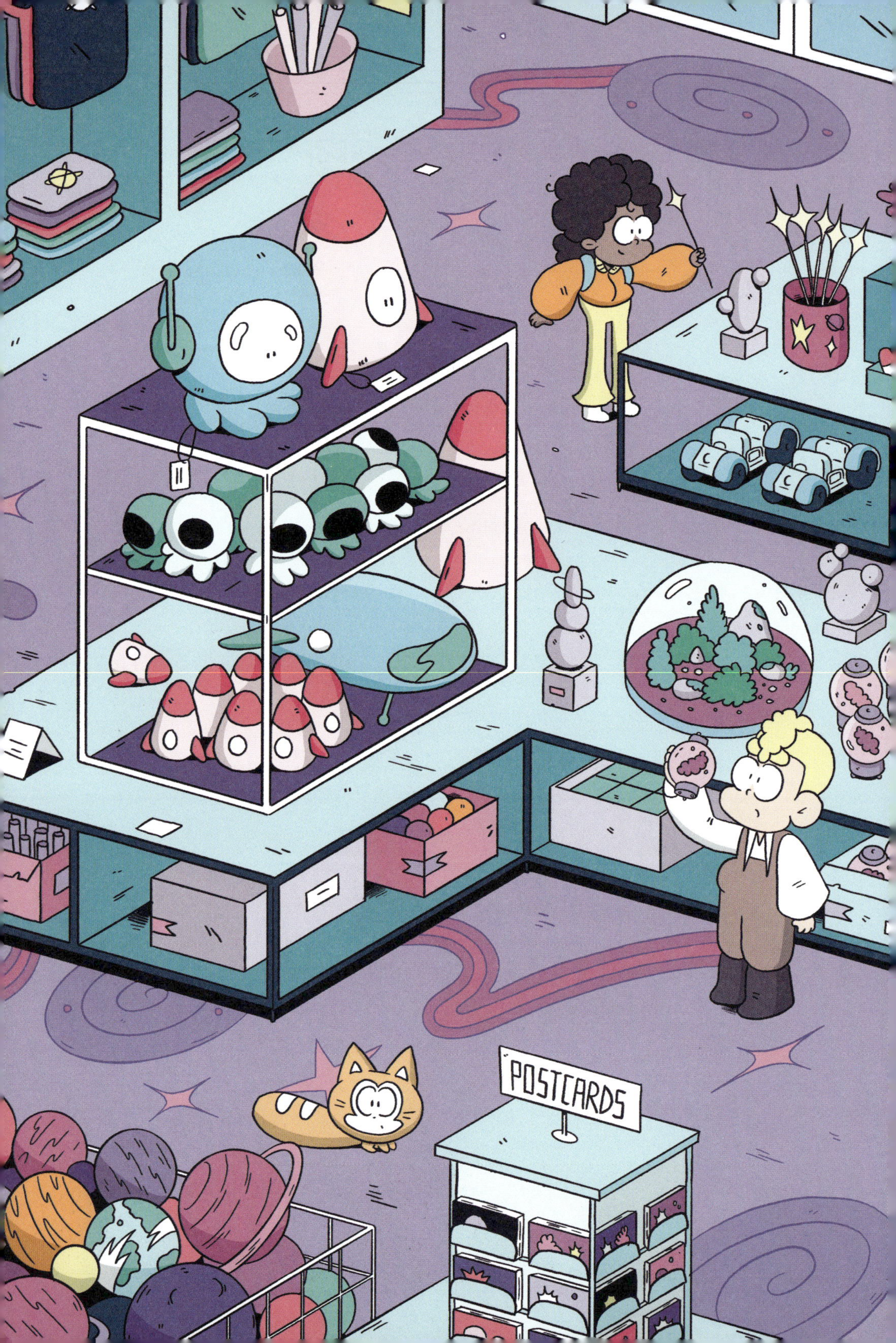
POSTCARDS

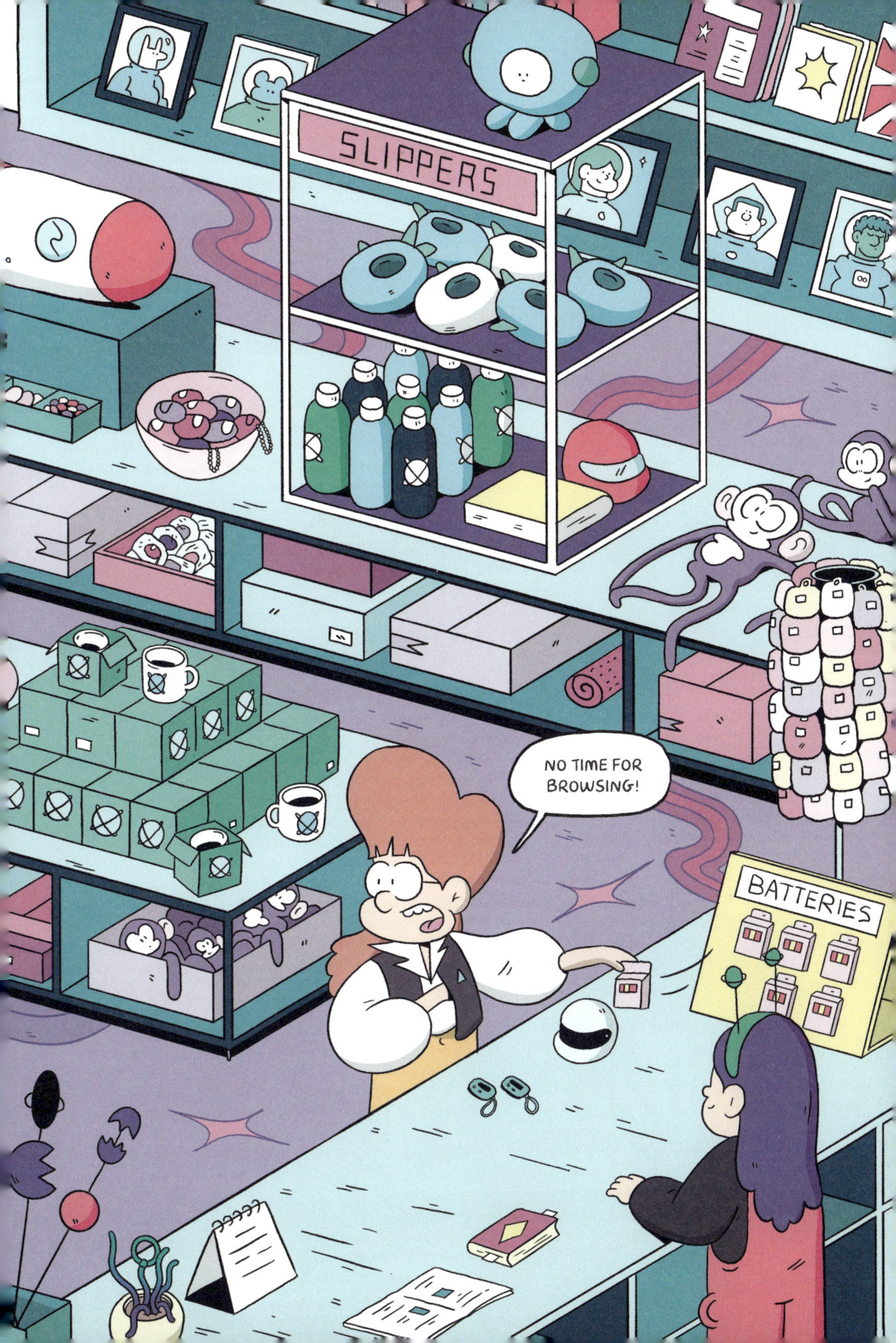
SLIPPERS
NO TIME FOR BROWSING!
BATTERIES

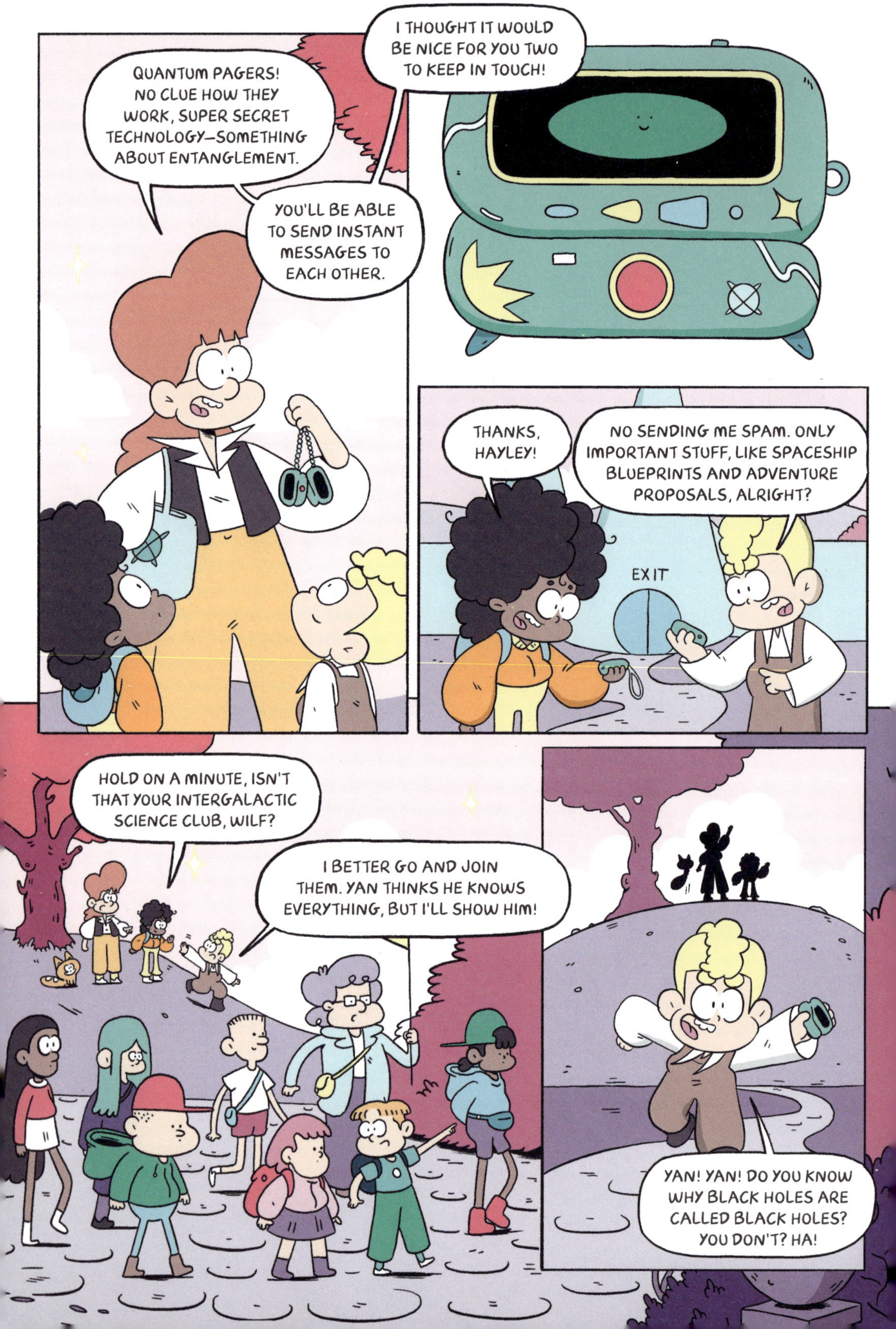
QUANTUM PAGERS! NO CLUE HOW THEY WORK, SUPER SECRET TECHNOLOGY—SOMETHING ABOUT ENTANGLEMENT.
YOU'LL BE ABLE TO SEND INSTANT MESSAGES TO EACH OTHER.
I THOUGHT IT WOULD BE NICE FOR YOU TWO TO KEEP IN TOUCH!
THANKS, HAYLEY!
NO SENDING ME SPAM. ONLY IMPORTANT STUFF, LIKE SPACESHIP BLUEPRINTS AND ADVENTURE PROPOSALS, ALRIGHT?
EXIT
HOLD ON A MINUTE, ISN'T THAT YOUR INTERGALACTIC SCIENCE CLUB, WILF?
I BETTER GO AND JOIN THEM. YAN THINKS HE KNOWS EVERYTHING, BUT I'LL SHOW HIM!
YAN! YAN! DO YOU KNOW WHY BLACK HOLES ARE CALLED BLACK HOLES? YOU DON'T? HA!

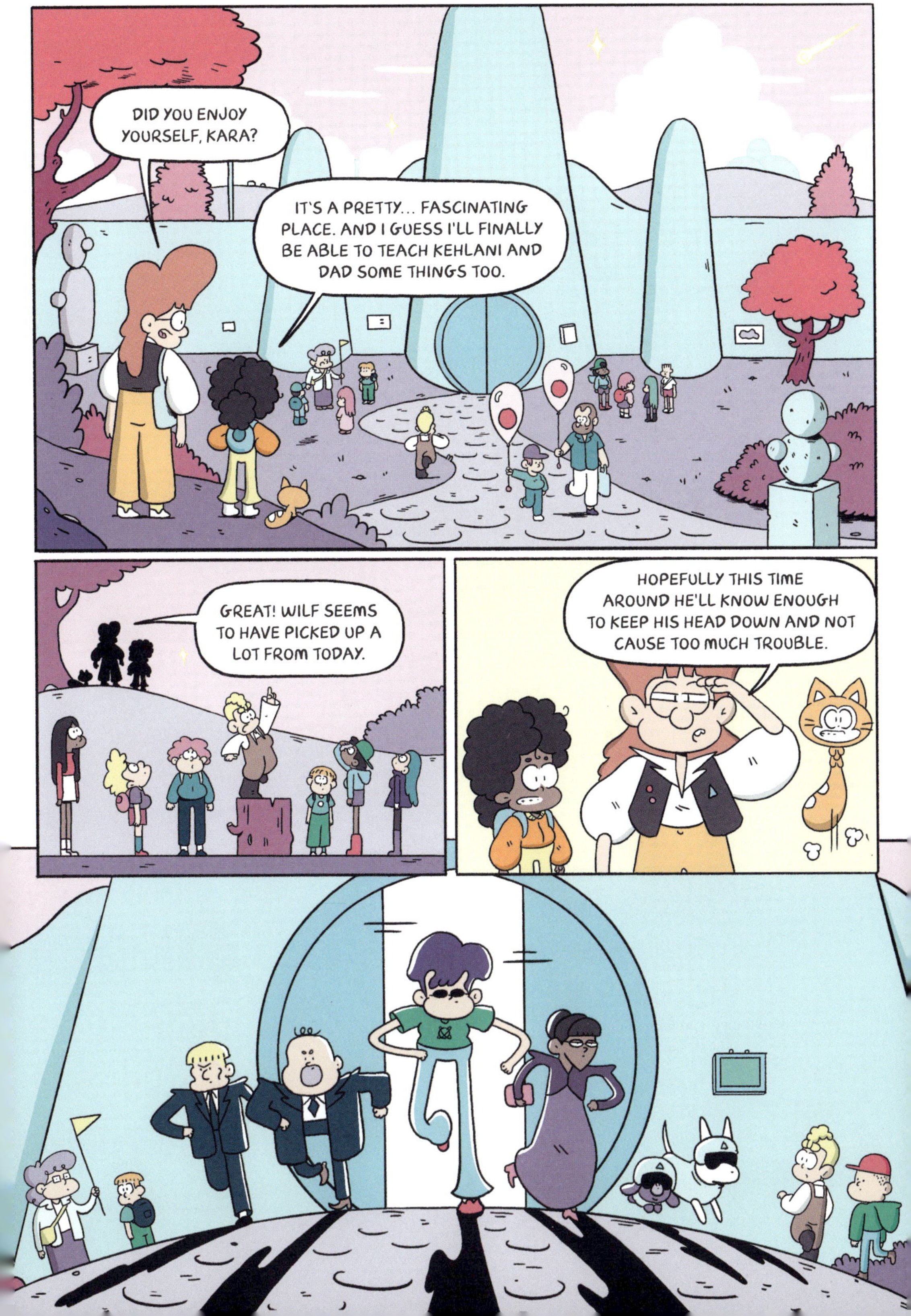
DID YOU ENJOY YOURSELF, KARA?
IT'S A PRETTY... FASCINATING PLACE. AND I GUESS I'LL FINALLY BE ABLE TO TEACH KEHLANI AND DAD SOME THINGS TOO.
GREAT! WILF SEEMS TO HAVE PICKED UP A LOT FROM TODAY.
HOPEFULLY THIS TIME AROUND HE'LL KNOW ENOUGH TO KEEP HIS HEAD DOWN AND NOT CAUSE TOO MUCH TROUBLE.

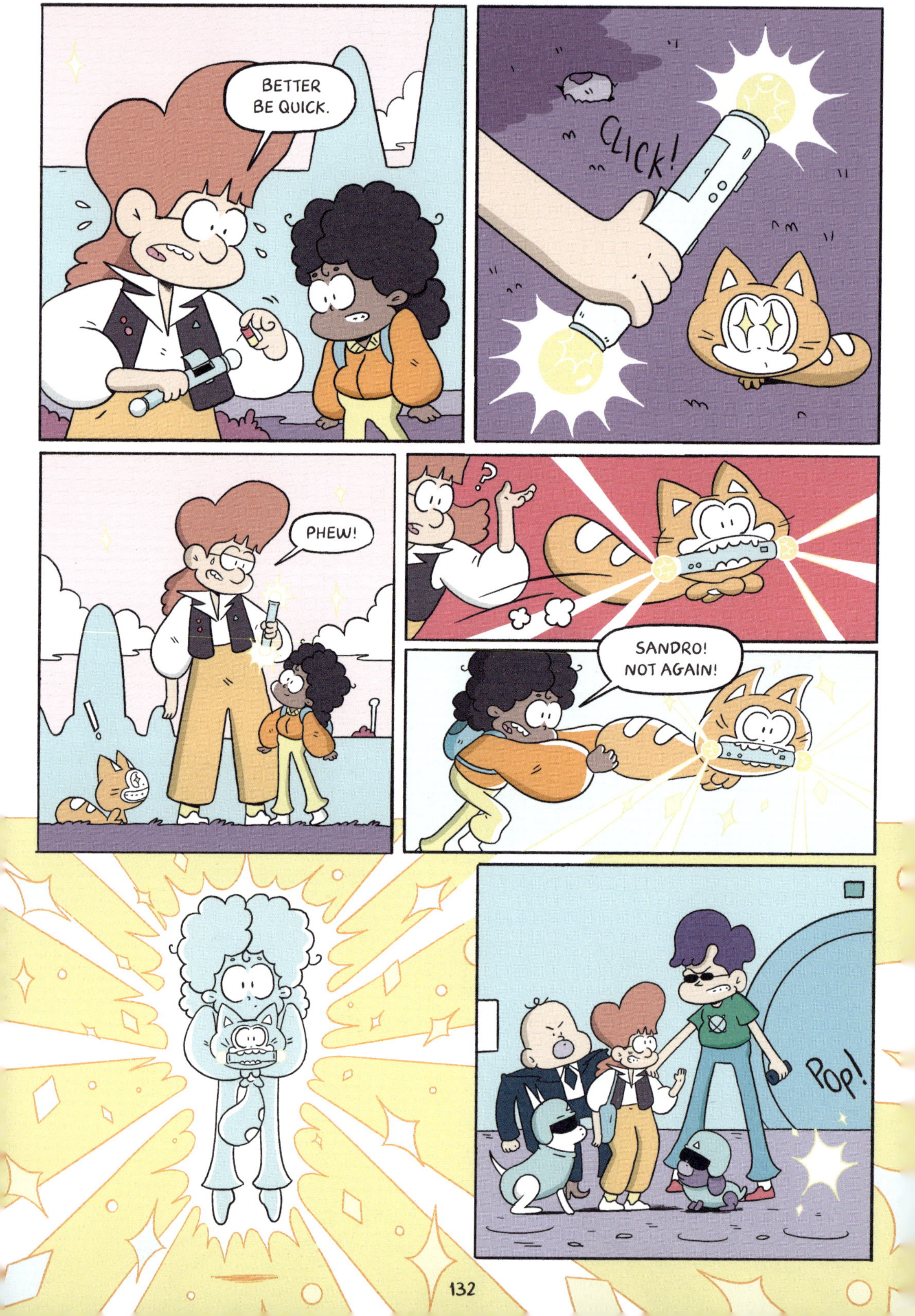
BETTER BE QUICK.
CLICK!
PHEW!
!
?
SANDRO! NOT AGAIN!
POP!

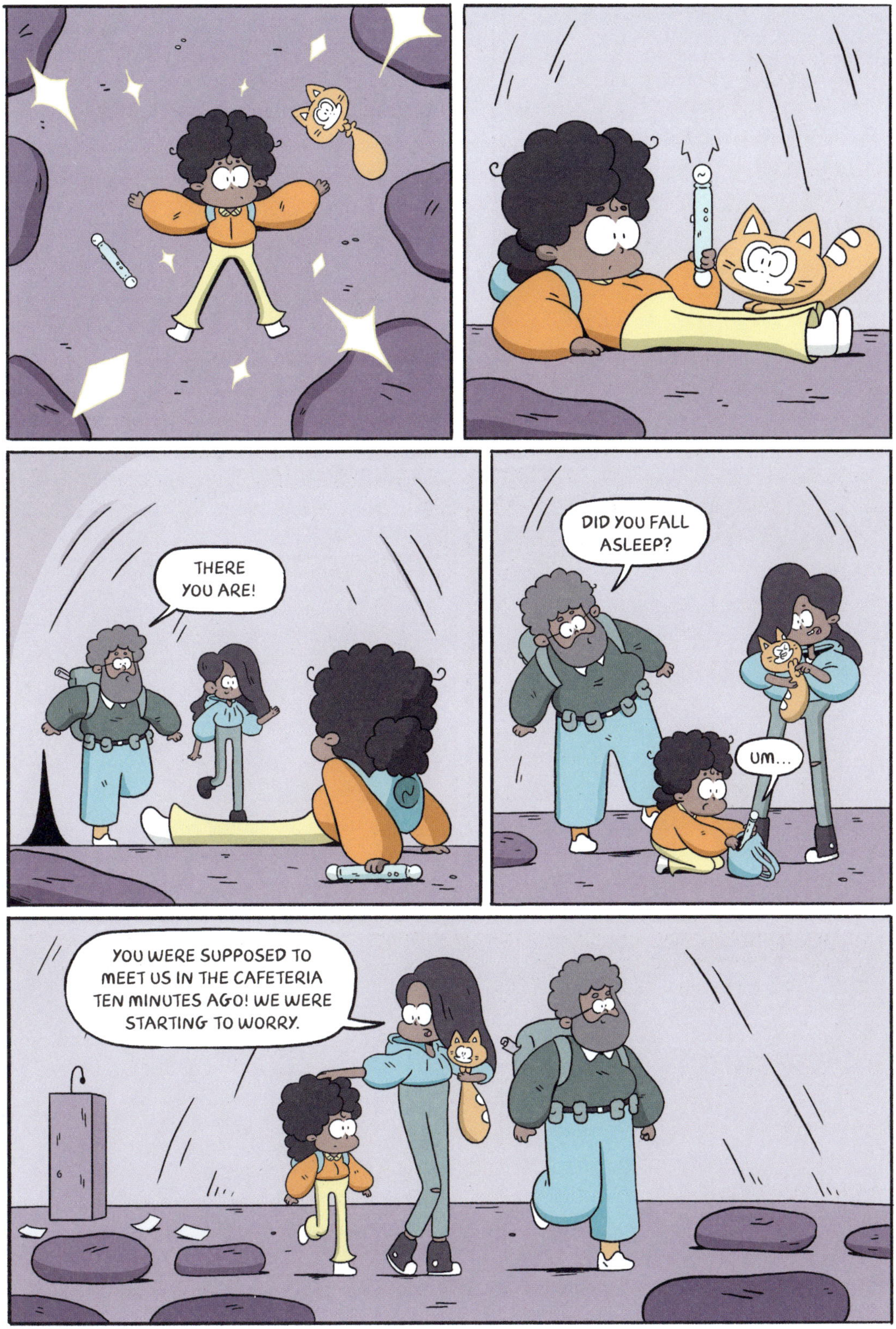
THERE YOU ARE!
DID YOU FALL ASLEEP?
UM...
YOU WERE SUPPOSED TO MEET US IN THE CAFETERIA TEN MINUTES AGO! WE WERE STARTING TO WORRY.

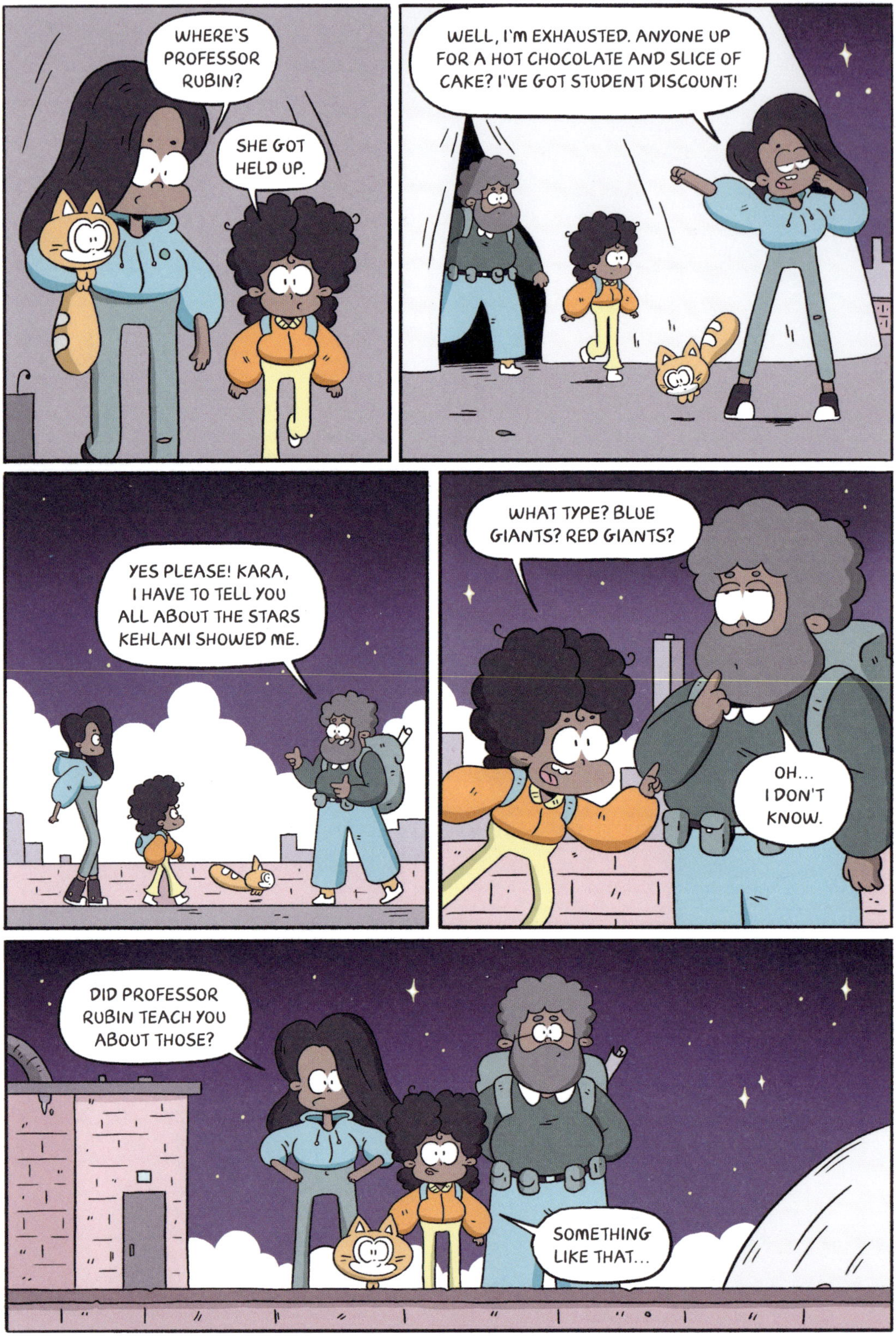
WHERE'S PROFESSOR RUBIN?
SHE GOT HELD UP.
WELL, I'M EXHAUSTED. ANYONE UP FOR A HOT CHOCOLATE AND SLICE OF CAKE? I'VE GOT STUDENT DISCOUNT!
YES PLEASE! KARA, I HAVE TO TELL YOU ALL ABOUT THE STARS KEHLANI SHOWED ME.
WHAT TYPE? BLUE GIANTS? RED GIANTS?
OH... I DON'T KNOW.
DID PROFESSOR RUBIN TEACH YOU ABOUT THOSE?
SOMETHING LIKE THAT...

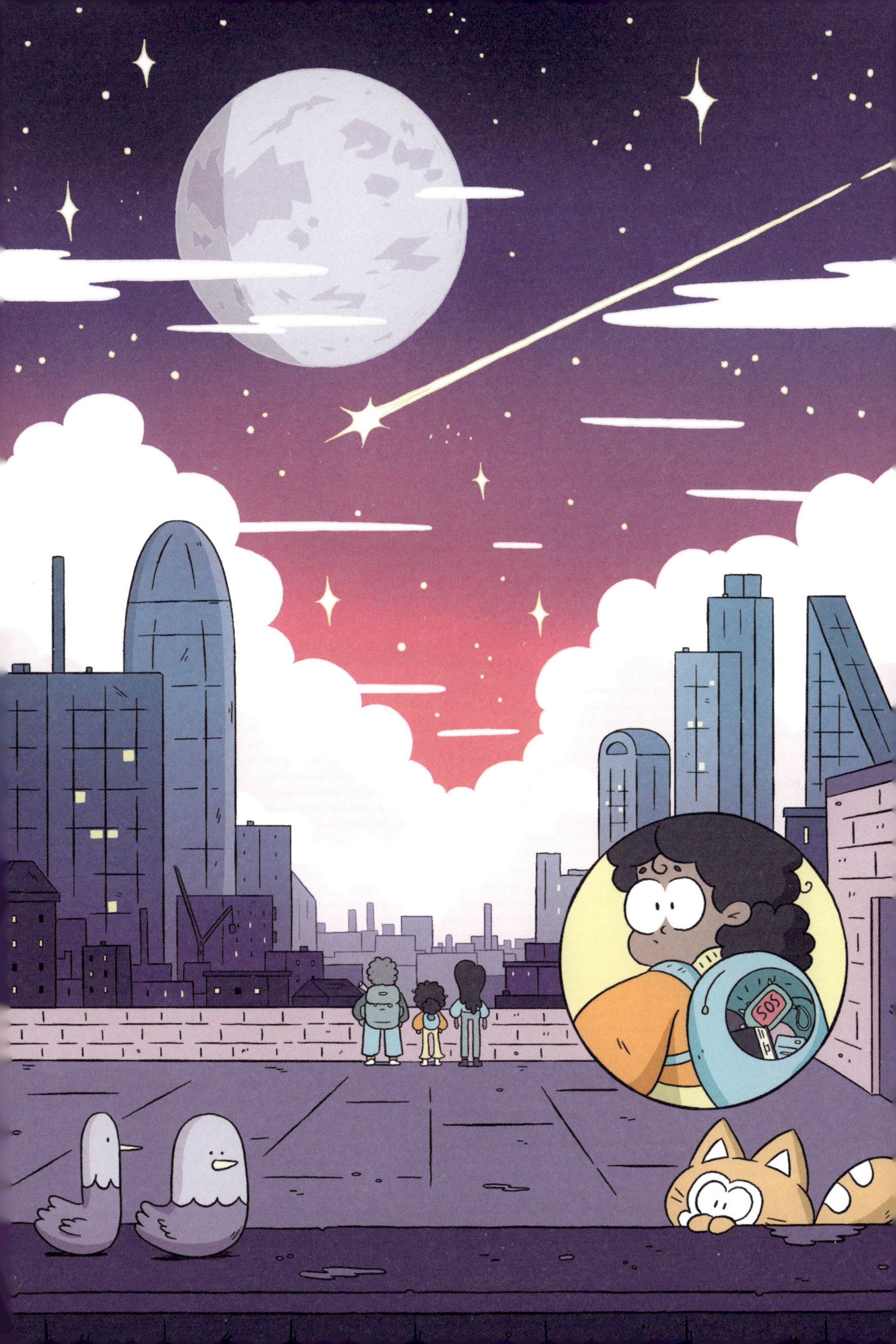
SOS

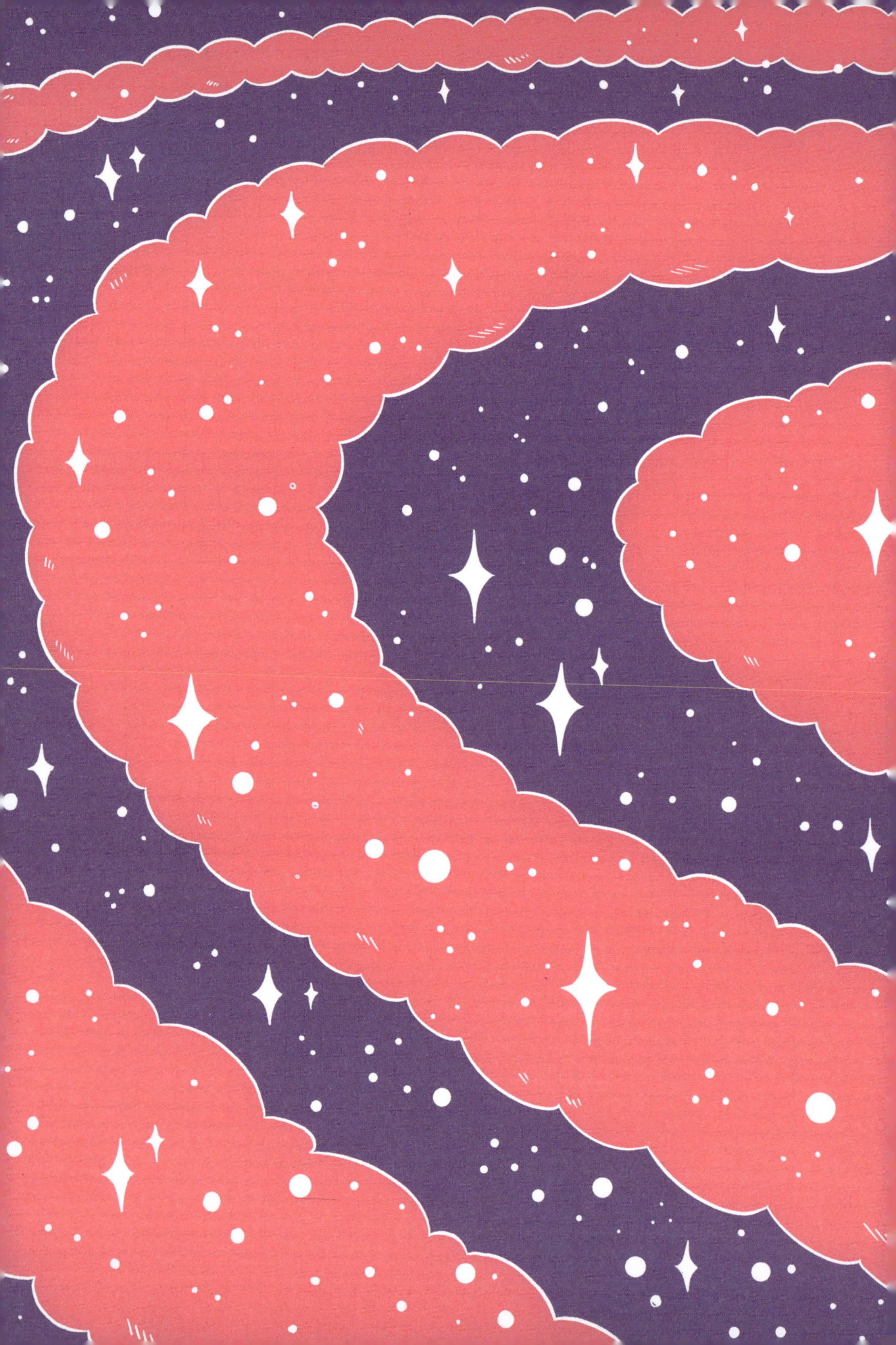